TURNS OF FATE

By the same author

HOSTILITIES ONLY

TURNS OF FATE

The Drama of HMS Cornwall

KEN DIMBLEBY

WILLIAM KIMBER · LONDON

First published in 1984 by
WILLIAM KIMBER & CO. LIMITED
100 Jermyn Street, London, SW1Y 6EE

© Ken Dimbleby, 1984

ISBN 0–7183–0523–X

Typeset by Grove Graphics, Tring
and printed in Great Britain by
The Garden City Press Limited,
Letchworth, Hertfordshire, SG6 1JS

To
HMS CORNWALL 1939–42
and all who sailed in her

Contents

List of Maps

List of Illustrations

Author's Preface and Acknowledgments

Inevitably fate played a big part in the lives of those who served in the cruiser HMS *Cornwall* in the Second World War. This is true of the men who survived as well as those who died. In the course of the warship's career, fate had many turns – many opportunities – to take a hand in the destiny of the men who made up the ship's company.

It may also be said that there were fateful turns – changes of course – by enemy ships that affected vitally the fortunes of the cruiser and the enemy.

And so the vicissitudes of the ship and all who sailed in her from the outbreak of the Second World War in 1939 until she was sunk in 1942 are summed up in the title of this book, Turns of Fate.

The loss of HMS *Cornwall* in company with HMS *Dorsetshire* is dismissed in one sentence in some histories of the sea war e.g. 'The Japanese detected the returning *Dorsetshire* and *Cornwall* and destroyed them in a brief bombing attack.'

One account says the two warships were sailing north to Colombo; another says east. They are both wrong. Another says the cruisers were sunk in the Bay of Bengal and that 'most of their crews were picked up by circling British destroyers', as though destroyers were on the spot and survivors were rescued immediately. Again wrong.

One dramatic account says *Cornwall* and *Dorsetshire* were 'cautiously approaching Ceylon when, on Easter Sunday morning, they sighted the enemy force steaming straight at them. Escape was impossible but they concentrated attention on themselves while the Eastern Fleet got away'. Yet again wrong.

It was in an effort to present an accurate account not only of the sinking but other aspects of HMS *Cornwall*'s wartime career, including her encounter with a German raider, that I undertook to write this book. I was encouraged by the co-operation of fellow survivors and should like to thank them, officers and other ranks, for their assistance in gathering material that has enabled me to tell something of the human drama in the actions in which the cruiser was involved.

I should also like to express my gratitude to the publishers who gave

me permission to use material from their books. In particular I must
mention the United States Naval Institute which was very co-operative
and helpful, and gave permission for material to be used or quoted from
the book *Midway: The Battle That Doomed Japan*, by Mitsuo Fuchida
and Masatake Okumiya. Captain Fuchida was an outstanding Japanese airman who was in command of the attack from carriers on Pearl
Harbor and Ceylon. Commander Okumiya also served in an aircraft-
carrier and both men later had access to Japanese records and reports.
The English version of their book is not merely a translation of the
original edition written in Japanese. It was edited meticulously by
Clarke H. Kawakami and Roger Pineau who checked the information
against all available American as well as Japanese documents.

The full list of acknowledgments is *Midway: The Battle That
Doomed Japan* by Mitsuo Fuchida and Masatake Okumiya. Copy-
right © 1955, US Naval Institute, Annapolis, Maryland; *The Second
World War by Winston Churchill* (Cassell Ltd., London, 1948–51);
War In The Southern Oceans 1939–45. Extracts reproduced under
Government Printer's Copyright Authority 7851 of 1.9.1982; *The War
At Sea 1939–45* by Captain S. W. Roskill, 1954–6 and *The War Against
Japan* by Major-General S. Woodburn Kirby, 1957–8 (with permis-
sion of the Controller of Her Majesty's Stationery Office); *Fighting
Admiral* by Captain Donald Macintyre (Evans Brothers Ltd., London,
1961); *Ghost Cruiser HK33* by H. J. Brennecke (William Kimber and
Co. Ltd., London, 1954); *Beyond The Laager* by Louis Duffus (Hurst
and Blackett Ltd., London, 1947); *Footprints In The Sea* by Captain
Augustus Agar VC (Evans Brothers Ltd., London, 1959); *The Most
Dangerous Moment* by Michael Tomlinson (William Kimber and Co.
Ltd., London, 1976); *Admiral Of The Pacific* by John Deane Potter
(William Heinemann Ltd., London, 1965); *The Turn Of The Tide* by
Arthur Bryant (Collins, London, 1957); *A Man Called Intrepid* by
William Stevenson (Macmillan, London, 1976).

PART ONE

The Rising Sun

I

'Dawn action stations . . .' The 10,000-ton County class cruiser HMS *Cornwall* had entered the Mozambique Channel and was sailing south, bound for Durban. It was a typically muggy morning in the tropics – humid even before the sun had risen, especially down below on the mess decks with all portholes closed because the warship had to be blacked out.

Having had the middle watch (midnight to 4 a.m.), which meant little more than an hour's sleep since getting back to my hammock, I was not feeling particularly bright when the hands were called a few minutes before closing up at action stations on that December morning in 1941. I slid out of my hammock and was still half asleep while standing on the mess deck, wearily lashing up. One went through the motions automatically because hammocks had to be stowed before going to dawn action stations. While in this semi-comatose state, I vaguely heard snatches of excited conversation . . . 'Pearl Harbor' . . . 'Yankee ships' . . . 'battleships sunk' . . . 'dirty Japs' . . . 'Roosevelt'.

There was no time to ask questions. The assault-at-arms bugle call sounded over the loudspeakers, followed by the pipe : 'Hands to dawn action stations.' Clad only in a pair of shorts, I dashed off to my action station which was then on the air defence platform above and behind the compass platform on the bridge.

The call to dawn action stations was an essential precaution every day when a warship was at sea. In the darkness one did not know if an enemy ship was nearby. Everyone closed up about twenty minutes before dawn so that the ship was in a state of readiness to go into action immediately, and stayed closed up until full light after sunrise. In those days warships did not have the benefits of the modern technology in this computer and electronics age. *Cornwall* was not even equipped with radar, so it was all the more essential to have dawn action stations because the ship depended entirely on human eyesight, even for gunnery.

Until one became accustomed to it, going to dawn action stations was an eerie start to the day. 'Action stations' was always a call one responded to without a moment's hesitation or delay. There was a general rush as everyone made for his position as fast as possible. Some had to go up, some down into the bowels of the ship. The cruiser was blacked out and there was only a subdued light below decks. Dark forms with lifebelts and gas masks slung at their sides clattered up and down ladders, going through hatchways to exposed positions on the upper decks or down to the engine-rooms, munitions sections or communications and control positions. A lone figure could be seen climbing up the long ladder to the masthead look-out position. The men manning the guns and in fire and repair parties looked hideous with their large anti-flash headgear and gloves.

Communication circuits and all the intricate mechanism connected with the ship's armament were tested. Reports on the state of readiness were made to the control positions. The bearing and elevation of the guns were tested. The barrels of the large twin eight-inch guns on the turrets, A and B forward, and X and Y aft, swung to port and starboard and then up to a surprisingly high angle. In the dim light before dawn the long barrels looked like prehistoric monsters groping in the darkness for some prey.

At their various vantage points, look-outs peered into the darkness through special powerful binoculars. On the compass platform on the bridge the Captain and other officers were also looking through binoculars. Scores of eyes were trying to penetrate the darkness before dawn. Would the morning light reveal anything? What was that dark blotch on the horizon – a ship or merely a cloud?

The men down below in the shell rooms, the cordite handling rooms, magazines and numerous other compartments became impatient. It was hot and stuffy. The smell of the cordite was sickening and gave one a headache. They wondered what was going on 'up top' and how much longer they would be closed up.

The sun rose, flooding light into a new day. The 'secure' was sounded to end dawn action stations.

While we were at action stations that December morning, the shrill note of the bosun's whistle was followed by the call 'Do you hear there?' which always preceded an important announcement. We all listened intently and heard the following message : 'Orders were received during the night to commence hostilities with Japan.'

So the balloon had gone up. Japanese naval aircraft had launched a devastating surprise attack on the United States fleet at Pearl Harbor on 7 December. America was in the war with Britain and her allies, and ranged against them were Japan, Germany and Italy. I recalled that a few weeks earlier, the Commanding Officer of *Cornwall*, Captain P. C. W. Manwaring, had told the ship's company he had been assured by the Commander-in-Chief East Indies that if Japan entered the war, we would be in the thick of it.

Standing on the air defence platform (ADP) I instinctively looked towards the east. The rising sun, red in the early morning summer haze, was just peeping over the horizon, sending crimson streaks across the calm, blue water of the Mozambique Channel. What was normally a lovely sight seemed to be a sinister setting for the news that Japan had entered the war. The rising sun, emblem of the Japanese flag, and the red streaks, symbolic of blood, did not make a pretty picture that day. I remembered my wife's foreboding that *Cornwall* was doomed if Japan came into the war.

Since leaving Simonstown at the end of February, *Cornwall* had enjoyed very little relief from hot weather. Most of the time had been spent in the tropics. When a member of the crew became seriously ill, it prompted a wag to circulate a joke that he had been in the tropics so long his blood had turned into water.

There had been much rejoicing when *Cornwall* left Aden on 1 December and it was announced that we were due to arrive at Durban on the 11th. But one afternoon at about five o'clock, while cruising slowly in a calm sea just north of the Mozambique Channel, the ship suddenly altered course about 180 degrees and headed north.

'Another blasted raider report, I'll bet,' muttered my friend, Bill Barrett, a Royal Marine bandsman. 'Just our luck.'

Cornwall had done many abortive patrols as a result of raider reports, especially false alarms from merchant ships, and the men were in no mood for a diversion now that the ship was on its way to Durban. There was a general groan when the bosun's mate piped : 'The ship has altered course to go to the assistance of a merchant ship that has reported being followed by a suspicious vessel.'

Two hours later, while at supper, we felt the ship slew acutely and change course to south again. To everyone's joy, it was piped that the 'suspicious vessel' had proved to be friendly and the distress signal had been cancelled.

Japan's entry into the war came a couple of days later to put a damper on things, but there was the consolation that our immediate destination was still Durban.

It was while we were closed up at dawn action stations that there was an amusing incident with Joe, the Geordie, whose north country accent was at times indecipherable, especially when it came over a voice pipe. He was a real character, his large bullet-shaped head almost bald although he was only thirty-two. When called up for war service, he chose the Royal Navy because his father served in it during the First World War. On this account he bore his father a grudge. After signing on for naval service, he learnt that while it was true that his father had served in the Navy, he had never been to sea. He only served in a 'stone frigate' – a shore establishment. Nevertheless, Joe could often be heard singing old naval songs that his father had taught him.

Joe's action station was also on the ADP. In the course of conversation, the officer in charge asked him: 'What were you before you joined the Navy?'

Without a moment's hesitation, Joe replied: 'A happy man.'

2

A happy man . . . Joe's quick retort set me thinking. Only a fool can really enjoy going on active war service, especially if one is married with a child. But there are times when one has to obey the call of duty and face whatever it might bring. My mind went back to joining up – volunteering because there was no conscription in South Africa. My first inclination was to answer a call for volunteers to join an anti-aircraft unit in the army and to go up north for service in the Western Desert. The first tentative step was taken to sign up. But then I changed my mind and decided to join the Royal Navy, influenced no doubt by the thought that I might as well see something of the world. If I had joined the army anti-aircraft unit, I should almost certainly have been taken prisoner at Tobruk if I had survived the battles in North Africa. Such are the quirks of fate.

My home was in Cape Town but arrangements were made to do the four weeks' training at the Royal Naval Volunteer Reserve base in Port Elizabeth where my wife, young son and I could stay with my parents and see something of them before going off on active service. So duly I reported to the base in the harbour and officially became an Ordinary Seaman, usually referred to as an OD and often with the Navy's favourite adjective preceding the O.

The eighteen recruits on the training course ranged from teenagers to a 36-year-old man and represented a variety of walks of life. Some were youngsters who had just left school, two had worked on dredgers and tugs in the harbour service while the others included apprentices, clerks, a carpenter and a mechanic. The big surprise was the 36-year-old T. C. Thorp, BA, BSc, who was a master at the Grey High School in Port Elizabeth when I was a pupil there and only a couple of months before becoming an Ordinary Seaman had been addressed as 'Sir' at school by some of the youngsters who were now his fellow recruits.

Because one of his eyes was well below standard, Tommy Thorp had been rejected for national service in South Africa in his younger days. Under war conditions, however, his close friend, Lieutenant-Commander Russel Paterson, RNVR, who was then Commanding Officer of the Port Elizabeth base, overcame the problem of the eye and Tommy was able to join the Royal Navy. Later the defective eye was to bar him from promotion in the executive branch. He was greatly admired for the way he accepted life on the lower deck during his service at sea.

Our instructor on the training course was Chief Gunner's Mate Edward Black, a Royal Navy man who settled in South Africa and later was awarded national colours as a marksman. Known to everyone as the 'Chief', he was strict, efficient and popular. We could not have wished for a better instructor. He had survived three sinkings in the 'bloody cold' northern waters in the First World War.

'If your ship goes down, wear as much clothing as possible,' he advised us. 'It keeps one warm in the water.'

We had an intensive training course, being at the base from 0800 to 1630 Navy time (8 a.m. to 4.30 p.m.) every weekday, and writing an examination on Saturday mornings. We were also mistaken for having the first nudist club in Port Elizabeth. The RNVR base opened on to a small beach in the harbour and at the end of a day's training, recruits often dived into the sea to cool off. Those who did not have costumes handy swam in the nude. But the 'club' was short-lived because the Commanding Officer received a complaint that some women who visited the docks had seen men bathing in the nude. Henceforth those who did not have costumes had to swim in their underpants.

There was an excellent spirit among the recruits and our training at the RNVR base was a happy time. But the four weeks soon passed and we were sent off by train to Simonstown which was a Royal Navy base. We were taken a couple of miles beyond the town to a camp that in peacetime was sponsored by a Cape Town newspaper to provide seaside holidays for poorer children from the hinterland. Now it was a naval transit camp named Froggy Pond and filled with sailors from several parts of Britain and South Africa waiting to be drafted to warships.

We arrived at Froggy Pond still wearing civilian clothes so on our
first day we were taken to the 'slops' (clothing store) in Simonstown to
be kitted up. We were each given a kitbag and the Supply Petty Officer
reeled off a list of articles as he threw them into it. It was not very
satisfactory 'shopping', as we discovered when we tried on the various
items of clothing. The jumper issued to me was a much darker blue than
the trousers so I took them back to the 'slops'.

'Do they fit?' asked the Petty Officer.

'Yes, but . . .'

Before I could complete the sentence, he said : 'Then what the hell
are you worrying about? Run along.'

I am reminded of the story told by Engine Room Artificer Cyril
Wood about his first day at Chatham Barracks in April 1940, when an
old three-badge Able Seaman showed him how to sling a hammock
and then how to lash it up. The AB said : 'Seven turns, one for each
day of the week. Your hammock is the best friend you'll ever have in
the Navy, and if it is lashed up properly it will keep you afloat for 24
hours.' He paused, then asked : 'Tell me, son, did you volunteer?'

'Yes,' replied Wood.

'Tut-tut, never volunteer,' said the old AB with typical tongue-in-
cheek humour.

At Simonstown the next day, wearing our newly-acquired suits
(sailors did not refer to uniforms), we were taken to the Sick Bay to be
inoculated and vaccinated. The naval doctor was an old chap who
must have been retrieved from a long-standing retired list. When it
came to vaccination, instead of just a small scratch, he seemed to take
a delight in the old-fashioned method of scratching one's arm exten-
sively. Indeed, I thought he was playing noughts and crosses on mine
and it irritated, to put it mildly. I certainly suffered later. When I was
a child vaccination was not compulsory and my mother did not have
me done. So this, my first time, 'took' with a vengeance. I spent a most
uncomfortable night with my temperature shooting up and then suddenly dropping as I broke out in a sweat. A few days later I had a
painful sore the size of half-a-crown on my arm.

One did not have to be in Simonstown long to learn that to sailors
it was known as Snoekie. They hardly ever referred to Simonstown –
just Snoekie, which was affectionately derived from Snoektown. Fishing
boats put out from Simonstown and other smaller harbours in False
Bay to catch the tasty fish, snoek. As far as I can gather, the name
Snoektown was coined in 1935 by the late Cecil Wightman when he
started what became a famous weekly indigenous radio programme,

'Snoektown Calling – the craziest radio station south of the line'. It was introduced every week with a blast of a typical Cape sound, the fish-horn. The programme, which was full of wit, humour and satire, became the most popular in South Africa. It was closed down in 1943 but was resumed in Italy when Wightman, an honorary Captain helping to run a radio station with programmes for the troops, broadcast 'Snoektown – the craziest radio station north of the line'.

When our batch of eighteen recruits arrived at Froggy Pond, we were told by the other matelots there that we would have to wait weeks, even months, before getting a draft to a ship. After we had been there only three days, however, Tommy Thorp and I were summoned by the Commanding Officer of the camp and told that we would be included in a draft joining HMS *Cornwall*. We had to be ready to leave at a moment's notice.

This unexpected decision came as a shock and I felt both thrilled and a bit apprehensive. We had seen *Cornwall* from a distance in the docks, knew she had been at Simonstown for some time undergoing a refit, but never for a moment thought that we would be drafted to her. The first thing I did was to telephone my wife in Cape Town and ask her to draw some money. As an Ordinary Seaman RNVR my pay was two shillings and sixpence a day – seventeen shillings and sixpence a week of which twelve shillings and sixpence had to be allotted to my wife, so I was left with five shillings a week. Fortunately the *Cape Argus*, the Cape Town newspaper which employed me, paid half salary to my wife while I was on service otherwise it would have been financially impossible to join up.

As a schoolmaster, Tommy Thorp had the difference between his naval pay and salary made up so he did not consider it necessary to make an allotment. The Petty Officer in the Pay Office at Simonstown informed him, however, that if he wanted his widow to receive a pension, he would have to make an allotment and twelve shillings and sixpence was the minimum.

'If you don't support your wife when you are alive, laddie, the service won't support your widow if you cop it,' he told Tommy, and added that ODs were not supposed to be married.

Early in the afternoon the next day Tommy and I said farewell to the sixteen men with whom we had trained in Port Elizabeth, boarded a lorry with several other 'HO' sailors and were driven to the docks to go aboard *Cornwall*. ('HO' was an abbreviation for hostilities only i.e. those serving only for the duration of the war.)

3

Cornwall was one of several County Class cruisers built to comply with the Washington Naval Treaty of 1922 which limited cruisers to 10,000 tons and guns not exceeding eight inches calibre. She was built at Devonport, being launched on 11 March 1926, and completed in November the following year at a cost of £1,970,000. There was no limit to the length of these ships. When we stood on the quayside where *Cornwall* was berthed at Simonstown, the thing that struck me most was her length. The cruiser was 630 feet long, which was only thirty feet short of twice the length of a rugby field from posts to posts. *Cornwall* was actually longer than some of the older battleships in the Royal Navy, including *Warspite* and the four R-Class battlewagons she was to serve with in the Eastern Fleet in 1942. I was quite awed by the size of the cruiser when at close quarters. When seen at a distance a ship looks deceptively smaller than its dimensions.

Because of the limitation on the tonnage of these cruisers, the designers used light metals and several other weight-saving devices. They did not have much in the way of protective bulges and narrow beams – $68\frac{1}{2}$ feet in the case of *Cornwall* compared with *Warspite*'s 104 feet. They were in effect large versions of destroyers, having a maximum speed of a little more than 30 knots when in top condition. *Cornwall* was built to do 31.5 knots, but in the last stages of her service could not manage more than 27.5 even when going flat out in an effort to save her life.

Although long and slender, the County Class cruisers were designed to pack a powerful punch, which they did with their four turrets of eight 8-inch guns (A and B turrets forward, X and Y aft). The weight of the shell they fired was 256 pounds, and soon after the ships were built a single broadside cost as much as £408. The big guns had exceptional elevation, even as much as 65 degrees. It was also reported that as a result of improved ammunition supply, the rate of fire of four rounds per gun per minute could be maintained.

We were impressed and walked up the gangway in single file carrying our kitbags and hammocks. We were lined up on the deck where Commander John Fair, the second in command in *Cornwall*, addressed us. He was a very tall, thin man, with light-coloured hair, and gave the impression of being a bit shy. He welcomed us as South Africans and said we had a reputation to uphold because the many other South Africans in the ship had acquitted themselves with distinction.

In the course of being shown over the warship, we noted the armament in addition to the main 8-inch turrets. There were four 4-inch mountings (each with two guns) – two on the starboard side and two on the port side – two mountings of multiple pom-poms, each mounting having eight guns, and several smaller machine guns.

A visit to the Regulating Office and Gunnery Office gave us cards bearing essential information such as which watch one was in, the number of one's mess and locker, one's cruising and action stations and also abandon ship station. The last item was a bit of a joke. My abandon ship station was No 1 Carley float which, I noticed, had not been completed and would not be of much use. When I remarked on this fact to the Regulating Petty Officer, he replied cheerfully: 'Never mind, when it comes to abandoning ship all the boats and floats will be smashed, so it won't make any difference.'

He was wrong. In due course No 1 Carley float was completed and was a godsend for several survivors.

When we had completed the formalities connected with joining the ship, it was time for afternoon tea which included liberal supplies of bread and jam. It was virtually a fourth meal.

I had never been aboard a warship and everything was strange. My first impressions that afternoon were a perpetual smell of oil, innumerable watertight doors, hatchways, ladders, an incessant noise and a large number of men in a limited space. With the arrival of our draft that day, the ship's company had been increased to close on 800.

We had been given all-night leave and I was glad to get ashore with the first libertyboat later that afternoon – always called libertyboat even when one just had to walk down the gangway to go ashore.

Back on board the next morning, there was a bugle call after breakfast followed by the pipe: 'Both watches for exercise, fall in.'

'What's that mean, for exercise?' I asked another seaman.

'Follow me,' he shouted as he dashed off along the deck, but did not ask which watch I was in.

I followed him at the double and found seamen lining up in double ranks.

'Which watch are you in?' asked the Buffer (Chief Bosun's Mate).

'Starboard,' I replied.

'Well, what the hell are you doing on this side?' he bellowed. 'Don't you know the difference between port and starboard?'

I learnt that 'For exercise' had nothing to do with PT. The exercise was what work had to be done that day, and on this particular day the order was: 'Paint ship'. I was paired off with an English HO rating and we spent the day painting a side of the large box-like hangar that had been added some time after *Cornwall* was built to house the couple of Walrus seaplanes she carried.

Within a few days *Cornwall*'s refit had been completed and she had been cleaned, painted and carried out trials in False Bay, including surface and anti-aircraft gunnery practices. When the ship 'made fast' at Simonstown on Thursday, 27 February, a gunnery programme had been arranged for the next day and it was generally accepted, on the strength of a strong buzz, that after target practice in False Bay, she would sail round Cape Point to spend the weekend at Cape Town before going to sea on service. The buzzes about where she would go from Cape Town ranged from Britain to Singapore.

But we soon learnt that the Navy is full of surprises. *Cornwall* duly left Simonstown harbour the next morning as the sun started breaking through the mist and clouds. A sharp breeze was blowing and water whipped up on to the deck as the ship gathered speed and ploughed through the swells. It was bracing and I was feeling quite cheerful. It was more pleasant to spend the day at sea before going to Cape Town than messing around with a paint brush in dock. On the lower deck we were all looking forward to the weekend in Cape Town.

Then came the bombshell. The loudspeaker near where I was scraping the quarterdeck crackled and the high note of the bosun's whistle was followed by the call: 'Do you hear there?' I stopped working and stood up to listen carefully to what he had to say. To my amazement, instead of saying that *Cornwall* was going round to Cape Town for the weekend, he announced: 'The ship is now proceeding on service to the South Atlantic to search for a German raider.'

I stood spellbound, struck by a feeling of shock and despair. It had seemed so certain that we would have the weekend at Cape Town for a proper farewell. Now the white trail of the cruiser's wake stretched farther and farther back. It seemed heartless the way the ship cut through the sea past Cape Point, heading west, the Cape Peninsula becoming fainter and fainter. Soon all we could see was the South Atlantic Ocean.

In the afternoon while on watch as a look-out on the bridge, I asked a Chief Petty Officer what he thought our chances were of finding the raider.

'Very small,' he replied. 'We've spent months looking for raiders. Most people don't realise how big the oceans are. Looking for a raider in the South Atlantic is like looking for the proverbial needle in a haystack.'

He had a good point. The Atlantic Ocean covers 31,800,000 square miles and the Indian Ocean (including the Red Sea and Persian Gulf) 28,400,000. Those are very vast areas, especially when it is remembered that in the years of the Second World War there were not such things as space satellites with highly sensitive cameras capable of observing and pinpointing what was going on at sea and on land. *Cornwall* and many other ships did not even have radar to extend their vision. Unless a ship had an aircraft and conditions were favourable for using it, her range of vision was limited to the horizon, a matter of ten to twelve miles, when searching for another vessel at sea.

That night the only place I could find on the seamen's mess deck to sling my hammock was next to a noisy electric fan. I had not yet learnt how to make a hammock comfortable, and when I lay down the sides almost overlapped above me. It was uncomfortable and the noise was disturbing, but I was exhausted after the emotional strain of the unexpected departure and first day at sea. I fell asleep and it seemed I had not slept very long before I was awakened by a bugle call, known as 'Charlie', over the loud-speaker system, followed by the pipe :

> All hands, all hands,
> Heave ho, heave ho, heave ho,
> Lash up and stow.

It was still dark when, a couple of minutes later, there was another bugle call and the pipe : 'Hands to dawn action stations.'

The cruiser was back in service at sea.

The second last question on our Service Certificates was : 'Can he swim ?'

Fortunately the answer was : 'Yes.'

PART TWO

Rampant Raider

I

HMS *Cornwall* and the German ship *Pinguin* were destined to have an encounter in the Indian Ocean. But much water was to pass under their keels before they met on that fateful day in May 1941. Both were to steam many thousands of miles.

Cornwall, the County Class cruiser, and *Pinguin*, the German auxiliary cruiser, had one thing in common : they were both doomed. Destiny had ordained that they would finish their careers in the depths of the Indian Ocean. Ironically, their sea-bed graves are not so very far apart in almost the same latitude just north of the equator.

The Germans called ships like *Pinguin* auxiliary cruisers, but they were more correctly labelled raiders by the Allies. They were disguised ships of war – merchant ships that had been fitted out with impressive armament. They plied the oceans with their guns concealed and in the guise of harmless merchantmen while they searched for and sank or captured Allied ships.

It was a campaign loaded with deceit, in sharp contrast to Britain's Armed Merchant Cruisers which were passenger ships converted to serve as warships, were not disguised, operated openly as warships and flew the white ensign of the Royal Navy all the time. The operations of the German raiders were described by Captain Augustus Agar vc, Commanding Officer of HMS *Dorsetshire*, as 'a loathsome and horrible form of sea warfare contrary to all the traditions of humanity among seamen'.

After the outbreak of the Second World War on 3 September 1939, Nazi Germany wasted no time in converting merchant ships to serve as what they so euphemistically called auxiliary cruisers. The plans were obviously made well before war broke out. Altogether ten ships were converted to serve as raiders. One of them returned to Brest after operating for a few months in the North Atlantic in 1940, during which it sank or captured ten ships. Another was damaged by aircraft in the English Channel shortly after the start of its voyage in February 1943, and was recalled to Germany. The remaining eight all operated in the southern oceans – the South Atlantic or Indian – but mostly in both.

Within a few days of the start of the war the Hansa Line freighter *Kandelfels* (7766 tons), which had been launched in 1936 and had just returned from a trade voyage to India, was requisitioned and sent to Bremen to be converted into an auxiliary cruiser. Protected by the utmost secrecy while she was in the hands of the dockyard workers, she was given the code name of *Ship 33* and became known as *HK 33*, the letters being an abbreviation of the German word *Hilfskreutzer* (auxiliary cruiser). The Royal Navy labelled her *Raider F*.

The captains and crews of the raiders were chosen carefully. They had to be men who could cope with trying conditions for a long time at sea. The captains had an onerous task that demanded efficiency, discipline, courage, resourcefulness and the ability to make sudden difficult decisions.

Captain Ernst Felix Krüder was well suited by both ability and personality to command *Ship 33*. He was a product of the German Imperial Navy. Born on 6 December 1897, he was still a teenager when he joined the Navy in the First World War. He saw action while serving as a Leading Seaman in the battleship *König* in the Battle of Jutland. Later he successfully completed various courses and was promoted to junior commissioned rank before the war ended. After the war he had a variety of naval experience and became a specialist in mining operations, something that stood him in good stead as captain of a raider. He held the rank of Commander when the Second World War broke out.

Captain Krüder went on board *Ship 33* on 11 November 1939, less than a month before his forty-second birthday, while the ship was being converted at Bremen for service as a raider. She was officially commissioned as an auxiliary cruiser on 6 February 1940, but there were still months of work to be done to the ship. After the conversion was completed, she was painted grey and had dummy wooden guns as a disguise to make her look like a warship when she sailed to Gotenhafen, near Danzig in the Baltic, where gunnery trials were carried out. The dummy guns were removed before the raider eventually set off from Gotenhafen at 1 a.m. on 15 June 1940.

It was apparently left to the captains to choose the names of raiders. Before sailing, Krüder had decided on the name of *Pinguin* for his ship. The fifth raider to sail from Germany, *Pinguin* was very well equipped for her piratic assignment. She had a maximum speed of 18 knots and carried two seaplanes for reconnaissance to help her scour the oceans.

When conditions were suitable the seaplanes, which were stowed in a hold, could be lifted out by crane and lowered over the side on to the water.

Like the other German raiders, *Pinguin* was heavily armed. The main armament consisted of six 5.9-inch guns and four torpedo tubes. Four of these guns were situated amidships – two on the port side and two on the starboard side – another was just forward of the bridge and the sixth was on the stern. It was thus possible to fire broadsides with four of the guns on either side. The torpedo tubes were just below the single funnel, two on each side of the ship. In addition, there was a 3-inch gun on the bow, which was used for firing warning shots across merchant ships' bows to help persuade them to comply with a signal to stop, a double-barrelled $1\frac{1}{2}$-inch gun just aft of the mainmast and a few smaller anti-aircraft guns. In the stern were two doors for releasing mines.

The armament was cleverly concealed, much ingenuity being used to ensure that the raider, although carrying a powerful punch, looked like an ordinary merchantman. Only the one gun on the stern was visible – the normal defensive armament of a merchant ship. When a raider went into action, the flaps concealing guns went up and they were brought into operation in a few seconds. The $1\frac{1}{2}$-inch gun was in what looked like a big box. When the box opened for action, the men manning the gun were already inside.

The gunnery officer, who controlled the firing, was in a place out of sight, such as a dummy ventilator. Rangefinders placed above the bridge were camouflaged to look like a water tank.

Pinguin carried a large crew and highly explosive 'cargo'. The crew of 346 included 21 officers and the extra men who would be needed to put on board captured ships as prize crews. In addition to ammunition for her guns, torpedoes and 300 mines for her own use, she had stowed on board 80 mines and 25 torpedoes to deliver to U-boats to replenish their supplies.

2

Germany's sea raiders received instructions from the SKL, the abbreviation for Seekriegsleitung (operational staff of the High Command German Navy). The SKL's intentions for these disguised ships were contained in the instructions given to Captain Bernhard Rogge, who

was in command of the *Atlantis*, the first of the raiders to leave Germany
and the one that had the longest time at sea. (The cruise of the *Atlantis*
lasted almost twenty months from 31 March 1940 to 22 November
1941.) The orders included the following:

E. Task

The chief aim of the task lies in the attempt to divert enemy naval
forces from home waters and to inflict damage on the enemy,

(a) by forcing the enemy to form convoys and to make strong protection available for his overseas trade even in remote waters,

(b) by forcing the enemy to employ his naval forces as much as possible,

(c) by scaring away neutral shipping,

(d) by creating a situation harmful to the enemy from an economic
and financial point of view.

To achieve this, it is more important to keep the enemy on the
alert and occupied over a long period than to sink a large number of
ships, which would lead to the shortening of the life of the auxiliary
cruiser. The sinking of enemy ships or of neutral vessels sailing in
the service of the enemy constitutes the means of attaining the
strategical aim.

F. Instructions as to carrying out of task

1. Surprise operations will be carried out in various seas with a
view to forcing frequent new situations on the enemy, and compel-
ling him to employ numerous units to protect his trade. This will
ease the situation on the home front and will slow down the enemy's
overseas trade considerably owing to the need for escorts.

2. The disguises adopted and the tactics employed when attacking
enemy merchantmen will be as varied as possible. Every imaginable
means should be employed, and stratagems and resourcefulness will
play an important part.

It will depend on perfect disguise and its skilful use whether an
auxiliary cruiser will be able to operate undetected in one area for
some time and whether the ship will succeed in making surprise
attacks, rendering it impossible for the enemy to give the alarm.

3. As soon as the enemy has learnt of the presence of an auxiliary
cruiser in one area, the cruiser will leave and move to an area which
is sufficiently remote from her previous one to ensure that the protective measures taken by the enemy cannot possibly have any effect
on the new area. An adequate period of suspension of operations will
be observed.

This period of suspension must be so timed that the enemy defensive measures cannot fully develop. The enemy must not be allowed to cut short his defensive measures in the old area and switch over to the new area, which would certainly happen if the auxiliary cruiser disclosed her presence in the new area at too early a stage.

A periodic disappearance of the auxiliary cruiser to remote areas for a longer time may therefore be advisable : the auxiliary cruiser would not only avoid enemy defensive measures but would also create a feeling of insecurity for the enemy.

4. Actions with enemy naval forces, including auxiliary cruisers, should be avoided. If, however, such action becomes unavoidable, full use of disguise will be made to secure surprise, and all available means will be ruthlessly employed to destroy the enemy or to inflict damage on him.

Escorted convoys will be left alone. Passenger ships should be avoided as enemy liners are usually superior in speed and armament. Even in a successful action, the number of the liner's crew and passengers would embarrass the auxiliary cruiser considerably.

The captains of raiders were ordered to wage war according to the German Prize Law. As far as surface ships were concerned, this law conformed fairly closely to international treaties and conventions. But it seems the Germans were determined not to have their hands tied too much by this law, and that there should be no qualms about disregarding it if necessary because the instructions added :

As, however, the war has to be waged in such a way as best to further the war effort as a whole, it goes without saying that the employment of effective weapons and of certain tactics cannot fall away because one or other international rule or regulation is against it. The political repercussion of measures which go beyond the accepted law can be appreciated and judged only by SKL : for this reason SKL reserves to itself the right to order the carrying out of such measures.

3

After leaving Gotenhafen and steaming into the Baltic Sea, *Pinguin* was escorted through the Kattegat by motor torpedo boats and aircraft. Four days later she anchored in the seclusion of Soergulen Fjord on the coast of Norway and spent a couple of days being disguised. The Germans were very adept at changing the appearance of raiders while at sea. They used a variety of devices such as dummy ventilators, collapsible deck-houses and bulwarks, telescopic funnels and masts, hinged samson-posts and, of course, plenty of repainting. In a few days the appearance of a ship could be completely changed. Thus the grey *Pinguin* that had sailed from Gotenhafen was to all intents and purposes the black Russian cargo ship *Pechura*, when she got under way from Soergulen Fjord on 22 June 1940.

Had British intelligence got wind of the raider's secret departure? The question is inevitably raised because not long after sailing from the fjord, she encountered a British submarine. Despite her camouflage as a Russian ship, the raider was attacked by the submarine which had surfaced and fired a couple of torpedoes. But the submarine was hampered by heavy seas, the torpedoes did not reach their target and *Pinguin* was able to draw away and continue on her northerly course some distance off the Norwegian coast into the Arctic Circle.

A change of course to the north-west took her into the ice barrier to the west of Jan Mayen Island where she hove to and waited for suitable weather to sail through the Denmark Strait between Iceland and Greenland. Suitable in this case meant misty, dirty weather with a minimum of visibility to enable the ship to elude the British blockade of this escape route and break out undetected into the North Atlantic Ocean. This was accomplished without incident, but not without discomfort in a boisterous Arctic storm. By 1 July the raider was in the open sea and, after passing appropriately-named Cape Farewell at the tip of Greenland on her starboard side, she set a course due south.

On 10 July when south of the Azores, the islands about 1,000 miles due west of Lisbon in Portugal, *Pinguin* hove to while the crew got to work over the sides with paint and brushes and also altered the appearance of the superstructure. By the time they had finished, *Pinguin* had changed her appearance from the black Russian freighter *Pechura* to the light blue and white Greek ship *Kassos*.

The disguised raider continued on the due south course and eight days later had her first assignment since leaving Gotenhafen – a rendezvous on 18 July with a U-boat to tranship oil and torpedoes. The operation was delayed for some days by rough seas. When the supplies of oil and torpedoes had been transferred to the U-boat, *Pinguin* took it in tow on 25 July and headed towards Freetown, an important British convoy port on the coast of West Africa.

That night a tanker was sighted and the U-boat cast off the tow to launch an attack, but the torpedo it fired went haywire. Instead of going straight to its target, it completed a circle, narrowly missing the U-boat itself. So the tanker went on its way, blissfully unaware that it had almost become a victim of the German U-boat campaign.

A couple of days later, on 28 July, *Pinguin* and the U-boat said farewell to each other and went on their respective ways. The raider altered course to south-east to keep roughly midway between the bulges of Africa and South America and crossed the equator. The stage was set for *Pinguin* to go into action and claim her first victim.*

4

When war broke out between Britain and Nazi Germany on 3 September 1939, HMS *Cornwall* was serving on the China Station together with three other cruisers, *Dorsetshire*, *Kent* and *Birmingham*, the aircraft carrier *Eagle*, one division of destroyers, the submarine depot ship *Medway*, and fifteen submarines.

It was a coincidence of fate that the two County Class cruisers *Cornwall* and *Dorsetshire* were together at the start of the war, often during the war and they ended their war service together in tragic circumstances.

A few days before the declaration of war, *Cornwall* was at Shanghai helping to quell disturbances connected with the Sino-Japanese War which had started in July 1937. With the crisis in Europe worsening, the cruiser was ordered to sail at full speed to Hong Kong where she received orders to top up with fuel and carry on to Singapore.

Cornwall filled up with fuel and stores at the naval base at Singapore and stood by ready to sail at a moment's notice. She received orders on 3 September to put to sea at noon local time, which was some hours ahead of Britain's time, so she was at sea when the formal declaration of war was announced.

Orders were received to round up German merchant ships, an operation that entailed much patrolling and being at sea for long spells, sometimes twenty-three days without putting into port. It also meant checking all ships intercepted, including Allied and neutral vessels because German ships were not averse to flying colours that were not their own. A boarding party was always ready to be sent over in a boat to a ship that had been ordered to stop for its identity to be verified.

Cornwall was now attached to the East Indies Station with Colombo

* See Appendix on page 220.

as its base. Within three days of the start of the war, the cruiser intercepted two German ships, *Olinda* and *Carlfritzen*, but when ordered
to stop the crews took to the lifeboats and the freighters were scuttled.

Searches for enemy shipping took *Cornwall* to several groups of
islands – the Nicobar and Andaman Islands in the Bay of Bengal, the
Lacadives on the other side of India, the Maldive Islands south-west
of India and the Seychelles, Amirante and Chagos groups between
India and Madagascar. When weather permitted, the cruiser's little
Walrus flying boats were used for extended searches.

In addition to checking all merchant ships encountered, British ships
had at times to be escorted. Sometimes *Cornwall* operated with the
aircraft carrier *Eagle*. It was tedious but essential wartime service,
during which every opportunity was used to step up the training and
efficiency of the ships' companies. They carried out gunnery drills and
practice shoots, both surface with the main and secondary armament
and anti-aircraft at a sleeve target towed by a plane.

They practised closing up at action stations (on one occasion spending all night closed up), dealing with casualties, breakdowns, fires,
damage and collisions, and carried out night action exercises, once with
Eagle acting as a raider. Every morning there was dawn action stations.

When *Cornwall* arrived at Colombo after a long spell at sea to be
cleaned up and have some defects put right, an old salt remarked : 'The
bottom of the ship must look like a fur coat.'

By the beginning of October it had become apparent that a powerful
German warship was in the South Atlantic. Actually there were two
German pocket battleships at large and they had been sent into the
Atlantic before the declaration of war. The *Admiral Graf Spee* had
sailed from Wilhelmshaven on 21 August 1939, and her sister ship,
Deutschland, had followed three days later.

Pocket battleships had been built by Germany ostensibly to comply
with the Treaty of Versailles after the First World War, which placed
a limit of 10,000 tons on the size of her warships. Actually they exceeded
the limitation by at least 2,000 tons and were particularly powerfully
armed with six 11-inch and eight 5.9-inch guns, plus eight torpedo
tubes.

The two German warships marked time and did not take offensive
action for more than a month, *Deutschland* in the North Atlantic and
Graf Spee in the South Atlantic, because even after the outbreak of war
Hitler hoped that when he had overrun Poland, Britain and France
would agree to make peace.

But towards the end of September, Grand Admiral Raeder, head of the High Command of the German Navy, urged that *Deutschland* and *Graf Spee* should go into action and, with Hitler's agreement, the pocket battleships were ordered on 26 September to attack British shipping. There was, however, some concern about *Deutschland* because of her name (Germany) and the effect on the morale of the German people if she was sunk. So after sinking only two ships on 5 and 14 October in the North Atlantic between the Azores and the United States, *Deutschland* was recalled and renamed *Lützow* on arrival back in Germany on 15 November. She was not used again to attack merchant shipping.

Meanwhile *Graf Spee* had sunk her first victim, the British ship *Clement* (5,051 tons), off Brazil in the South Atlantic on 30 September. When the crew, who were picked up by another ship, landed on the South American coast the next day, they mistakenly identified the raider as *Admiral Scheer*.

This confirmed the Admiralty's suspicion that at least one pocket battleship was at large. The presence of the second one was not known until 21 October when the crew of the Norwegian ship *Lorentz W.* *Hansen*, which had been sunk by *Deutschland* a week earlier 400 miles east of Newfoundland, reached the Orkney Island in another ship that had rescued them.

5

To combat the activities of the powerful German warship raiders, Royal Navy units, augmented by a few French warships, had been formed into hunting groups in different areas. *Cornwall, Dorsetshire* and *Eagle* were designated as Force I to look after the Indian Ocean. The Commanding Officer of *Cornwall*, Captain C. F. Hammill, addressed the ship's company in October and told them there was a good chance of encountering a pocket battleship with superior armament. It was a case of continuing with the tiring routine of long patrols, escorting British ships and searching for German supply ships.

'We are sweeping the entire length of the Indian Ocean as they seem quite sure there is something loafing around,' noted the Chief Yeoman of Signals, E. A. (Sam) Langford. 'We have crossed the line so many times in this war that the bump is hardly noticeable. Haven't had time for any ceremony.'

These efforts were not unrewarded. At the end of October four

German ships were captured south of the Chagos Islands, boarded and sent to Colombo under escort. A fifth ship scuttled herself.

After sinking *Clement*, *Graf Spee* moved eastwards across the South Atlantic, sank four ships and then, as a feint to confuse the Royal Navy, steamed south and round the Cape of Good Hope, passing about 400 miles off Cape Agulhas. She revealed her presence in the Indian Ocean on 15 November by sinking the small tanker *Africa Shell* (706 tons) 160 miles north-east of Lourenco Marques and only ten miles off the Southern African coast. The next day she gave further evidence of her position in the Indian Ocean by stopping a neutral Dutch ship, *Mapia*, in the same area and then returned quickly to the South Atlantic, again giving the Cape a wide berth.

The Royal Navy's Force H (the County Class cruisers *Sussex* and *Shropshire*) and Force K (the battle-cruiser *Renown* and aircraft carrier *Ark Royal*) had patrolled south of the Cape of Good Hope from 28 November to 2 December 1939, to try to intercept *Graf Spee* if she doubled back from the Indian Ocean, but were too late. The raider had already returned to the South Atlantic and on 27 November had a rendezvous in mid-ocean north-east of Tristan da Cunha with the tanker *Altmark*, from which she had refuelled several times during her foray. It was the *Altmark* that became notorious as a prison ship, which carried survivors from British ships captured or sunk by the raiders.

Graf Spee went into action again north-west of Walvis Bay, sinking *Doric Star* (10,086 tons) on 2 December and the *Tairoa* (7,983 tons) the next day. *Doric Star* had managed to send out an RRRR (warship raider) distress signal so the German ship left this area little more than 500 miles from the African coast and sped west. (The QQQQ radio signal to report 'Armed merchantman wishes to stop me' was introduced early in the war by the Admiralty. The signal to report an enemy warship was RRRR and SSSS was used to report a U-boat.) On 7 December *Graf Spee* claimed her ninth and last victim, *Streonshalh* (3,895 tons), which had sailed from the River Plate in South America.

Catching a sea raider may be said to depend on three factors : luck, intelligence reports based on information received from ships attacked, and intelligent anticipation. The interception of *Graf Spee* and the memorable battle that ended her career were due to two of these factors – the report from the *Doric Star* and intelligent anticipation on the part of Commodore H. Harwood, who was in command of Force G which had been assigned to operate off South America. The force consisted of four cruisers, *Exeter*, *Cumberland*, *Ajax* and *Achilles*.

Harwood had always considered that a pocket battleship raider would make for the River Plate area where ships carrying valuable cargoes would be rich prizes. In his despatch he wrote :

The British ship *Doric Star* had reported being attacked by a pocket battleship in position 19 degrees 15 south, 5 degrees 5 east during the afternoon of 2 December 1939, and a similar report had been sent by an unknown vessel (*Tairoa*) 170 miles south-west of that position at 0500 GMT on 3 December.

From this data I estimated that at a cruising speed of 15 knots the raider could reach the Rio de Janeiro focal area a.m. 12 December, the River Plate focal area p.m. 12 December or a.m. 13 December and the Falkland Islands area 14 December.

I decided that the Plate, with its larger number of ships and its very valuable grain and meat trade, was the vital area to be defended.

The most powerful ship under Harwood's command, *Cumberland*, with eight 8-inch guns, was not available immediately as she was refitting in Port Stanley at the Falkland Islands. Flying his broad Commodore's pennant in *Ajax*, he ordered *Exeter* and the New Zealand cruiser *Achilles* to join him, and early on 12 December the three warships were in a position about 150 miles off the entrance to the River Plate.

Harwood had formulated his tactics well in advance for just such an encounter and explained his plans to the captains of the three cruisers. His forecast of the *Graf Spee*'s movements proved to be incredibly accurate. Early on the morning of 13 December while they were steaming in line ahead, with *Ajax* leading *Achilles* and *Exeter*, smoke was sighted. *Exeter* was ordered to investigate at 6.14 a.m. and within a couple of minutes signalled : 'I think it is a pocket battleship.'

The cruisers raced towards the formidable enemy warship. Studying them through his binoculars, the German Commanding Officer, Captain Langsdorff, at first understandably mistook the two smaller cruisers for destroyers. He decided to attack and for a time the two forces were racing towards each other at a closing speed of about 50 knots. *Graf Spee* opened fire with her 11-inch guns at 6.18 a.m. The British ships went into action a couple of minutes later as the range closed rapidly.

In accordance with Harwood's rehearsed tactics, the cruisers split into two forces, *Exeter* turning to port to engage from the south with her six 8-inch guns while the smaller cruisers, *Ajax* and *Achilles*, attacked from the east with their 6-inch armament. This meant that *Graf Spee* had to decide whether to divide her superior guns to attack both divisions at the same time or concentrate on one of them. At first she fired at both divisions, but soon changed and concentrated on *Exeter*. She directed her secondary armament of eight 5.9-inch guns at *Ajax* and *Achilles*.

Exeter suffered serious damage, two of her three turrets being knocked out, her bridge and internal communications wrecked and her speed reduced. By 7.30 a.m. a fire was raging in the ship, she had a heavy list to starboard and had to turn away to effect repairs. She had tried to carry on the fight with only one turret.

Concentrated fire by *Ajax* and *Achilles* plus torpedoes from *Exeter* and *Ajax* had forced *Graf Spee* to seek refuge behind smoke screens more than once, but Commodore Harwood commented : 'We might as well be bombarding her with snowballs.'

Hits by heavy shells put both of *Ajax*'s after turrets out of action and smashed her topmast. *Achilles* was also damaged and Harwood turned away under cover of smoke. He decided at 7.40 a.m. to end the day action and shadow *Graf Spee* until after dark.

But the German raider had by no means escaped unscathed. She had been hit by two eight-inch and 18 six-inch shells, losing one officer and 35 ratings killed and 60 wounded. Firing only occasional salvoes at the pursuing *Ajax* and *Achilles*, she made for the sanctuary of the neutral water at Montevideo in the River Plate where she arrived shortly after midnight.

Exeter, which had fought so valiantly, was limping south to the Falkland Islands to await a decision about repairs. Her casualties were 61 killed and 23 wounded. Churchill reported that she had been hit more than 100 times and had 'fought one of the finest and most resolute actions against superior range and metal on record'.

Ajax (seven killed and fifteen wounded) and *Achilles* (four killed, nine wounded) were on guard just outside neutral waters, ready to resume the action if *Graf Spee* ventured out. They were joined on the evening of 14 December by *Cumberland* which had raced up from the Falklands.

Several other powerful British warships were ordered to make for the River Plate but they could not get there before 19 December. These ships included *Renown* and *Ark Royal* coming from the north, *Dorsetshire* from Cape Town 3,650 miles due east of Montevideo, and a couple of days later *Shropshire*, also from the Cape.

The Captain of *Graf Spee* had successfully applied to the Uruguayan Government for an extension of the 24 hours normally allowed to stay in a neutral port to repair damage, and the deadline was 8 p.m. on

17 December. He had been deceived by false reports put out by the British about the naval reinforcements and believed *Ark Royal* and *Renown* had joined the cruisers waiting off Montevideo. His Gunnery Officer had in fact told him on 15 December that he could see *Renown* from the *Graf Spee*'s control tower!

Time was running out and on 16 December Captain Langsdorff sent a signal to the German Admiralty in which he said that because of the naval blockade off Montevideo, 'escape into open sea and break-through to home waters hopeless'. He proposed to try to fight his way to Buenos Aires in Argentina, on the other bank of the River Plate, but asked whether, if necessary, he should scuttle the warship or allow her to be interned. Hitler and Admiral Raeder agreed to the attempt to break out, but ruled that scuttling would be preferable to internment.

The time for the climax on Sunday evening, 17 December, had come. There had been much activity on board *Graf Spee* and during the afternoon hundreds of men had been transferred from the warship to a German merchant ship in Montevideo harbour. Langsdorff had made his decision. Shortly after 6 p.m. he gave the order to weigh anchor and, watched by a large crowd, the ship moved out of the harbour and steamed slowly down the river, followed by the German vessel *Tacoma*.

The charges had been placed and the remaining crew in the pocket battleship were taken aboard the merchant ship. Suddenly, at 7.56 p.m., the suspense was broken by explosions in *Graf Spee*. One of *Ajax*'s aircraft flew over and reported : '*Graf Spee* has blown herself up.' Not long afterwards *Ajax*, *Achilles* and *Cumberland*, the three cruisers that had maintained the blockade, steamed past the fiery remains of the German raider.

'She was ablaze from end to end, flames reaching almost as high as the top of her control tower, a magnificent and most cheering sight,' wrote Rear-Admiral Harwood in his despatch. (Commodore Henry Harwood had been honoured for the brilliant part he played in the *Graf Spee* action by being promoted immediately to Rear-Admiral and knighted, Knight Commander of the Bath.)

His adversary, Captain Langsdorff, whom Churchill described as 'a high-class person', had an outstanding record. Captain Roskill says in *The War At Sea* : 'It must stand to the credit of Captain Langsdorff that not one British life was lost through his ship's action against defence-less merchantmen.'

The story is told that when a British officer apologised to him for the unruly behaviour of some of the firemen prisoners, Langsdorff smiled and replied : 'Don't worry, I know these Liverpool stiffs.'

But now, humiliated and broken-hearted by the loss of his ship, he wrote on 19 December :

I alone bear the responsibility for scuttling the pocket-battleship *Admiral Graf Spee.* I am happy to pay with my life for any possible reflection on the honour of the flag.

He shot himself that night.

Churchill, who was then First Lord of the Admiralty, was elated by the Battle of the River Plate and wrote :

The effects of the action off the Plate gave intense joy to the British nation and enhanced our prestige throughout the world. The spectacle of the three smaller British ships unhesitatingly attacking and putting to flight their far more heavily gunned and armoured antagonist was everywhere admired. . . . The impression was exhilarating and lightened the dreary and oppressive winter through which we were passing.

6

The Battle of the River Plate and ignominious scuttling of *Graf Spee* had some effect on the movements of *Cornwall. Dorsetshire* had been detached from Force I on 2 December and sailed to Cape Town en route to Britain. Her place had been taken by the cruiser *Gloucester.*

Cornwall, Gloucester and *Eagle* arrived at Durban on 12 December on the eve of the River Plate action. They were due to have a rest at this hospitable South African port. But then the *Graf Spee* crisis blew up, there was a late night recall of those members of the ship's company ashore on leave and *Cornwall* sailed at 2 a.m. full speed on a southerly course. When she reached the south coast, however, she was ordered to return to Durban.

The three ships in Force I were made available to the Commander-in-Chief South Atlantic as a precaution against the possibility of the pocket battleship escaping eastward from the River Plate. A few days after the scuttling of *Graf Spee*, they sailed from Durban. *Cornwall* was ordered to leave Force I and go to Simonstown. She spent Christmas at sea, arriving at Simonstown on 26 December 1939.

The fates were not kind to the four warships that served in Force I. *Gloucester*, which was transferred to the Mediterranean from the East Indies Station in May 1940, was damaged in a surface action against Italian warships off the Calabrian coast on 9 July that year. She was hit by a bomb in an air attack after taking troops to Malta in January 1941, and then sunk with heavy loss of life by German dive-bombers during the defence of Crete a few months later on the afternoon of 22 May. Destroyers searched for survivors that night but found none. The casualties included many South Africans. The aircraft carrier *Eagle*, which was a converted ex-Chilean battleship, also went to the Mediterranean where she was sunk by a U-boat on 11 August 1942. The story of the demise of *Cornwall* and *Dorsetshire* will be told later.

After leaving Force I, *Cornwall* sailed from Simonstown on 2 January 1940, and spent the next month patrolling and escorting convoys and individual ships. During this time she intercepted a German ship, which scuttled herself, and sixty-eight survivors had to be picked up.

She also intercepted a Swedish ship that was reported to have German military and air force personnel on board. After taking nine men and one woman off the ship and landing them at Cape Town, *Cornwall* docked at Simonstown to have her bottom scraped. It was described as being 'inches deep with fur and barnacles'.

Advantage was taken of the fortnight spent at Simonstown to give each watch three days' leave, which was spent on wine farms in the Western Province – a welcome break with warm hospitality away from the sea.

Rested and refreshed, the ship's company faced an arduous three months when *Cornwall* left Simonstown in company with another County Class cruiser, *Cumberland*. Most of the time was spent in tropical heat near the equator, with no shore leave when calling at ports on the west coast of Africa such as Freetown, which was known as 'white man's grave'. Routine daily dawn action stations, patrols, exercises and practice shoots were all part of the monotony of long weeks at sea between Africa and South America.

Early on, a German supply ship that was intercepted carried out the usual routine when ordered to heave to and scuttled herself, which meant that survivors had to be picked up. After *Cumberland* had parted company with *Cornwall* on 16 April, a collier was intercepted and sent to Freetown. Two tankers were captured and taken to Rio de Janeiro and Bermuda with prize crews on board.

It was while patrolling just outside the three-mile neutral limit off Brazil that *Cornwall* was involved in an amusing incident. It was a particularly tedious time patrolling up and down the coast in the hope that enemy ships sheltering in neutral ports might come out and be seized. Every day when the weather was suitable, the Walrus aircraft were catapulted off the ship to carry out reconnaissance flights. The two pilots took turns and one morning Pilot No 1 decided to relieve the monotony of his morning flight by nipping inside the three-mile limit and flying over Pernambuco. When he returned to the ship he told Pilot No 2 that he had clearly seen lovely senoritas, and that they had waved to him.

That was too much for Pilot No 2 who was by way of being a bit of a lady's man. When he took off for his flight, he also went inside the three-mile limit and flew over Pernambuco. But his luck was out. Before he had time to study the female population, he saw a Brazilian fighter plane diving at him.

'He turned and made for *Cornwall* as quickly as he could in the old Walrus with tthe fighter on his tail,' recalled one of the Able Seamen in the cruiser.

He flew round and round the ship, cutting corners in the slow plane and the Brazilian could not stick to him as his fighter was too fast to turn quickly. Our pilot did not look at all happy, but eventually the Brazilian made off and he was able to land alongside the ship and be hoisted inboard. We had all collected on deck to watch the fun and thoroughly enjoyed the incident. I have an idea the Brazilian pilot did, too.

The Chief Yeoman commented : 'Just a playful episode.'

There was another week of patrolling before orders were received to go back to Freetown where the men sweated in the humidity of West Africa for a few days. Then came cheering news. *Cornwall* sailed in company with *Dorsetshire* at 2.30 a.m. on 15 May with orders to 'proceed with all despatch to Gibraltar'. It raised hopes of getting to England at long last.

The two cruisers were escorted through the Straits by destroyers and aircraft and arrived at Gibraltar on the evening of 18 May. It was only a few days short of nine months since *Cornwall* had left the China Station at the outbreak of war and Chief Yeoman Sam Langford remarked : 'We had done the longest trip ever from China to Gibraltar. Usual distance 8,700 miles. Our distance 83,000 miles.'

But hopes of going to England were dashed. *Cornwall* and *Dorsetshire* sailed from Gibraltar at noon a few days later. When they parted

HMS *Cornwall* in Kilindini Creek at Mombasa shortly before sinking the German raider *Pinguin*.

One of HMS *Cornwall*'s Walrus seaplanes landing alongside the cruiser. The warship's two aircraft played an important part in the sinking of the *Pinguin*.

The German raider *Pinguin*, which was sunk by HMS *Cornwall* on 8 May 1941 after being at sea for 328 days as a disguised merchantman.

Pinguin's career ends in a huge explosion, leaving only debris and oil after her encounter with HMS *Cornwall* in the Indian Ocean on 8 May 1941.

company at midnight, however, *Cornwall* had to say a rather envious farewell as *Dorsetshire* was bound for Plymouth and *Cornwall* turned to go south to escort a convoy of troop transports from West Africa.

7

On 15 June 1940, the day *Pinguin* sailed from Gotenhafen to embark on her career as a raider, *Cornwall* was having an uncomfortable time being buffeted by a storm with hurricane force wind while rounding the Cape of Good Hope with the convoy of troopships. The storm blew up on 11 June which happened to be the day after Italy formally entered the war on Germany's side. That night was an ordeal with mountainous seas that did considerable damage on board.

The Chief Yeoman in *Cornwall*, who had long service and experience in different parts of the world, noted on 13 June :

Blew up to strong gale during the night. Terrible seas. Wind 90 miles an hour. Had to heave to in the early morning as we were unable to make any headway. Up to dusk it was still terrible and quite the worst I have ever been in.

Later the ships resumed 'steaming at half speed against the sea to keep going'. On 15 June the Chief Yeoman noted :

Terrible night again. Hurricane doesn't look like easing up. Icy cold and wind in gale force. Everything smashed to hell on the ship. We are now rounding the Cape at slow speed.

The next day :

We are round Port Elizabeth point and are now getting the full force of a south-easterly gale – and what a gale. This will be the seventh day without a rest.

Zigzagging as a precaution against possible submarine attacks, *Cornwall* and the convoy arrived at Durban on 18 June and heard the news that France had capitulated.

Two days later *Cornwall* sailed from Durban with another convoy, which it escorted via Cape Town to Freetown where they topped up with fuel and provisions. She got under way again on the afternoon of 6 July with orders to take the convoy to the United Kingdom. It was 'Home' at last for most men in the cruiser and the next morning the Royal Marine Band cheered them up by playing 'Rolling Home'.

When the raider *Pinguin* hove to south of the Azores on 10 July 1940 to change her disguise to the blue and white of a Greek ship, *Cornwall* was heading north with the convoy. The next day *Pinguin*, coming south, and *Cornwall* passed each other, each unaware of the other's presence in the same latitude in the same ocean, but separated by a few hundred miles.

On the morning of 16 July *Cornwall* left the convoy protected by destroyers, which had come out to provide an anti-submarine screen, and headed at full speed for Liverpool where she arrived that night. The cruiser was due to stay for at least a couple of weeks for degaussing – having a special electric cable fitted round the upper deck as a counter to the magnetic mines used by the Germans. There were also some defects that required urgent attention.

8

It was just a wisp of smoke on the horizon, but *Pinguin*'s masthead lookout spotted it. Soon it was identified as a ship. The previous day the raider had crossed the equator. Now, a few degrees south of the line on the last day of July 1940, the first of her victims, the British ship *Domingo de Larrinaga* (5,358 tons), was in sight.

Pinguin made the necessary alteration to her course and increased speed to overtake the freighter. When it became apparent that she was being chased, *Domingo de Larrinaga* radioed a QQQQ raider report and manned her stern gun. *Pinguin* hoisted her German naval ensign and opened fire, several shells crashing into the merchant ship. The crew took to the lifeboats, leaving four dead on deck. The thirty-two men in the boats, including eight wounded, were taken on board the raider as prisoners.

A boarding party from *Pinguin* placed scuttling charges in *Domingo de Larrinaga*, but they failed to explode and the raider had to use a torpedo to sink her.

It was almost a month before *Pinguin* went into action again. Her captain, Krüder, had been given permission by the operational staff of the High Command German Navy to lay mines off Cape St Francis, near Port Elizabeth on the southern coast of South Africa. He decided not to carry out this operation, however, because *Atlantis*, the first raider to sail from Germany, had already laid ninety-two mines off Cape Agulhas nearer Cape Town.

Instead he set a course round Southern Africa, keeping about 400 miles from the Cape of Good Hope, and then north-east into the Indian Ocean which was to be his main area of operations. By this time *Pinguin* had been at sea for more than two months and the crew were well accustomed to the routine, which was designed to avoid boredom and give them as much comfort and recreation as possible.

The men worked four-hour watches and most of the time wore normal naval uniforms. But when a ship was approached, only a few, not wearing naval uniforms, remained on the upper deck. When they went into action, however, those on deck wore their uniforms.

The facilities on board included a swimming pool, cinema, library, laundry and equipment to make cool drinks and fresh water from sea water. A doctor looked after the crew's health and arrangements were made for a few men at a time to have periodic leave periods of a week during which the only duty they had was if the alarm for action stations was sounded.

The crew helped to pass the time with a variety of activities. They taught one another different hobbies and made such things as presents for the captain's birthday and for Christmas. In addition to radio and musical programmes, sport and various competitions, meetings were held and lessons were given to members of the crew. To help keep up their morale, there were special regular broadcasts from Germany giving domestic news about the men's families. They were thus kept in touch even though operating at sea thousands of miles from home.

Officers and men had the same food. 'Everybody ate out of the same pot,' said Richard Tomczak, a Petty Officer who served in *Pinguin* and gave me information about the raider. He now lives in Cape Town.

Merchant ships' crews taken prisoner were kept locked in rooms below deck, with a constant guard outside. They were 'treated as human beings' and were allowed out twice a day to exercise on deck, the time depending on the number of prisoners and the weather. At one stage the number of prisoners exceeded the number of *Pinguin*'s crew.

One of the raider's seaplanes was lowered over the ship's side on to the water to make its first flight on 26 August when about 300 miles south of Madagascar and due east of Durban. It proved its value in the afternoon by sighting a tanker, the Norwegian *Filefjell* (7,616 tons), about 150 miles away. The tanker was bound for Cape Town from the Persian Gulf with petrol and oil.

This marked the start of a very rewarding 24 hours for *Pinguin*. The pilot of her aircraft dropped a message in English, purporting to come from a Royal Navy ship, telling *Filefjell* to alter course to avoid a German raider! The captain of the Norwegian tanker was not tricked by this ruse and made a radio report about the incident. Later, when it was dark, the aircraft returned to the tanker and forced her with the aid of machine-gun fire to stop and wait until *Pinguin* arrived, put a boarding party on board and captured the ship.

In the early hours of 27 August another tanker, *British Commander* (6,901 tons), which was sailing in ballast, was sighted. It was torpedoed and shelled, but before the radio cabin was put out of action, a raider report was transmitted. The crew joined the other prisoners on board *Pinguin*.

Later that morning *Pinguin* overtook the Norwegian freighter *Morviken* (5,008 tons) and sank her. Soon afterwards another cargo ship was sighted but, because the raider report made by *British Commander* had obviously been received and a warning radioed from Durban, Krüder decided to move out of the area and left the freighter alone. In the evening he gave orders to sink the well-laden *Filefjell*. Scuttling charges and gunfire set the tanker alight and the glow of the flames could still be seen when fifty miles away. Krüder was criticised by the operational staff of the High Command for over-hasty action in destroying the tanker with her valuable cargo of petrol and oil.

The time had come to alter the raider's appearance again. At the end of August, in a position south-east of the sinkings, the disguise of *Pinguin* was changed to resemble the Norwegian ship *Trafalgar*.

The successes were followed by an accident and almost a disaster. Heading north again, *Pinguin* lost one of her aircraft which crashed at take-off and caught fire on 5 September. A week later the British ship *Benavon* (5,872 tons) was intercepted off the south of Madagascar, but instead of submitting meekly, she put up a fight with her single gun on the stern. One of her shells ricocheted off the sea and crashed through the side of the raider but did not explode. If it had, *Pinguin* might well have been destroyed because of the mines she carried. A member of the crew named Streil – now a man in his eighties – picked up the shell and pushed it into the sea through the hole it had made.

Pinguin attacked the *Benavon* with her main armament, causing considerable damage and killing several men. The German boarding party found twenty-eight survivors out of a crew of forty-five, some of whom were wounded.

When the Norwegian ship *Nordvard* (4,111 tons) was captured four days later on 16 September, Krüder put about 200 of his prisoners together with a prize crew on board and sent the ship to a port in France.

9

HMS *Cornwall*'s arrival at Liverpool on 16 July 1940 was the ship's first visit to Britain since before the outbreak of war and the first time many members of the crew had been home for seventeen months. After the spell at Liverpool and being in dry dock at Birkenhead on the opposite shore of the estuary of the Mersey, the cruiser was at sea again early in August. She was southward bound, calling at Freetown on her way to the Cape of Good Hope where she arrived not long after *Pinguin* had passed there en route to the Indian Ocean.

While in South African waters, *Cornwall* was suddenly ordered to go to Freetown as fast as possible to take part in Operation Menace. This operation was sparked by a fear that the Germans would get into the French West African colonies with the consent of the Vichy Government – a move that would be a danger to Allied convoys on the vital route round Africa to the Middle East (hence the code name Operation Menace). It was therefore decided to try to get General De Gaulle's Free French movement installed in Senegal with its important strategic naval base at Dakar.

This involved a lot of naval activity to prevent French warships joining other Vichy naval units at Dakar. *Cornwall* was suddenly sent from Cape Town to help reinforce the naval force taking part in the operation off West Africa. Steaming at an average speed of almost 30 knots, the cruiser travelled 716 miles in a day. After a call of only a few hours at Freetown, she was ordered to search for a French cruiser, *Primauguet*, in the Atlantic. With the help of her Walrus aircraft, the French warship was intercepted and stopped on 19 September by *Cornwall* and the light cruiser, HMS *Delhi*.

Ken Collier, who was then an Able Seaman and communications number in *Cornwall*'s 'A' turret, recalled the tense situation that followed:

We argued with her until two o'clock in the afternoon when we sent her an ultimatum. This was that if she did not turn and come back with us by 4 p.m., we would open fire. At 3.45 p.m. we closed up at action stations and stood by. At 3.55 she had not moved. Then, with only three minutes to go, she got under way and came with us. We were to take her to Casablanca farther north on the African coast to keep her out of mischief and away from the Dakar operation.

This episode was not without an amusing sidelight in retrospect. It involved communications with the TS (Transmitting Station, a gunnery control position a few decks down in the ship) when an exercise was ordered. Collier had been at action stations in the turret for several hours with earphones on to receive and pass on orders :

After the anti-climax of the near action I suppose we were all a bit sleepy. When the order came from the bridge, 'For exercise, for exercise open fire', the TS communications rating must have asked for a couple of repeats before passing the signal on to me. I didn't catch what he said and also asked for a repeat. While this was going on the fire bell sounded off. The captain of the turret had the reflexes of a cat. To him the fire bell without warning of an exercise meant only one thing – open fire! He slammed the interceptors closed and when the director layer pulled the trigger, instead of an innocuous little (exercise) click, 'A' turret erupted in flame and two armour-piercing, high explosive shells weighing 256 pounds each and propelled by 120-odd pounds of cordite were on their way in the direction of *Primauguet*. Where they landed we never found out because the turret's crew was too busy dealing with another 160 pounds of exploding cordite in the shape of the Gunnery Officer.

Fortunately the shells did not hit the French cruiser.

In the words of Captain Roskill in *The War at Sea*, *Primauguet* 'was finally shepherded safely into Casablanca after five days of continuous shadowing and persuasive pressure'. During this shadowing the men in the British cruisers had very little sleep as the guns had to be manned all the time. At one stage the captain of the French warship complained in a signal that *Cornwall* was too close astern of his ship and said he did not like the 'cat and mouse game'. The Commanding Officer of *Cornwall*, Captain Hammill, replied that playing the role of cat was just as distasteful to him as it was for the Frenchman to be the mouse.

Cornwall was involved in another incident after shepherding *Primauguet* when she came across a Vichy French troopship 'taking troops to where we did not want them to go', as Ken Collier said.

We turned her round and at dawn the next day she tried to scuttle herself. I had had the middle watch (midnight to 4 a.m.) and was enjoying my lie in so the first thing I knew about it was when I was bounced out of my hammock and told to fall in with the boarding party.

When I fell in, still half asleep, a revolver was thrust into my hand and I was told to get into the cutter with all speed. The cutter had already been lowered so I had to go down a life-line. With the panic on, there was no time to climb down so I had to slide and, as I had no shoes on, I removed large chunks of my skin on the way down.

By this time the sea was full of boats and rafts crammed with the troops and crew of the scuttled ship. *Cornwall* had to open fire on the bridge with a pom pom to prevent further nonsense. It made a juicy mess of the bridge but fortunately no one was hit.

When the first part of the boarding party started going up the rope ladder, it broke – or was cut – and three of them fell into the sea. Our party got aboard safely and stopped up the sea cocks. The attempt to scuttle the ship had been badly done and water was coming in slowly so there wasn't much trouble. When the situation had been cleared up, we had to fish the crew and troops aboard again. The troops were all black, big and simple. They seemed completely bewildered and hadn't the faintest idea what it was all about. It was pitiful to see them coming up the ladder. A rope ladder isn't too easy to manage at the best of times, and these chaps were obviously terrified at the thought of an involuntary swim. Eventually we got them all aboard, got the ship under way and were escorted to port. With a couple of exceptions, the crew were quite friendly and supplied us with cigarettes and wine.

Incidentally, Operation Menace was a failure but, in any case, the menace it was planned to forestall never materialised because neither German surface raiders nor submarines ever used Dakar as a base of operations against Allied shipping.

After operating in the equatorial heat and humidity off West Africa, the ship's company in *Cornwall* had a marked change of temperature when the cruiser was ordered to go to Greenock and then north of Scotland late in October 1940, to look for the German pocket battleship *Admiral Scheer*. The weather was extremely cold and the seas the worst many of the crew had ever experienced. But when *Admiral Scheer* left Wilhelmshaven on 23 October, she put in at the Norwegian port of Stavanger and stayed there until the 28th before sailing for the North

Atlantic via the Denmark Strait. By that time *Cornwall* was back at
Greenock where she spent a couple of days before setting off south with
a convoy. When she called at Freetown on the way to the Cape, the
temperature had risen 60 degrees in a fortnight.

At Simonstown on 20 November 1940, Captain P. C. W. Manwaring
took over from Captain Hammill as Commanding Officer of *Cornwall*.
He was a well-built, handsome man, rather aloof and known as 'a
tough guy'. His nickname among his fellow officers was Bats because
he did not have much rest at night. He popped up on the bridge at all
hours (to be more specific I should say compass platform, the part of
the bridge where the officer of the watch and look-outs were on duty).
As an Ordinary (later Able) Seaman I recall that Captain Manwaring
invariably appeared, irrespective of whether it was the first watch
(8 p.m. to midnight), middle (midnight to 4 a.m.) or morning (4 a.m.
to 8 a.m.).

The new Captain's first assignment was to escort the convoy on to
Aden and then return to Simonstown where *Cornwall* was due for a
refit.

10

After capturing the *Nordvard* almost midway between South Africa
and Australia on 16 September, *Pinguin* sailed east and then north-east
towards Java, three weeks passing before she got another victim. It was
well worth waiting for because the ship, captured without any trouble
on 7 October, was the Norwegian tanker *Storstad* (8,998 tons), which
was destined to play an important part in mining operations planned
by Krüder. *Pinguin*'s tanks were filled from the 12,000 tons of diesel
oil carried by *Storstad* which had been on her way from Borneo to
Melbourne.

Alterations were made to *Storstad* so that she could be used to lay
mines and her name was changed to *Passat*. Stocked with 110 mines
loaded from the raider, *Passat* set off on 12 October with a prize crew
from the raider plus a few volunteers from her original Norwegian crew
to operate in conjunction with *Pinguin* in Australian waters.

Pinguin got under way the next day and there was rejoicing when a
signal was received announcing that Captain Krüder had been awarded
the Iron Cross of the First Class and that fifty Iron Crosses of the
Second Class were available to be awarded to members of the crew.
Four days later the crew celebrated having travelled 21,600 miles since

leaving Germany – the equivalent of circumnavigating the earth.

Operating separately, *Pinguin* and *Passat* mined the approaches to the more important Australian ports. *Pinguin* operated off Sydney, Newcastle, Hobart (Tasmania) and Adelaide, while *Passat* concentrated on the Bank and Bass Straits between Tasmania and the mainland, these mines covering both the east and west approaches to Melbourne.

It was an audacious operation by the two ships. On the night of 28 October *Pinguin* approached to within two miles of the coast between Newcastle and Sydney, laying mines sometimes in the beam of a lighthouse. While *Passat* was laying mines in the Bass Strait area, an Australian patrol boat steamed round her without becoming suspicious, and a lighthouse which signalled to ask her identity was satisfied when she replied that she was the Norwegian tanker *Storstad*.

By the time both ships had completed the operation early in November, 230 mines had been laid. The ships met at their rendezvous position 800 miles west of Fremantle on 15 November, by which time their mines had claimed a few victims. *Passat*'s mines were responsible for the sinking of the British ship *Cambridge* (10,855 tons) and the *City of Rayville* (5,883 tons), the first United States ship lost in the Second Word War. *Pinguin*'s mines were less successful, claiming only the coaster *Nimbin* (1,052 tons), sunk off Sydney, and *Hertford* (10,923 tons), which was damaged near Adelaide.

The minefields did, however, have considerable nuisance value, necessitating sweeping operations and the closing of the Bass Strait and the port of Melbourne for a week.

Krüder decided not to use *Passat* again for laying mines and she reverted to her proper name of *Storstad*. But he had another job in mind for her, and during the next few weeks she provided extra eyes for *Pinguin*. The two ships sailed on a parallel course about forty miles apart on the Australia–Durban route. *Pinguin* captured the British ship *Nowshera* (7,920 tons) on the night of 17 November and scuttled her the next morning.

Two days later the British refrigerator ship *Maimoa* (10,123 tons) was chased. *Pinguin*'s aircraft was flown off with orders to tear down the merchantman's aerials to prevent her sending a wireless report and to use bombs to stop her. But she ignored the bomb attack, got a signal off on an auxiliary radio set and damaged the aircraft's floats with machine-gun fire. The plane had to ditch in the sea and wait to be picked up after the *Pinguin* had overhauled the *Maimoa* and sunk her.

It was on the night of 21 November that *Pinguin* had a surprise. After opening fire on and sinking the *Port Brisbane* (8,739 tons), it was discovered that among the prisoners taken was a woman wearing a coat over her night attire.

But there was a bigger surprise to come. *Pinguin* and *Storstad* continued on a westerly course and the latter reported sighting another ship on the morning of 30 November. On the grounds that he could presume a darkened ship to be a warship and attack it without warning, Krüder shadowed the vessel and deferred taking action until that night. At 10.30 p.m. he opened fire on the victim, another refrigerator ship, *Port Wellington* (8,301 tons), which caught alight. She burned throughout the night and had to be sunk the next morning. This time the prisoners included seven women passengers. One of them was a very pretty, high-spirited young woman with a ready smile that revealed 'a set of teeth that many a film star might have envied'.

'You're on top for the moment, but you haven't won by a long chalk yet,' she told the captain of *Pinguin*.

Krüder grinned and replied : 'I know. He laughs best who laughs last. Well, we'll see.'

It was reported that the young woman was the daughter of a British general who was one of the other passengers taken prisoner. It transpired, however, that he was a brigadier in the Salvation Army.

Although the women prisoners were an embarrassment to the extent that they had to have separate quarters, the German raider was not unprepared for accommodating them as comfortably as possible. With typical Teutonic thoroughness, *Pinguin* had been prepared for all eventualities. Apart from women's clothing, even a pram was on board in case the prisoners should include a baby.

There was much enthusiasm on 8 December when *Pinguin* had a rendezvous with the raider *Atlantis* almost 1,000 miles south-east of Madagascar. The crews lined the decks and cheered, and the two captains, Krüder and Rogge, took advantage of the opportunity to discuss their experiences and plans. Rogge gave the captain of *Pinguin* valuable charts and books dealing with the whaling areas of the Antarctic which he had acquired when the *Atlantis* captured the tanker *Teddy* on 9 November. *Teddy* had been supply tanker to the whaling fleet in 1939.

Both raiders replenished their fuel tanks from *Storstad*, which was to sail for Bordeaux on the night of 9 December, and also transferred to the tanker hundreds of prisoners. *Pinguin* got rid of 405, including the eight women, and *Atlantis* 124, all of whom arrived safely in France. The two raiders then went their separate ways, *Pinguin* on a southerly course.

11

Christmas Day, 1940 . . . HMS *Cornwall* was on a southerly course in the Mozambique Channel. It was a typical midsummer's day, the heat and humidity relieved only by the slight breeze made by the ship as she sliced her way through the calm tropical sea at a moderate, fuel-conserving cruising speed.

Not only those on watch had been up early (the morning watch had been on duty since 4 a.m.). The rest of the ship's company had been called as usual to dawn action stations. There could be no relaxing precautions, even on Christmas Day. They had been awakened while it was still dark with the call over the public address system to 'lash up and stow'. A few minutes later the bo'sun's mate piped : 'Hands to dawn action stations.'

There was the usual feeling of urgency as the men hurriedly responded to this order. And so they exchanged festive greetings while closed up at their action stations. 'Merry Christmas, mate', was heard all over the warship.

Those in exposed positions up top felt the slight chill that heralds the break of a new day. The rim of the sun appeared over the horizon. It seemed to come quickly out of the sea, its rays streaking across the calm water in the wide channel between Madagascar and Africa. Daylight took over from the dark hours. No ships were in sight. It was all quiet on this front on that Wednesday in December 1940, so the 'secure' was sounded and the ship's company reverted to cruising stations. Those not on watch hurried to the bathrooms to have a quick wash before falling in to carry out the routine work on board before going to breakfast.

There was a cheerful mood in *Cornwall*. Despite the overlaying damper of being at war and at sea, the spirit of Christmas pervaded the ship. The Captain would go on his customary Christmas Day rounds visiting all the messes and messdecks, there would be a special Christmas dinner . . . and the next day *Cornwall*, which had left Aden on 19 December, would arrive at Durban. Two days later, on Saturday, 28 December, she would dock at Simonstown, the popular naval base, to undergo a much-needed refit after steaming more than 100,000 miles since war had broken out just short of sixteen months earlier. The ship would remain at Simonstown in the warm summer sunshine for two months, which meant plenty of 'runs ashore' in Cape Town, which was little more than an hour's journey in an electric train from the naval base, 'Snoekie', and Cape Town ensured a lot of enjoyment for the ship's company – the next best thing, the British matelots said, 'to going home to the UK'.

It was also midsummer where *Pinguin* was spending Christmas with the ship's company being given a rest period of a few days by Captain Krüder. But in sharp and bitter contrast to the midsummer heat men in *Cornwall* were enjoying, dressed in tropical rig shorts, the Germans in the raider were muffled up in freezing weather. Instead of being fascinated by flying fish skimming the swells in the tropics as they got out of the way of the ship's bows, the Germans were watching icebergs. They celebrated Christmas in the polar sea about 2,000 miles due south of *Cornwall*. Although in the same midsummer season in the southern hemisphere, they seemed to be in a different world of grey sea, ice and snow.

After the meeting with *Atlantis* early in December, *Pinguin* had sailed on a south-westerly course for a few days and then headed due south, the days getting colder and colder. The ship entered the polar sea in mid-December and, with the temperature dropping to freezing point, the crew soon saw hundreds of icebergs.

Pinguin kept on its due south course until 19 December when she was almost 65 degrees from the equator and little more than 100 miles from the Antarctic Circle. Krüder then ordered a change of course to north-west. The previous day he had received a radio signal from Germany giving the approximate position of where a Norwegian whaling fleet was operating for the British. While on the new course, *Pinguin* encountered huge icebergs, Krüder noting that some of them were 'gigantic Table Mountains 900 metres long and 50 metres high'. It was during this prelude to surprising the whaling fleet, which must have felt safe so far south, that the men in *Pinguin* had their Christmas dinner and for the first time saw real penguins on the floes.

12

During the last week in December *Pinguin* heard radio telephone conversations in Norwegian from which Krüder learnt that the two factory ships, *Ole Wegger* (12,201 tons) and *Pelagos* (12,083 tons), were operating with six and seven whale-catchers respectively. Krüder did not want *Pinguin* to be seen by any of the catchers otherwise his chances of capturing the factory ships would be jeopardised.

His luck held and he started 1941 with a New Year's Day present when *Pelagos* broadcast her position about 150 miles away. He also learnt that the whaling fleets were awaiting the arrival of a tanker, and decided to wait until it arrived before going into action. During a snowstorm on 8 January he overheard on the radio that the supply tanker *Solglimt* (12,246 tons) was expected to rendezvous with *Ole Wegger* four days later.

Krüder planned to capture the two big ships while they were alongside each other and waited until the night of 13 January before closing on them through fields of floating ice. Aided by the bright lights illuminating the work on the two ships, he sighted them at 11.15 p.m. and, under cover of a snow squall, approached unseen. Shortly after midnight, as the weather cleared, *Pinguin*'s searchlight was suddenly trained on the two ships alongside each other, her boats carrying boarding parties were lowered and a signal flashed : 'Do not use wireless or telephone. We are sending boats.'

The ships were taken completely by surprise, there was no resistance and within twenty-five minutes they were in German hands. Four of *Ole Wegger*'s catchers were also captured, the other two escaping among the icebergs. It was a valuable haul. *Ole Wegger* was laden with 7,000 tons of whale oil and 5,500 tons of fuel oil, while *Solglimt* had 4,000 tons of whale oil and 4,000 tons of fuel.

The next night *Pinguin* added to her haul when she pounced on *Pelagos* and captured her in the same manner. The Captain was ordered to recall his seven catchers by radio and all of them were also seized. *Pelagos* was carrying 9,500 tons of whale oil and 800 tons of fuel.

The success of these slick operations in the Antarctic gave the raider a problem because she did not have sufficient prize crews to take the whaling fleets to a French port. Krüder had to ask headquarters in Germany to arrange for more prize crews, but as the radio message would almost certainly reveal to the British the presence of a German ship, he decided as a feint to make the signal from a position 500 miles north-west of where he had captured the ships. While *Pinguin* steamed north-west, the whaling fleets were sent to a rendezvous position farther south.

After sending the signal, *Pinguin* was delayed by bad weather and missed the prize ships on her return to the south. She continued going south into the Antarctic Circle, reaching the Ice Barrier just short of the 70th parallel before turning back and finding the ships on 25 January. The next day *Pelagos* and *Solglimt* were sent off to Bordeaux where they arrived safely in March.

Ole Wegger and eleven whale catchers, escorted by *Pinguin*, arrived

at a raiders' rendezvous area code-named Andalusien in mid-South
Atlantic (25 S 19 W) between South Africa and South America on
15 February. While at Andalusien, *Pinguin* met the German supply
ship *Nordmark*, which arrived towing the British refrigerator ship
Duquesa (8,651 tons). The coal-burning *Duquesa* had been captured
by the pocket battleship *Admiral Scheer* between Freetown and South
America on 18 December, but had run out of fuel.

One thing the refrigerator ship was not short of was eggs. *Pinguin*
topped up with provisions from her, taking 360,000 eggs in 1,000 cases
and 17 bags of oxtail. To add to the raider's joy, another German
supply ship, *Alstertor*, arrived with bags of mail as well as prize crews.

At one time there were sixteen ships at Andalusien, but they soon
dispersed. Prize crews from *Duquesa* were put on board *Ole Wegger*
and ten of the eleven whale-catchers, which were dispatched to Bordeaux, all but two of the catchers arriving safely. *Duquesa*, still well
stocked with eggs and other provisions, was then scuttled. The eleventh
catcher was renamed *Adjutant* to be used as a reconnaissance ship.

Pinguin, *Adjutant* and *Alstertor* got under way for Kerguelen
Island, between Africa and Australia in the south of the Indian Ocean,
but a couple of days later *Pinguin* was diverted north. She received
orders from Germany to rendezvous with *Kormoran*, the latest raider
to leave Germany, in a position about 1,000 miles off the coast of South-
West Africa between Luderitz and Walvis Bay. The captain of *Pinguin*
was to pass on advice about mining and help with repairs to *Kormoran*'s
engines, which had been giving serious trouble.

The two raiders met on 25 February, the day on which *Cornwall*
started trials in False Bay in preparation for sailing after her long refit
at Simonstown. The next day *Pinguin* left *Kormoran*, which was later
to be involved in one of the grimmest raider dramas of the war. *Pinguin*
resumed the course that was to take her round the Cape of Good Hope
to Kerguelen Island.

Meanwhile the pocket battleship *Admiral Scheer*, which had operated against shipping in the North and South Atlantic in November and
December, swept round wide of the Cape into the Indian Ocean in
February. She captured one and sank three ships north of Madagascar,
two of which managed to make RRRR raider signals, one of them
adding : 'Battle-cruiser chasing.'

The pocket battleship was sighted by an aircraft from the cruiser
HMS *Glasgow*, which was then ninety miles away. Although the
Commanding Officer of *Admiral Scheer*, Captain Krancke, did not

think the plane had seen his ship because it did not break radio silence to make a report, he decided to leave the Indian Ocean as quickly as possible. He managed to escape and passed south of Cape Town late on 2 March.

With *Pinguin* steaming south-easterly to pass the Cape, *Admiral Scheer* going north-westerly and *Cornwall* heading west from Simonstown, fate was beginning to set converging courses.

13

Soon after *Cornwall* sailed from Simonstown on the morning of Friday, 28 February 1941 – exactly two months after she had arrived at the naval base at the Cape to dock for a long refit – it was announced over the public address system that the cruiser was to search for a German raider in the South Atlantic. If at that moment a look-out on *Cornwall's* bridge could have had a telescope capable of seeing 900 miles and pointed it directly ahead, he would almost certainly have seen *Pinguin.*

This has become evident as a result of studying the track chart of the raider that became available only after the war. *Cornwall* was sailing west and would cross the course of the *Pinguin*, which was steaming south-east on her way back to the Indian Ocean. At that moment on 28 February *Pinguin's* position was just about where the two ships' courses would intersect. If *Cornwall* had sailed a couple of days earlier, she would most probably have encountered the raider that was to play a fateful part in her career. Instead *Pinguin* slipped past the Cape undetected and continued on her course to Kerguelen Island.

In terms of sea warfare at that time, and considering the vast expanse of the oceans, it could be rated as a comparatively near miss, especially as *Cornwall* had two Walrus aircraft that were used for extended reconnaissance in favourable weather conditions. These aircraft were later to have a vital role in the *Cornwall* versus *Pinguin* drama.

All this is known now. But when *Cornwall* sailed from Simonstown one heard the lament on the lower deck : 'Just another bloody patrol.' The ship had spent many weeks and months steaming thousands of miles on patrols, day after day seeing nothing but the sea.

It was while on watch as a look-out on patrols that I could not help singing in my thoughts the Irving Berlin song that Fred Astaire sang in the 1936 film *Follow the Fleet* :

> We joined the Navy to see the world,
> And what did we see? We saw the sea.

At the end of Sunday church parade on the quarterdeck two days after starting the patrol from Simonstown, the Commanding Officer, Captain Manwaring, addressed the ship's company and referred to the importance of having dawn action stations. He told us that a powerful German warship – probably a pocket battleship – and a strongly armed converted merchant ship were at large and, if we were lucky, we might find one of them. Later in the day we learnt that we had reached the area in which a German raider was known to have been recently. The look-outs were told to keep their eyes skinned. I was on watch as a look-out at this time and cannot help smiling when I recall the peculiar tricks imagination played. Magnified by the strong binoculars, swells on the horizon sometimes resembled warships.

Radio-direction finding, which was known by the abbreviation D/F, helped in getting information about enemy ships, particularly raiders. The latter reported by radio from time to time to the operational staff of the High Command of the Navy in Germany. Even though their messages could not be decoded, when they were intercepted by more than one Allied shore station it was possible, by taking bearings, to determine the position of the ship making the signal. This would be indicated by where the lines of two or more bearings intersected. But, of course, the enemy ship did not remain in the position from which she made the signal and it was not known in which direction she might be sailing. In any case, there was not always a warship available nearby to send to the area in which the enemy ship was known to have been when she used her wireless.

Those of us who had only recently joined *Cornwall* during the cruiser's refit at Simonstown did not have long to wait for our first taste of wartime excitement, even if it was only a light appetiser. On the day after the Sunday service, while having breakfast, I heard that a ship had been sighted and went up on the upper deck to join those off duty who were watching the fun. *Cornwall* was heading towards the ship, a passenger vessel, which ignored a signal telling her to stop. More signals were flashed, but the ship did not respond and continued

(Left) Members of HMS
Cornwall's crew gather on
the foc's'le after sinking the
German raider Pinguin. The
men bending over the
guardrail are looking at the
hole blown in Cornwall's
starboard side by a shell
from the raider.

(Below) The last shell fired
by Pinguin falls short
seconds after the German
ship had been blown up by
a salvo from HMS Cornwall.

Boats from HMS *Cornwall* pick up survivors among the debris which was all that remained to show where the German raider *Pinguin* blew up.

Photograph of a painting by Nils Andersen of survivors being picked up after the sinking of the German raider *Pinguin* by HMS *Cornwall* on 8 May 1941.

on her southerly course. By this time our 4-inch and pom pom guns had been manned and a blank 4-inch shell was fired to impress on the ship's captain that *Cornwall* meant business. He took the hint, stopped the ship and a boarding party under the command of Lieutenant-Commander J. S. Milner was sent across in a cutter.

The vessel we had intercepted was the Vichy French passenger ship *Ville de Majunga*, which was carrying black troops with white officers and was bound for Madagascar. Its destination was changed quickly. The boarding party had taken over the ship and a signal from the Captain of *Cornwall* told Milner to take the Vichy vessel to Simonstown. The French officers were not co-operative and the only charts on board were French ones which were of no use. Anyway, Milner got the ship under way on a course to Simonstown, and *Cornwall* resumed her westward patrol.

On arrival at Simonstown, Milner made a signal to the naval base identifying the *Ville de Majunga* and was promptly told to take the captured ship to Cape Town. Again he had the problem of not having charts. On the way from False Bay round Cape Point to Cape Town, a launch came out and expressed annoyance because the ship was not in the channel swept by minesweepers. The answer was that Milner and his boarding party did not know the position of the channel.

The ship was taken safely to Cape Town and became part of the Allies' merchant fleet – a useful acquisition at a time when U-boats were taking a heavy toll of merchant shipping and any additional vessel was most welcome. It is strange that the interception and capture of the *Ville de Majunga* does not seem to be mentioned in any of the official or unofficial histories of the war at sea. The only reference I could find to the ship was the fact that nearly two years after she was captured, she ran aground a few miles from Cape Town on 6 December 1942. Fortunately tugs managed to get her off at high tide.

After handing over the *Ville de Majunga* at Cape Town, Milner and the rest of his boarding party went to the Royal Navy base at Simonstown to be kitted out as they had only the clothing they were wearing when they boarded the Vichy French ship. Later they were sent by train to Durban where they rejoined *Cornwall*.

When *Cornwall*'s Captain addressed the ship's company on the Sunday, 2 March, we did not know how close we were to come to meeting the pocket battleship *Admiral Scheer*, which was on her homeward bound north-west course after rounding the Cape. We crossed the German warship's track not once but twice – first as we continued steaming west after intercepting the *Ville de Majunga*, and then again

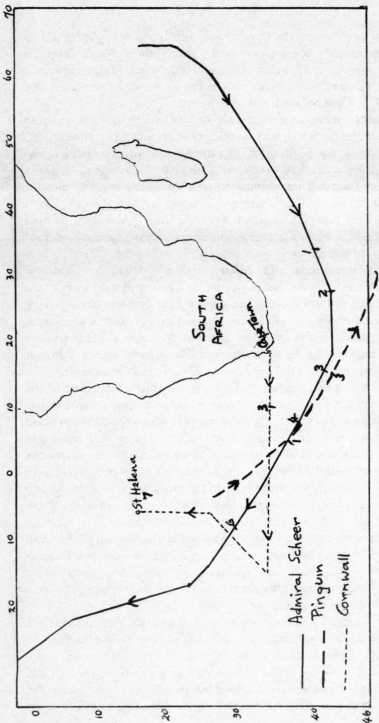

The converging courses of the German raider Pinguin, pocket battleship Admiral Scheer, and HMS Cornwall off the Cape of Good Hope early in March 1941. The figures give the dates on which the ships were at the various positions. Cornwall, which sailed from Simonstown on 28 February and captured the Vichy French ship Ville de Majunga, on 3 March, crossed Pinguin's track a couple of days after the raider sailed round the Cape. The British cruiser must have come very close to meeting Admiral Scheer, crossing her track twice.

when we changed course to north-east. Track charts show that this must have been a close shave and a lucky break for *Cornwall*, whose 8-inch armament could not have matched the more powerful pocket battleship with 11-inch guns.

But we steamed on blissfully unaware of how close we had been to an encounter that could have resulted in the end of *Cornwall*'s career. After carrying out the patrol without finding either *Pinguin* or *Admiral Scheer*, *Cornwall* was ordered to go north and we heard that we were bound for the island of St Helena.

Before arriving at the island, however, the monotony of seeing only the sea was broken unexpectedly one afternoon. Those of us off watch – we worked one in four while keeping ordinary sea watches – were resting after dinner when suddenly it was piped that a suspicious vessel had been sighted and that the hands would be required to go to action stations in five minutes' time.

There was an air of expectancy. Everyone dashed around collecting their gas masks and lifebelts and made their way to their various stations even before the 'action stations' buzzer was sounded. Deep down in the ship in one of the cordite handling rooms, which was my action station at the time, was not exactly a cheerful place. The proximity to the very powerful explosive seemed to depress people and engender morbid conversation, while the rather sickly smell of the cordite soon gave one a headache. On one side of the confined space was the ship's side which was not very thick in County Class cruisers. On the inside was the magazine. The only link with the handling room was a small hatch which was opened momentarily to pass the long round pieces of cordite for the 8-inch guns and then quickly closed. The cordite was placed in a cage that took it up to the gun turret and we were ready to go into action.

Then came the anti-climax. The 'secure' was sounded – the order to fall out from action stations – and it was announced that the suspicious vessel had turned out to be a British merchant ship. It was not an uncommon occurrence, but tardiness by merchant vessels in identifying themselves was understandable because of the German warships and raiders that were at large. It was a relief after the sickly atmosphere of the cordite handling room to get up top on the upper deck and breathe some fresh air while watching the 'suspicious' ship pass by fairly close to *Cornwall*.

By the next day we had left the green and rather turbulent water of the southern ocean and in the afternoon were sailing in a calm blue sea when St Helena was sighted. One's first impression of the island was of a rock rising sheer out of the sea – and that just about sums it up even when seen from closer after *Cornwall* had anchored in the rather exposed harbour. No wonder it was chosen for Napoleon's exile. The dull reddish-brown cliffs rose almost perpendicularly from the sea. Jamestown, with its green trees and white buildings, stood out in bold relief on the foreshore at the end of a narrow valley between two sheer cliffs. Perched on top of one of the cliffs were the Royal Marine barracks and leading up to them the famous Jacob's Ladder with its 699 steps. The so-called ladder, 923 feet long and 620 feet high, was built on the face of the cliff.

It was frustrating not being able to go ashore. Although very little vegetation could be seen from the harbour, we learnt that inland the island was pretty, with woods, meadows and streams. And, of course, there was the historical interest in the house in which Napoleon lived and his grave. Some of the islanders who came alongside *Cornwall*'s gangway in their boats were allowed to come aboard to sell their wares, mostly articles made of beans. They were fascinating people, in appearance similar to the light brown Cape Coloureds in South Africa. But in sharp contrast to the accent of the Afrikaans-speaking Cape Coloureds, they spoke with a marked English accent; in fact were inclined to 'put it on' and the womenfolk addressed everyone as 'My dear'.

That night the film *The Great Waltz* was shown on the hangar deck, but my luck was out. I was in the duty watch from 8 p.m. to midnight and, instead of enjoying the lovely Strauss music in the film, spent a very uncomfortable 2½ hours as one of the crew of *Cornwall*'s cutter. The cruiser had anchored near a tanker from which she refuelled, and the cutter had to ply to and from the tanker carrying empty oil drums. The sea had become choppy and the boat pitched and tossed furiously. What with the motion of the cutter and the nauseating smell from the oil drums, I felt seasick for the first time since joining the Navy. I only just managed to hold out and walked up the gangway with rubbery legs when our stint in the cutter ended and I had to go up to the bridge to spend the last hour of the watch as a look-out.

Late the next afternoon *Cornwall* weighed anchor and sailed on a northerly course. That night I had just settled in my hammock when it was piped that an aircraft from the battleship HMS *Malaya* had sighted the two German battle-cruisers *Scharnhorst* and *Gneisenau* between Gibraltar and Freetown, the direction in which we were heading. It was not exactly the sort of bedtime story conducive to a peaceful night's sleep. A short while earlier in February the German 8-inch cruiser *Admiral Hipper*, had sunk seven ships, totalling 32,806 tons, in an unescorted convoy from Freetown before retiring to the French port of Brest. We should have been even more disturbed if we had known that the *Admiral Scheer*, after a rendezvous with a supply ship from which she replenished in the mid-South Atlantic, was coming up astern of *Cornwall* on our port side on her way to the North Atlantic.

The danger north of us dissipated when it became known that *Scharnhorst* and *Gneisenau* had also retired to Brest. They had accounted for twenty-two ships totalling 115,622 tons. *Gneisenau* was damaged in a Royal Air Force bombing raid on Brest in April.

The *Admiral Scheer*, which had set out from Stavanger in Norway on 28 October 1940, completed a successful five-month cruise covering the North and South Atlantic and a sortie into the Indian Ocean when she arrived at the sanctuary of the Norwegian port of Bergen on 30 March 1941. During this time the German pocket battleship sailed 46,419 miles, sank or captured sixteen merchant ships (99,059 tons) as well as sinking the armed merchant cruiser *Jervis Bay*. Five of the merchant ships were in a convoy defended with outstanding gallantry against vastly superior odds by the *Jervis Bay*, whose Commanding Officer, Captain E. S. F. Fegen, was posthumously awarded the Victoria Cross.

Cornwall continued sailing north and on the morning of 11 March crossed the equator. Early that afternoon a forest of masts appeared on the horizon ahead of us. Gradually they became ships, more and more of them until we could see a fleet of thirty-two merchant ships escorted by two cruisers, HMS *Birmingham* and HMS *Phoebe*. It was a large southbound convoy that was to be *Cornwall*'s responsibility for a long way and a long time. *Cornwall* did a 180-degree turn and, as senior escorting warship, took up station at the head of the convoy.

There was not a breath of wind and the calm, deep-blue tropical sea helped to make the large convoy a picturesque and impressive sight as it steamed in lines astern of *Cornwall*. Among the thirty-two merchant ships were old cargo vessels, large passenger liners, a couple of intermediate Union-Castle ships and a proper troop transport built especially for this wartime work. A number of the ships were crammed with troops bound for the Middle East to take part in the North African desert warfare. Others carried stores and machines. A railway engine and truck were secured on the deck of one ship, motor torpedo boats on another while tanks and armoured cars could be seen on others. It was obviously an extremely valuable convoy in terms of men and material and had to be protected at all costs.

Escorting the convoy was welcomed as a break from the monotony of patrolling on our own and seeing only the sea day after day. As a look-out one could study the ships as well as just the sea as far as the horizon. But there were disadvantages, too, and one soon learnt that being a convoy escort could become very tedious. The speed of a convoy was limited to the speed of the slowest ship and the speed of the slowest ship in that big convoy was *very* slow. There were times when it seemed that we were just drifting along in a slow-moving current.

So the glamorous gloss of the convoy soon wore off and, as we followed a zigzag course, we wished we could get a move on and finish the job of delivering the ships safely to their destination. The convoy had to be 'mothered' all the time. At night the task of those on duty on the bridge, including look-outs, was made more arduous because they had to keep a keen eye on the merchant ships lest any of them lagged behind and became lost.

In the evenings as the sun was setting, *Cornwall* sped ahead and made a wide sweep to ensure that no raiders were lurking nearby, and also to check later that all the ships in the convoy were properly blacked out with no lights showing. We looked forward to this precautionary measure because it meant cracking on some speed which gave us a bit of breeze. Similarly when any other ships were sighted during the day, we raced ahead to investigate and make sure that they were friendly.

Day after day, as we sailed slowly down the west coast of Africa, we sweated in the humid tropical heat. We lower deck ratings wore only a pair of shorts, shoes and cap. During the day the sun beat down relentlessly. After sunset, when the ship was darkened and all the portholes sealed, the heat became almost unbearable in the decks below. Lying in one's hammock, it was difficult at times to get to sleep as a result of the irritation of perspiration trickling down one's body. Even on watch in the open up top at night we remained almost naked.

It was a relief when we ran into cool weather as we approached the Cape of Good Hope. The cruiser *Birmingham* left us as we rounded the Cape and we sailed on with the convoy to Durban where we arrived on 26 March for a few days' breather before carrying on up the east coast of Africa. After twenty-seven days at sea, sixteen of them with the convoy in trying conditions, it was a tonic to be able to step on land again and, above all, to receive mail from home. The ship's company made the most of the opportunity to go ashore and enjoy the hospitality of the people of Durban. One day when I was in the duty watch and could not go ashore, I sat in the sun on deck and lazily studied the libertymen as they went down the gangway to the quayside. Some of them were met by people with motor-cars, but one of our Royal Marines was met by two young women on bicycles. The next minute I noticed a third bicycle. The Marine mounted it and rode off with the two women. Later I met the Marine, who was known as Jock, and he told me he had bought the bicycle on arrival at Durban and sold it a few days later.

During *Cornwall*'s sojourn at Durban an announcement was made over the public address system : 'Captain's requestmen fall in.' An old hand who had twelve years' service in the Navy explained to me : 'If you want to see the Captain about something, you first have to give the Chief Petty Officer of your division a written request applying to see the Captain. This request then goes to the Divisional Officer, who decides whether it is worth passing on for consideration by more senior officers. If he decides it is, it goes to the Commander and, if he approves, it goes to the Captain and one becomes a Captain's requestman. But that does not mean you see the Captain in private. Oh, no, there is a big turn-out when the Captain sees requestmen. Those present include the Commander, all the Divisional Officers, the Captain's secretary, the Master at Arms and the Regulating Petty Officer.'

The old hand smiled and added : 'There is more red tape in the Navy than there are red flags in Russia !'

14

While *Cornwall* was sweating in tropical heat with the big convoy off West Africa, *Pinguin*'s crew had donned winter uniforms again because they were 50 degrees south of the equator. After sailing south-east past South Africa, the raider had turned east and on 11 March, the day *Cornwall* joined the convoy, she sighted Kerguelen Island about 4,000 miles due south of India. She had joined up again with the supply ship *Alstertor* and the captured whale-catcher *Adjutant*, which had gone on ahead together after the rendezvous at Andalusien. The next day they met the raider *Komet* 120 miles east of Kerguelen. In bad weather the four ships sailed to Kerguelen and anchored in a sheltered bay on 13 March. After taking on supplies from the *Alstertor*, *Komet* left the following day to operate west of Australia.

During a twelve-day stay at Kerguelen, *Adjutant* was converted for use as a minelayer and *Pinguin* took on supplies brought by *Alstertor*, including a new aircraft, ammunition, torpedoes and provisions. The raider's engines were overhauled and the ship was careened to clean her hull. At the same time she was repainted yet again, this time grey to look like the Norwegian ship *Tamerlane*. It was to be her last disguise.

With some ingenuity, advantage was also taken of the opportunity to replenish the ship's supply of fresh water from a stream that flowed from the high ground on the island down to the shore. A pipe was laid from the stream to *Pinguin*'s boats which were filled with water and then towed back to the raider which pumped the water aboard. In this way 900 tons of fresh water were taken aboard.

The members of the crew were allowed to go ashore to stretch their legs and shoot rabbits which abounded on the island. With typical thoroughness, great care was taken to ensure that they left no evidence of their visit. Then, replenished, refitted and repainted, *Pinguin* weighed anchor on 25 March – the day before *Cornwall* arrived at Durban with the convoy – and sailed north with *Adjutant* to resume operations against Allied shipping. *Alstertor* left to rendezvous with the raider *Orion* about 1,100 miles east of Mauritius.

Using *Adjutant* for reconnaissance, the Captain of *Pinguin* hoped to intercept ships on the route between Australia and South Africa which had earlier been a rewarding area, but this time he searched in vain. Flights by the raider's aircraft did not help. There were no ships to be seen. On 1 April, the day *Cornwall* sailed from Durban to resume her voyage with the northbound convoy, *Pinguin* was in the middle of the Indian Ocean due east of the South African port and sailing on a northerly course. She was due to have an arranged rendezvous the next day with two tankers, *Ole Jacob* and *Ketty Brövig*. *Ketty Brövig*, a Norwegian ship, had been captured by the raider *Atlantis*, and naval headquarters in Germany had ordered that she should be used to assist in mining Indian ports, chiefly Karachi.

When *Pinguin* and *Adjutant* arrived at the appointed position, however, only *Ole Jacob* appeared. *Pinguin* took about 1,300 tons of diesel fuel from *Ole Jacob* and set off to spend some days searching for the *Ketty Brövig*. When no trace of the tanker had been found by 13 April, it was accepted that she had been lost. (She had in fact been scuttled on 4 March after being sighted by an aircraft from the Australian cruiser *Canberra*.)

Encouraged by the successful use of the tanker renamed *Passat* for mining operations off Australia late in 1940, *Pinguin*'s Captain, Krüder, decided to try to capture one for use as a mine-layer around India. Accompanied by *Adjutant*, he searched east of the Seychelles but did not find any ships, and moved even farther north in the last week in April to try his luck on the India–Mozambique Channel route.

This helped to bring the raider on course to nemesis.

15

Cornwall's departure from Durban on the morning of 1 April engraved itself in my mind as an example of the glamour of the Navy, particularly in times of war. When a ship entered or left harbour, there was always a certain amount of ceremony which aroused an emotional response. The ship's company was dressed in blue or white uniforms, depending on the weather, and fell in smartly in the different parts of ship – the men in the Forecastle Division on the foc's'le, the Topmen amidships and the Quarterdeck Division on the quarterdeck with the Royal Marine Band which played stirring music.

Durban harbour in the Bay of Natal is like an inland sea with a fairly narrow opening to the Indian Ocean at the Bluff. *Cornwall* was berthed at Maydon Wharf, well up the harbour which was a restricted area during the war and thus not open to the general public. But there were several people on the quayside as the warship drew slowly away. They waved and some of the women blew kisses. Girls working at a canteen on the wharf came out on to the front steps and waved handkerchiefs. A woman taxi-driver jumped into her car and drove slowly abreast of the ship along the road running close to Maydon Wharf, waving all the time. A merchant ship dipped its red ensign in salute as we passed and its crew clapped. When we passed a naval ship flying the white ensign, we were called to attention. HM ships always salute each other.

As *Cornwall* approached the exit to the harbour, the Royal Marine Band struck up with the music of the popular South African song, 'Sarie Marais'. A group of people at a vantage point waved frantically and cheered. We passed the Bluff and sailed out to sea alongside a breakwater. The driver of a railway engine on the breakwater gave two blasts on his whistle as a farewell gesture and cheerily waved an empty beer bottle.

It was all very stirring. In the Navy it was called 'flannel', but we were soon out in the roadstead and back to the usual sea routine. The convoy we had escorted from West Africa was already formed up and we set off north accompanied by another cruiser, HMS *Phoebe.* Our destination was obviously Aden and within a couple of days we were sweating again in the tropics as we sailed up the Mozambique Channel between Mozambique and Madagascar. On the fourth day out from Durban a man fell overboard from one of the ships in the convoy, but was picked up none the worse for his ducking. It was a very hot day and a wag in *Cornwall* said : 'I'll bet he jumped overboard on purpose to cool off.' But in the evening some days later a young soldier fell overboard from a troopship in the convoy and was lost. The chances of finding him in the darkness were nil. The convoy was blacked out and sailed in complete darkness.

We had an entertaining interlude on the Sunday afternoon six days after leaving Durban. *Cornwall* sailed up and down the lines of the convoy while the Royal Marine Band, boosted by specially rigged loudspeakers, provided a programme of light music to relieve the monotony of the long voyage and keep up the spirits of the crews and troops in the ships. The sailors and soldiers on board the merchant ships cheered lustily as we passed, while those of us off watch lined the decks of *Cornwall* and waved and whistled to them. The Captain stood on the bridge and waved his cap to the ships. He obviously enjoyed the interlude and repeated it the following Sunday.

The cruiser *Phoebe* had left us on 7 April and we carried on alone with the convoy. Two days later we heard that a raider had been reported a few hundred miles east of us. It was no doubt *Pinguin* which was also on a northerly course in the Indian Ocean. The next day we crossed the equator and were joined by another cruiser, HMS *Glasgow*, which helped to escort the convoy for a few days until past what was the dangerous area. A couple of ships we sighted apparently did not identify themselves satisfactorily and boarding parties were sent across to them. Their papers were, however, in order and they were allowed to carry on.

Two weeks after leaving Durban we rounded the 'horn' of Africa at Cape Guardafui and turned west into the Gulf of Aden. The next day, as the sun was setting, we passed the island of Perim and led the convoy through the narrow entrance to the Red Sea which was very blue. It was an impressive spectacle with the ships formed into two long columns. Land was in sight on both sides, Africa on the left and Arabia on the right. The Italians had been cleaned up in Abyssinia and the Red Sea was now a safe area. The United States was still officially neutral, but President Roosevelt had declared on 11 April that the Red Sea was no longer a 'combat zone' and was therefore open to American ships.

Cornwall stayed with the convoy for one more night, then bade it farewell and good luck and left it to carry on unescorted to Suez. It had been a long and arduous job. We had escorted about 300,000 tons of shipping carrying troops and valuable supplies for thirty-three days, during which time we sailed 8,672 miles – quite a few more than the convoy itself because of our zigzag course and diversions to investigate ships.

By the time *Cornwall* arrived at Aden and moored in the harbour on the afternoon of 17 April, she had travelled 13,652 miles since leaving Simonstown a month and a half earlier. The cruiser was to spend most of its time in the tropics and members of the ship's company could claim that they contributed their fair share of at least two items of Mr Churchill's promise of 'blood, toil, tears and sweat'. The blood and tears were to come later.

16

Cornwall had topped up with fuel and we had been able to stretch our legs a couple of times in the Arabian heat on the barren shore when the aircraft-carrier HMS *Eagle* arrived at Aden on the morning of 21 April. *Cornwall* sailed in the afternoon and it was piped that we were 'proceeding to Mombasa in company with *Eagle*', which joined us about an hour later. There was a strong buzz in *Cornwall* that after calling at Mombasa we would go on to Cape Town. It was a cheering thought, and in the evening the next day it was good to feel the ship doing a turn of more than 90 degrees to starboard to round the horn of Africa and set a southerly course. We did not know that fate would intervene and change the plans for *Cornwall*.

We were back to the monotonous sea routine – up before daylight for dawn action stations, sweeping and scrubbing decks or painting parts of the ship when not on watch during the day, PT in the afternoon and then the weary watches after dark. But on this voyage the monotony was broken to some extent by exercises *Cornwall* carried out with the aircraft-carrier. Planes from *Eagle* made dummy dive-bombing and torpedo attacks on the cruiser which provided useful practice for the pilots of the aircraft and *Cornwall*'s gunners.

During the day *Eagle* was on *Cornwall*'s starboard beam, but at night she sailed astern of us. *Eagle* also sent planes on reconnaissance flights during the day. A few days out from Aden one of her aircraft failed to return from a reconnaissance flight. *Cornwall* put out smoke screens to indicate our position and carried out a search, during which our two Walrus seaplanes were used. No trace could be found of *Eagle*'s plane, but that night it was announced that the crew from the aircraft had been picked up by a British merchant ship bound for Aden.

When *Cornwall* and *Eagle* crossed the equator going south on the night of 24 April, *Pinguin* was heading north just about due east of them. After fruitless searches, during which she made extensive use of her aircraft, *Pinguin* was close to the route from India to the Mozambique Channel. The raider's extra 'eye', *Adjutant*, sighted a merchant ship on the horizon north of the equator that morning. She called up *Pinguin* by radio and shadowed the ship, *Empire Light* (6,828 tons), all day. The raider caught up at 5.15 the next morning, took 70 prisoners from the *Empire Light* and sank her by gunfire. The merchant ship did not make a radio QQQQ signal to report that she had been intercepted by an armed merchantman raider so her fate and the position of *Pinguin* on 25 April were not known.

It was a misty morning on 26 April when *Cornwall* and *Eagle* arrived off Mombasa, but by the time we sailed up the river-like harbour the mist had cleared and a hot sun shone on the beautiful, green country. By the time we had made fast at the wharf there was a small fleet in the harbour. Besides the aircraft-carrier and *Cornwall*, there were two other cruisers and an armed merchant cruiser. Later in the day two destroyers arrived, but they stayed only a few hours.

Our arrival at Mombasa was a good illustration of the saying that in the Navy one is paid for twenty-four hours' work a day, but works at least twenty-five. While at sea clocks were often changed. Depending on whether the ship was sailing east or west, clocks were either advanced or put back. During our long spell in the tropics in the east in the Indian Ocean, clocks in *Cornwall* were often five or more hours ahead of Greenwich mean time. But the manner in which the clocks were changed was considered a bit of a racket. They were invariably advanced during the night, which meant a loss of sleep. When they had to be put back, however, it was usually done during the forenoon working hours so that we had to work extra time. According to the ship's time, we arrived at Mombasa at 9.30 a.m. Mombasa time was 7.45 a.m., so during the forenoon clocks were put back an hour and three-quarters. That meant we had to work an extra 105 minutes before dinner. It hit hard those of us who had been on the morning watch (4 a.m. to 8 a.m.) because when the clocks were put back it meant that according to local time we had been on duty since 2.15 a.m.

Despite the long and tiresome forenoon, we were able to appreciate the beauty of Mombasa, which contrasted sharply with barren Aden. It looked so lush and fresh, with colourful trees and the tropical touch of palms, coconut trees and banana groves. I was surprised to learn that Mombasa is situated on a coral island three miles long and two-and-a-half broad. It is because the town is built on an island in a bay of the mainland that when a ship sails to the harbour it is like sailing up a river. Sailing up what was known as Kilindini Creek was a real joy. One bank abounded with coconut trees and palms, with attractive houses built at the water's edge. On the other side was a carpet of lovely green grass, rolling hills and slightly inland one could see the residential outskirts of the town. The harbour was a mile or two from the town. On the way up Kilindini Creek we passed a picturesque golf course laid out along the shore with green fairways down to the water's edge. We saw no sandy beaches.

There was an old harbour at Mombasa which teemed with small craft, including dhows, rowing boats and canoes. The new harbour, where *Cornwall* berthed, was one of the largest and safest on the east coast of Africa. Port watch was on duty that day and I was in starboard so was able to go ashore in the afternoon with a couple of friends. After an enjoyable bus ride to the town, our first consideration was to change our money into East African currency. We had no difficulty in finding a place to do this because every second shop had a large notice outside : 'Money exchanger'.

It was a hot afternoon and after the extra-long morning we decided that a cold beer would go down well. We found a hotel nearby, but discovered that in Mombasa all bars closed between 2 and 6 p.m. Just as we were bemoaning our bad luck a rascally-looking black man came up and, as though he had read our thoughts, asked : 'Does Jack want a beer?' We told him 'Jack' wanted a beer but did not want to go to a *shebeen*.

'Oh, no,' he replied. 'You have beer in barber-shop. Go take a seat in barber-shop.' He pointed to a hairdressing saloon a few doors away.

We duly took a seat in the barber-shop and waited. A few minutes later our good Samaritan returned with three bottles of cold beer and glasses. While patrons had their hair cut by a large, corpulent barber, we relaxed and drank our beer. The 'barman' got his commission on the sale, so everyone was happy.

The next morning *Cornwall* left the wharf and anchored in mid-stream farther down Kilindini Creek. We heard that we were due to stay at Mombasa for some days as we had to wait for the aircraft-carrier which was having some of her boilers cleaned. But life can be full of surprises in the Navy in wartime, and we got one while in Kilindini Creek.

Early in the morning of 28 April, the British merchant ship *Clan Buchanan*, which was bound for India with a cargo of military stores, was intercepted and attacked by *Pinguin*. Although the German raider's guns destroyed the ship's radio cabin with the first salvo, the wireless operator managed to send a feeble signal on an auxiliary set. He was one of the 110 prisoners taken by *Pinguin* when the *Clan Buchanan* sank. The War Diary of *Adjutant*, which was still helping *Pinguin* to look for ships, recorded that among the debris after the sinking of the *Clan Buchanan*, several documents were found, including two bags of secret mail, the War Diary of the cruiser HMS *Hawkins*, and coding keys for British warships.

The captain of *Pinguin* had asked for a rendezvous with the supply ship *Alstertor*, in the middle of the Indian Ocean about 500 miles south of Diego Garcia. On 29 April he dispatched *Adjutant* south with the secret documents and some of the prisoners to meet *Alstertor* while *Pinguin* headed north-west to continue the search for a tanker. Krüder did not think the weak distress signal from *Clan Buchanan* had been received, but although 'incomplete and partly unreadable', it had been picked up and a fairly accurate estimate of the longitude in which the ship was attacked had been made. Thus it came about that at 10 a.m. on 29 April *Cornwall* suddenly weighed anchor in Kilindini Creek and set off in a hurry.

As soon as we were clear of the Creek, *Cornwall* increased speed to 25 knots. It was obvious that there was something in the wind because of the sudden change of plans. We were all naturally curious as the cruiser sped east. We did not have long to wait to learn the reason for *Cornwall*'s hasty departure from Mombasa. There was the shrill note of the bo'sun's whistle, followed by the familiar call: 'Do you hear there?' Everyone stopped working and listened. 'The ship has put to sea,' piped the bo'sun's mate, 'to look for a raider that has been interfering with ships on the main shipping route between India and the Cape.' Later in the day we heard that a British ship (*Clan Buchanan*) had reported being shelled by a raider and it was her report that had caused us to sail so unexpectedly and in such haste.

'I hope we get the bastard this time,' muttered a sailor working near me. We all hoped we would catch the raider this time. *Cornwall* had done many weary patrols without luck. I had a feeling we would – sort of felt it in my bones – but most of the sailors were sceptical.

For two days *Cornwall* sped along at 25 knots, but shortly after crossing the equator northwards on 1 May – more than 1,000 miles from Mombasa – we slowed down to 12 knots and started to patrol the area we had been ordered to search. We changed course frequently and made extensive use of our Walrus aircraft for reconnaissance. Those two tough little seaplanes were to prove invaluable.

That afternoon hopes were raised and there was a buzz of excitement when a ship we sighted did not obey a signal to stop. *Cornwall* increased speed and drew nearer to it. A blank was fired to show that we were serious. Still the ship did not stop. One of our 4-inch guns fired a shot that fell just ahead of the vessel. This had the desired effect and it stopped very promptly.

A boarding party was sent across and ascertained that it was a British merchant ship with a very foolish captain.

Cornwall's Captain sent a signal : 'In future when ordered to stop do so immediately.'

'Why ?' the skipper of the merchant ship signalled.

'Because I insist on it,' curtly replied our Captain.

While chatting on the foc's'le during this interlude and anti-climax, the conversation in a group of us turned to raiders and the chances of our being in action. This prompted one of the older hands, a Leading Seaman with several years' service, to ask me if I knew why the Royal Marine Band always provided music during 'quarters clean guns'. Twice a week, on Wednesdays and Saturdays, the hands were piped to what was called quarters clean guns. This entailed spending about an hour cleaning the guns and all the instruments connected with gunnery. It was a time when much brightwork was polished.

While the hands were engaged on this cleaning routine, the Royal Marine Band fell in on the upper deck and provided light music. The reason for having music, the Leading Seaman told me, dated back to the old days when, after a ship had been in action, the hands were mustered to clean the guns, clear up the sanguinary mess and identify messmates who had been killed. The decks were bespattered with blood and dead and mutilated bodies were lying around. It was a grim time so the band provided music to keep up the men's spirits. It had become a tradition and the band still played even though 'quarters clean guns' had become a routine of 'spit and polish'.

The days dragged by as *Cornwall* patrolled, meandering on different courses to cover the area where it was hoped to intercept the raider. On Sunday, 4 May, the Captain addressed the ship's company after church parade on the quarterdeck. He explained that *Cornwall* had a

certain area to patrol and that we would refuel at the Seychelles. He
told us our stores were low and we might have to go short of food. As
we were likely to have a dull time on patrol, a day of games would be
arranged to relieve the monotony. The Captain pointed out, however,
that there was a distinct possibility of our meeting the raider. He said
he was pressing for *Cornwall* to be sent to the Cape as soon as possible
as the ship had been in the tropics for a long time and a spell of cool
weather would do us good. He added that we were originally to have
escorted the aircraft-carrier *Eagle* to Cape Town, but owing to the
raider report the cruiser *Hawkins* had been given the job. So the buzz
about our going to the Cape from Mombasa had been correct after all.

Two days later it was piped that the ship would leave the patrol area
that evening and go to the Seychelles to refuel. We crossed the equator
yet again when we duly changed to a southerly course – and again the
unexpected took a hand.

17

When *Cornwall* changed to the southerly course on 6 May, *Pinguin*
was a few hundred miles to the north and heading north-west in the
hope of catching a tanker coming from the Persian Gulf. At dawn the
next day the raider sighted the tanker *British Emperor* (3,663 tons),
which Krüder hoped to capture undamaged so that it could be used
as an auxiliary minelayer. But the Captain of the British tanker ignored
Pinguin's warning shots and the second wireless officer repeatedly
made very clear signals reporting the interception by the raider and
giving its position. Krüder had to give up any hope of capturing the
tanker without damaging it and gave orders to sink the ship by gunfire.

Despite the gunfire, which was aimed at the bridge and especially
the radio cabin, and the fact that he was mortally wounded, the wireless
officer continued tapping out the emergency signal until it was impossible to carry on. He was a very brave man who played a crucial part
in the operation against the German raider. The fierce gunfire attack
started fires in the ship and the crew had to abandon her. The members
of the crew taken prisoner in boats from *Pinguin* included the wounded
radio operator, who had been treated by the raider's doctor.

The British tanker proved to be a tough and obstinate adversary.
Smoke billowed from the ship as a result of the shells that tore into her,
but still she refused to sink. A grim Captain Krüder, realising his parlous

position because of the clear radio signals made from the tanker and the smoke as a result of it staying afloat, ordered that a torpedo be used to sink the ship. The tanker had to be disposed of quickly.

A torpedo was fired at the *British Emperor* but, instead of going straight to its target, it began to travel in a circle. It soon became obvious that when the torpedo completed its circular course, *Pinguin* would very likely be the target to be hit by her own missile. Desperate avoiding action was taken, the helmsman being ordered: 'Hard a'starboard.' The torpedo crossed the bows of *Pinguin* not more than twenty yards away, much to the relief of everyone on board. The torpedo continued on its haywire course for a short distance, then disappeared in the sea. Krüder ordered that a second torpedo be fired at the tanker. This one behaved normally and went straight but missed its target, so a third one had to be fired. This time the *British Emperor* was hit amidships and finally sank.

The emergency signal from *British Emperor* was received by *Cornwall* as soon as it was made in the early hours of 7 May. We were then operating under the Commander-in-Chief East Indies, whose headquarters were at Colombo in Ceylon, but without waiting for instructions the Commanding Officer of *Cornwall* took immediate action. While we were closed up at dawn action stations, it was piped that the raider had been reported within an area of 500 miles of us and that we would start searching for it immediately. *Cornwall* slewed round from a southerly course, increased speed and raced northwards at 26 knots.

The *British Emperor* had been sunk 400 miles south-east of Socotra, an island off the horn of Africa. Naval Headquarters at Colombo also sprang into action and ordered *Cornwall* and two other cruisers on the East Indies Station, *Glasgow* and *Leander*, to start hunting. The raider would obviously not stay in the area in which it sank *British Emperor*, but the question was which course Krüder would choose. It was arranged to have air patrols from Socotra and at 8.15 a.m. *Cornwall* was ordered to cover an area north of the gap between the Seychelles and Chagos groups of islands. This entailed making a slight alteration of course to the east.

Both of *Cornwall*'s Walrus aircraft were launched at 4 p.m. to carry out a co-ordinated search on our port side and ahead of us, which the Admiralty later commended as having been 'well designed'. The planes were in the air for three hours and, although they did not sight anything, the one searching ahead of *Cornwall* was only about thirty-five miles from *Pinguin* at 6.08 p.m. when it had to return to the cruiser.

Krüder had chosen to go south-east and when *Cornwall* altered its patrol course at 9.30 p.m. to east-south-east, the two ships were on converging courses.

All the activity had built up an atmosphere of expectancy in *Cornwall*. There was a feeling that we might locate the enemy ship during the night. I had the middle watch (midnight to 4 a.m.) as a look-out and recall how all of us on the bridge were told to be particularly alert on the port side. The keenness of the look-outs was no doubt also stimulated by the knowledge that sighting an enemy warship – and that included an armed merchant raider – would earn a reward of £5. Look-out awards were paid at the end of every month and, depending on the quality of the 'sight', varied from one to three shillings for friendly ships to £1 for an enemy merchant ship or mine, or £5 for an enemy warship or submarine.

Nothing was sighted from *Cornwall* that night but our course had taken us closer to *Pinguin* and at 3.30 a.m., when we were slightly ahead of her and were making a small alteration of course to south-east, we were sighted against the setting moon by the men on watch in *Pinguin*. Ulrich Harder, who was a gunner in the *Pinguin* and whom I met when he visited South Africa forty-two years later, told me the sighting appeared like a shadow and was not identified as *Cornwall*. But they knew warships must be searching for *Pinguin* as a result of the sinking of *British Emperor* and were perturbed by seeing something on the horizon.

It was at this point that the Captain of the raider made a fateful decision. Krüder decided on a 90-degree turn from south-east to south-west astern of *Cornwall*, which at that time had altered course slightly to south-east. During the rest of the night *Cornwall* was thus steaming at right angles to, and away from, *Pinguin*.

When we closed up at dawn action stations the next day, 8 May, there was an undercurrent of excitement. But when the sun rose and bathed the calm tropical sea in its light, no ship was in sight. Both of *Cornwall*'s aircraft were catapulted off at about 6.30 a.m. to carry out an extended search. A few minutes after 7 a.m. the Walrus that had been ordered to fly on a north-westerly course sighted a ship steaming south-west at speed about sixty-five miles from *Cornwall*. This was reported when the aircraft returned to *Cornwall* at 8 a.m., but the cruiser had to wait for the return of the second plane, which had searched in vain to the south, before altering course and increasing speed to 23 knots at 8.25 a.m. As *Cornwall* had been sailing east, she had to do almost a 180-degree turn to get on a westerly course to overtake the ship that had been sighted.

The First Lieutenant in *Cornwall*, Lieutenant-Commander G. M. E. Grove, had volunteered to fly as an observer so that both aircraft could be used because the cruiser had two pilots but only one observer. He was in a Walrus that was flown off again at 10.15 a.m. to check further on the ship that had been sighted. The raider was steaming at full speed (about 18 knots).

Tension had been building up in *Pinguin* since the sighting of the 'shadow' at 3.30 a.m. The uneasiness had increased when the Walrus, a Royal Navy plane, was sighted shortly after 7 a.m. and it was obvious that the raider had been spotted. Then came the Walrus that had been catapulted from *Cornwall* at 10.15. It reached *Pinguin* at about 11.20, circled over the raider and, using its signal lamp, asked the ship to identify herself.

Krüder adopted the ruse of posing as an ordinary merchant vessel on its way from Bombay to the Mozambique Channel and told his signalman to hoist the flags giving the signal letters of the Norwegian ship *Tamerlane*, which *Pinguin* had been painted to resemble at Kerguelen Island. The raider had been cleverly disguised to look like the *Tamerlane*, but Grove's suspicion was aroused by the reaction of the few members of the crew who could be seen on board *Pinguin*. Nobody waved whereas usually the appearance of an aircraft created much interest on board a friendly ship.

'We had never flown round a ship without someone waving,' said Grove. He heard later that in *Pinguin* 'they debated whether to shoot us down'.

The Walrus shadowed *Pinguin* for about twenty minutes and then returned to *Cornwall* to be hoisted on board at 12.23 p.m. When Grove made his report to the Captain, the cruiser's speed was increased to 26 knots and then later to 28 at 1.43 p.m. when the second Walrus was sent off to keep an eye on the suspicious vessel. *Cornwall* was gradually overtaking the ship on the slightly converging courses.

On the lower deck we ratings were not fully acquainted with everything that was going on. It was evident that something was in the offing, but during the morning different stories circulated. Some ratings said the raider had been sighted; others said it was a false alarm. As I had had the middle watch and not much sleep, I was tired and stretched out on the upper deck after dinner to have a rest.

After being asleep for some time I was awakened by loud, excited voices and water splashing on the deck as *Cornwall* crashed through the swells at 28 knots. I was told that the ship our aircraft had sighted was almost certainly the raider and that we were racing to overtake it. The time was about 3 p.m. Shortly afterwards it was piped that the hands would go to tea at 3.30 instead of 4.15.

I had the first dog watch (4 to 6 p.m.) as a look-out and when we closed up on the bridge, extra look-outs were posted on the starboard side to scan the horizon for the ship. The Walrus that had gone off earlier in the afternoon was still shadowing the ship so we knew its approximate bearing. We strained our eyes to catch sight of it. A few minutes after 4 p.m. a report was received from the masthead look-out in the crow's nest that he could see the ship from his elevated position. We were all excited and impatient to see what could be the raider. Shortly afterwards two masts became visible above the horizon, then the funnel and finally the whole ship. It was quite eerie watching it gradually come into full view.

At this stage action stations was sounded off and I had to go up to a position as look-out on the air defence platform. As those of us up there were not involved in a surface action, we donned steel helmets and took up positions on the starboard side to watch the proceedings.

As soon as the German ship sighted *Cornwall*, which altered course to close, she turned to starboard and kept steaming away. Krüder had not given up and made another move to confuse *Cornwall*. He made an RRRR (warship raider) wireless signal in English as from the Norwegian ship *Tamerlane*, and said : 'Suspicious vessel following' (*Cornwall* being the raider!). To add further credibility to his disguise and signal, the message was made on a captured British wireless set which could be identified and distinguished from a German set.

This must have increased any doubts there were in the mind of the Captain of *Cornwall*. The cruiser's boarding party, under the command of Lieutenant-Commander Milner, was piped to muster on deck and gathered at the cutter. We heard that the plan was for *Cornwall* to steam ahead of the ship, launched the boarding party in the cutter and then signal the ship to stop so that it could be boarded and its identity checked. Fortunately this scheme was abandoned. It would have taken *Cornwall* even more dangerously close to the raider and, in any case, one could not imagine the Germans not resisting and taking action against a boarding party from an enemy ship.

Pinguin's crew had been sent to action stations. Her guns and torpedo tubes were manned and ready for firing at a moment's notice. Krüder knew that any seeds of doubt he had sown about the identity of his ship gave him the big advantage of having the option to open fire first. He was also drawing *Cornwall* closer and closer into his range, which was shorter than that of the British cruiser's 8-inch guns.

Cornwall flashed signals to the raider to stop. *Pinguin* ignored them and carried on steaming with its stern to *Cornwall*. On the bridge of the raider the German captain had his binoculars fixed on *Cornwall*. The British captain had his binoculars trained on *Pinguin*. The two captains, who had seen action as young men on opposing sides in the Battle of Jutland in the First World War, were now facing each other for a fight to the death.

One of *Cornwall*'s guns roared and an 8-inch shell was fired to the port side of *Pinguin* as a warning. Still the German ship ignored signals to heave to, so another warning shot was fired. Krüder put on his naval cap and jacket, and gave the order to hoist the German flag and open fire. Up went the flaps concealing the guns.

It was a dramatic moment. When *Cornwall*'s second warning shell was fired, the raider turned very deliberately to port and then, suddenly at 5.14 p.m., there were four flashes and four puffs of dirty brown smoke as the German ship fired a broadside at *Cornwall* which was only 10,500 yards away. Two torpedoes were also fired and the three-inch gun on the foc's'le joined the four 5.9-inch guns that could bear on the port side. What had been an innocent-looking merchant ship erupted into a fearsome weapon of war.

A *Cornwall* signalman had been repeatedly flashing in Morse to the raider the signal 'OL – K' which meant : 'Heave to or I will open fire. Stop instantly.' He was in the process of flashing 'OL – K' again when the Germans opened fire. The signalman was so taken aback by seeing the sudden broadside that he forgot the 'L' and merely flashed 'OK'.

Cornwall's large battle ensign had been hoisted and the fight was on. The roar of guns shattered the peace of a tropical day in the soft light of late afternoon just north of the equator. As those of us on the air defence platform were in an exposed position, the officer in charge told us to get down and stay down. Shells whistled through the air as they straddled the cruiser and splashed into the sea nearby, sending up surprisingly high columns of water. There was the tinkling of falling insulators on wires severed by shrapnel which also made holes in the forward funnel. Broadsides from *Cornwall*'s guns jarred the ship with their strong recoil. But it was disturbing at first. Whereas the raider was firing rapid, accurate salvoes, our more powerful turrets were aiming a long way off the target.

The Captain turned to the Chief Yeoman of Signals standing nearby and exclaimed : 'What the hell's going on ?' Then he spoke into a voicepipe, presumably to the Gunnery Officer, and repeated: 'What the hell's going on?'

Cornwall was in trouble. One of the first shells fired by the Germans had hit the cruiser on the starboard side, blasting a hole on the water-line large enough for a motor-car to drive through and upsetting our gunnery control. As it was explained to me, a screw came out of the hunting gear in the Transmitting Station (TS), the gunnery control position well below the bridge and not far from where the shell exploded. As a result, the communication circuits between the TS and turrets were dislocated and training indicators on the guns showed incorrect bearings. Our guns were thus trained many degrees off the target. During the breakdown the turrets had to go into independent local control, known as quarters firing.

But this was not the only trouble. The German shell had also put the forward steering-gear out of action temporarily and the Captain told the Chief Yeoman to open a communication line to the after deck to repeat orders to the hand-steering compartment.

All this happened within minutes, but in the heat of the battle it seemed very much longer. Four minutes after *Pinguin* opened fire, our gunnery control was back to normal and the eight guns in the four turrets were straddling the enemy ship with their 8-inch shells. It was comforting to feel the thud in the cruiser every time a salvo was fired. *Cornwall* had altered course away to open the range, which was to her advantage.

During the action *Pinguin* sent a radio message to naval headquarters in Germany. It was the raider's last signal and read: 'After sinking 136,550 tons gross of enemy shippping, apart from the results of mine-laying, am engaging British heavy cruiser *Cornwall*.'

With *Cornwall*'s gunnery on target, Krüder knew it was the end for *Pinguin*. He had played all his cards in a desperate effort at deception and to deliver a vital blow with his opening attack. But his torpedoes had failed to score a hit, though the Germans claimed one of them missed the cruiser's stern by only a few yards, and the salvoes from his guns had caused only a brief dislocation of *Cornwall*'s gunnery.

Krüder gave his last order – to release the prisoners in *Pinguin* and abandon ship. Before it could be carried out, however, a salvo of four shells from *Cornwall* crashed into the raider at 5.26 p.m. One hit the forward aircraft hold, one exploded in the meteorological office below the port side of the bridge, one tore into the engine-room and the fourth – the most devastating – hit the hold in which were stored the 130 mines it had been planned to lay off the Indian port of Karachi.

It was an unforgettable sight. On the air defence platform we heard a sudden cheer and jumped up in time to have a grandstand view of the end of *Pinguin*. The raider disintegrated in a terrific explosion. Most of the ship, from the bridge to the stern, just disappeared and a huge cloud of smoke shot up to a height of about 2,000 feet. The bows, still moving forward, went up at an angle of about 45 degrees and then, in a matter of a few seconds, slid back under the sea. All that remained to mark the grave of 554 men killed in the explosive end of the raider were dark oil patches, debris and some survivors. A few seconds after the sinking, one of *Pinguin*'s last shots splashed in the sea short of *Cornwall*.

Shortly before the action started, Captain Manwaring made an emergency signal to naval headquarters at Colombo reporting that *Cornwall* was about six miles from an armed raider and giving the cruiser's position. When the firing started, he signalled, 'Am engaging', and after *Pinguin* had blown up he reported : 'Enemy sunk. Am closing for survivors.'

The Commander-in-Chief East Indies sent a signal to *Cornwall* : 'Well done.' He then made one to all ships on the East Indies Station referring to the 'R' distress message made by a vessel calling herself *Tamerlane*. The C-in-C's signal continued : 'Norwegian ship *Tamerlane* is not on East Indies Station. Ship which made message is considered to be armed merchant raider sunk by HMS *Cornwall*.'

The exact position of the sinking is recorded as 3 degrees 27 north 56 degrees 38 east. It was a short, sharp engagement, lasting only twelve minutes, but they were long minutes. The Germans claimed that they fired 200 shells, while it was reported that *Cornwall* fired 112.

Cornwall was by no means unscathed and the end of the raider was not the end of the cruiser's troubles that day.

18

Cornwall's Walrus aircraft that had been flown off at 1.43 p.m. had stayed up all the time to report the fall of shot of the cruiser's shells and had also spotted the two torpedoes. The second aircraft was on the catapult, loaded with bombs and ready to be launched with the aid of a cordite charge. Lieutenant-Commander Grove, who was flying as observer that day, urged the Captain to let the plane go off and bomb the ship that was ignoring signals to stop. Eventually the Captain agreed and said to Grove : 'Off you go and bomb the bugger if he won't stop.'

Grove made his way aft to the aircraft, but by the time he and the
pilot were clambering aboard *Pinguin* had opened fire. Shell splinters
smashed the tail and propeller and cut ailerons so they had to climb
out and abandon their venture. They got out just in time to be soaked
by the splash from another shell that burst alongside the cruiser.

Grove recalled this incident in a letter to his father-in-law, the late
Mr Richard Stuttaford, a leading businessman in South Africa who
was a Member of Parliament from 1924 to 1942, and Cabinet Minister
during the last nine of those years. He was Minister of Commerce and
Industries in General Smuts' wartime cabinet from the outbreak of the
Second World War in 1939 until he retired in 1942. Grove wrote :

> It was rather eerie watching the flashes of the enemy's guns and
> knowing that there was a salvo on its way to you. It was not very nice
> when you had time to sit and think about it, but one soon gets used
> to it. In fact, generally speaking it was not as frightening as I ex-
> pected it to be.

Referring to the whole action, Grove wrote that considering the number
of splinters flying around, 'we got off pretty lightly'.

In addition to the big shell hole on the water-line, *Cornwall* had a
smaller one higher up amidships made by another shell. This shell
exploded in the Chief Petty Officers' pantry, making rather a mess of it.
Fortunately no one was in the pantry at the time.

It was fortunate, too, that the shell that blasted the big hole on the
water-line landed in the flour and biscuit store and was deflected so
that it exploded upwards, otherwise the damage would have been more
severe. As it was, it ripped into the Marines' mess deck and the explosion sent shrapnel flying into the lower steering position. It was there
that the Quartermaster and one or two others were wounded. Their
injuries were not serious but the shrapnel was unkind and two of the
wounded had difficulty in sitting down for some time after the action.

What was more serious was electrical damage that caused *Cornwall*
to become immobilised. A piece of shell severed the ring main, which
cut off the power supply and put all ventilation fans and communications
between the bridge and the engine-room out of action. The temperature
rose alarmingly and the engine-room had to be evacuated as the heat
became unbearable. Several men flaked out and had to be carried to
the upper deck to recover in the fresh air. But an Engineer Lieutenant,
who was overcome by heat, was too severely burnt by the time he
could be dragged out and died. He was the only fatality in *Cornwall* as

a result of the action, compared with the 554 who, German sources say, lost their lives when the raider was sunk. The 554 included 18 German officers, 323 other ranks, and 213 prisoners, mostly Lascars.

Meanwhile boats had been launched by *Cornwall* to rescue survivors from *Pinguin*, most of whom had been in the foc's'le. Some of them just spilled out when the foremost part of the ship was ripped off the rest of it which was blown up. Ulrich Harder, who was a 20-year-old gunner manning the 3-inch gun on the bows, told me his gun fired the very last shot. He said his range-finder had half of his face blown off. Harder himself was knocked unconscious in the explosion that destroyed *Pinguin* and came to in the water.

The members of *Pinguin*'s crew had become very fond of Captain Krüder. They resented the fact that another raider captain, Bernhard Rogge, of *Atlantis*, was made senior to Krüder. The first thing they asked when they found themselves alive in the sea after the sinking of *Pinguin* was: 'Where's the Captain?' The Captain was killed; he disappeared in the mighty explosion while he was on the bridge.

One of the survivors did not wait to be picked up by a boat from *Cornwall*. He was an old Lascar seaman who dog-paddled to the cruiser. As he drew nearer and nearer he was encouraged by a crowd of our sailors who gathered along the guard-rails. A cheer went up when the old Lascar eventually reached the ship's side. A rope was lowered to him and he was hoisted inboard. He was one of the first survivors to come aboard and received an enthusiastic welcome. A number of British seamen survivors had collected on a piece of wreckage and were cheerfully singing the popular wartime song 'Roll Out The Barrel' when they were picked up.

When the German survivors were brought up the gangway, one ardent admirer of Hitler gave the Nazi salute as he stepped on deck. But for the most part they were not arrogant and got on well with *Cornwall*'s sailors. They certainly did not lack for such things as cigarettes, fruit and chocolates.

Altogether 84 survivors were rescued – 60 German members of the crew of the raider and 24 prisoners (9 British seamen and 15 Lascars). The Germans included three officers, one of them the ship's assistant surgeon, Dr Hasselmann, and another the meteorological officer, Lieutenant Hans Roll. One of the British survivors was the second wireless officer of the *British Emperor*, the last ship to be sunk by *Pinguin*, who had made the signals that led to the cornering and destruction of the raider. He had a serious wound and Dr Hasselmann reported that he was on drugs and would require immediate attention.

Dr Hasselmann, who spoke excellent English, was given facilities to have a wash and a clean tropical white uniform to wear. When Lieutenant-Commander Milner saw him, he thought Dr Hasselmann was one of the British survivors and took him down to the wardroom to have a drink. The doctor then went to *Cornwall's* Sick Bay to help attend to the wounded survivors.

Ordinary Seaman Tommy Thorp, the schoolmaster in peace-time, had been summoned to be interpreter when the Germans came aboard *Cornwall*. Tommy's mother was German and he spoke the language fluently. The first formalities of getting the basic details such as the names, rank etc were held on the quarterdeck. The positions had been reversed now, the Germans being the prisoners.

It was almost dark before the last of the survivors was brought on board. As a result of the engine-room having to be temporarily evacuated, it was a few hours before *Cornwall* could get under way again. It was 8 p.m. before we could have supper, during which the Captain gave the order, 'Splice the main brace', the traditional custom in the Navy to celebrate a victory. So rum was issued to everyone over the age of twenty, but after one sip I gave mine to a regular rum drinker. As a result of the electrical damage, the ship's cooling system was out of action and the water mixed with the rum was warm. We had to be satisfied with drinking warm water for some days.

Part of the lighting system had also been put out of action and emergency leads had to be rigged. Heat coming up from the engine-room had made the interior of the ship exceptionally warm and everyone had to suffer extreme discomfort that night. I was detailed to work throughout the night carrying leads for the torpedo party which was responsible for electrical repairs. It was like working in a Turkish bath and the perspiration ran down one's body. All I wore was a pair of shorts and tackies. My shorts were soon sodden and the tackies became waterlogged. It was just as though I had walked in water. Eventually I was told to knock off at 5.40 a.m. and just stretched out as I was on the lower deck next to my locker for a little sleep before having to turn out for dawn action stations. We had crossed the equator again and were bound for the Seychelle Islands where the German prisoners and other survivors from the raider were to be landed.

Tommy Thorp had been kept busy interpreting at the interrogation of the Germans which carried on until after midnight and was resumed the next morning. One thing that surprised them was to learn that *Cornwall's* ship's company included more than 100 South Africans. They had been led to believe that all South Africans were on their side.

It was also evident that when *Pinguin* sailed from Gotenhaven in mid-June 1940, they thought they would be home by Christmas that year. The French under Marshal Pétain signed the surrender on 22 June and the Germans were confident that after this collapse, Britain would link up with Germany and France against Russia.

In the course of the interrogation Thorp noticed that one of the German seamen, Richard Markucik, had an arm in plaster. When asked when and how he had injured it, he pointed to a date written on the plaster of paris. It was the day *Pinguin* had loaded 360,000 eggs from the captured refrigerator ship *Duquesa* at the rendezvous area in the South Atlantic known as Andalusien. While loading the cases of eggs, he and another seaman had fallen into a refrigerator room. The other seaman broke his nose but Markucik came off worst with his arm broken in two places. And to add to his misery *Pinguin* was sunk on his twenty-first birthday. I learnt from Ulrich Harder that Markucik died shortly before Christmas in 1982.

The German seamen complained about the food they were given in *Cornwall*, maintaining that they were accustomed to better fare. It was made plain to them that they were getting the same food as *Cornwall's* ship's company. The fact was that, as mentioned earlier, our stores were low and we were not exactly getting five-star menus. And it was going to get worse before it improved.

The day after the raider action was a busy one. There was a lot of cleaning up to be done what with damage from the shell hits and shrapnel. Able Seaman Ken Collier recalls that there was also some damage for which *Pinguin* could not be held directly responsible. Before he recounts how this came about, it should be explained that what was named the Heads Flat was the foremost part of the superstructure on the upper deck of *Cornwall*. It was situated above the seamen's mess deck and gave access to the upper deck just aft of 'A' turret. Two passages led to doors opening on to the upper deck, one to the port side and the other to the starboard side.

The Heads were the toilets for the lower deck ratings and the name gave rise to the old naval story about the rating who wrote to his parents that he had been promoted and was now Captain of the Heads. (This was the name of the job of looking after the toilets and keeping them clean.) I never inquired why they were called Heads for fear that showing any interest might give the impression I was keen on promotion.

Anyway, back to Ken Collier who, it will be recalled, was a communications number in 'A' turret at the time of the incident with the

French cruiser *Primaguet*. In the encounter with the German raider he was local layer in the turret which was situated on the foc's'le just forward of the Heads Flat. He said :

When the director circuits went out of action and the order for quarters firing was given, the local turret layers had to take over. As soon as the order was given, the captain of the turret started shouting at me to open fire.

You will remember that at this stage our guns were aiming on the wrong side of the raider and, as the only thing I could see through the telescopic sights was a small section of empty horizon, there was nothing I could do. Meanwhile the trainer was swivelling the turret round as fast as he could until eventually he picked up the enemy ship in our sights. I then commenced firing and was told afterwards that my rate of fire of the eight-inch guns was about the same speed as the pom poms !

Cornwall was taking evasive action and, as she swung away to port, 'A' turret had to bear farther and farther aft until the guns seemed to be aiming almost directly at our own ship. We had long passed the indicator for 'Cease firing' but I could still see the raider clearly in my sights and her guns were flashing far too rapidly for my liking. Technicalities like blast damage to our own ship seemed very small compared with collecting a salvo of German shells so I continued firing as if I were sending dots on a Morse key.

When eventually *Pinguin* blew up and the cheering crew poured out of the turret, the upper deck was a shambles. The blast from 'A' turret's guns had blown the steel door of the Heads Flat clean off its hinges. The steel was thick enough to withstand anything the sea could do to it or any normal enemy action, but the blast of 120 pounds of cordite at very short range was a bit much. Fortunately, as we had the direct hit just below the Heads Flat and just above the water-line, it was assumed that the damage had been done by the enemy. I was happy to let that sleeping dog lie.

That day we also had to muster on the quarterdeck for the funeral of the engineer officer who had died. He was buried at sea in the traditional manner, the body being sewn and weighted in canvas.

In the afternoon some of us were detailed to work in the flour and biscuit store from which we had a fine view out of the ship at sea level thanks to the German shell that had blasted a hole about eight feet in diameter. As the bottom of the hole was just about level with the sea, which splashed in, we put on bathing trunks. Our job was to toss out sodden bags of flour. Fortunately the sea was calm and the ship was travelling at a moderate speed so the inflow of water was not a serious problem.

The wireless officer who had sent the vital signals from the tanker *British Emperor* had undergone an operation but his wound proved too severe and we were all sorry to hear that he died in *Cornwall*'s sick bay before we arrived at the Seychelles the next day. I do not know if his bravery was officially recognised, but if ever a man deserved a posthumous award, he did. He was buried at the Seychelles, some sailors from *Cornwall* going ashore to be mourners at the funeral and lower his body into the grave on the island.

Cornwall arrived at the Seychelles at noon and, as soon as she had anchored off the main island of Mahé, a tanker came alongside to top up the warship's fuel tanks. At the same time our shipwrights got busy with temporary repairs to close the hole on the water-line. They built a concrete wall and a steel plate found in a field on the island was attached to the ship's side to cover the outside of the hole. A Sub-Lieutenant, a Petty Officer and an Able Seaman, who had his own construction company in peace-time, were in charge of putting on the plate. When the ship eventually got to Durban a couple of weeks later, the Able Seaman was congratulated on the job done quickly with limited facilities in difficult circumstances.

As interpreter, Tommy Thorp became involved in a problem that the Officer Commanding the Seychelles had with accommodating the German officers. The local jail, it appeared, was small, functional and ill-equipped to put up the three officers. But it was the only alternative to the Germans agreeing to be put on some form of parole.

It was strange to hear a call over the ship's public address system for 'Ordinary Seaman Thorp to report to the Captain's cabin' – most unusual for an Ordinary Seaman to see the Captain in his cabin.

The Lieutenant-Colonel, who was the senior officer ashore, had met the Germans and had come aboard to discuss his problem of the prisoners with our Captain. He was not satisfied that he, or they, clearly understood the position and Thorp was asked to discuss it with the German officers who were in another cabin. After he had done so, Thorp explained that it was a question of whether the officers should be put on parole and be trusted not to try to escape. They appeared to be quibbling about the meaning of the word they were prepared to give – they would give their word as gentlemen but were not prepared to give an oath.

'What would you do?' the Lieutenant-Colonel asked Thorp when he reported this.

'Put them in jail,' he replied.

The Ordinary Seaman's advice was taken, and that is where they stayed for some time until they went in a ship to Mombasa and then to Port Elizabeth in South Africa.

All our passengers – the German prisoners and the British and Lascar seamen who survived the sinking of *Pinguin* – were put ashore at the Seychelles.

In a letter *Pinguin*'s meteorological officer, Lieutenant Hans Roll, wrote some years later:

It may interest you to know that the 60 survivors of *Pinguin* disembarked in Port Elizabeth on 18.6.41 from the British transport *Strathmore*, and then were moved by train to Durban where they stayed in a tented camp near the racecourse of Clairwood from 21 to 28.6.41. I am happy to have this opportunity to make it known that during the journey and our stay in the Union (South Africa),

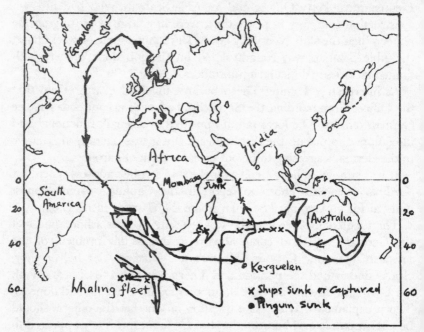

The voyage of the German raider Pinguin, *from 15 June 1940, until she was sunk by HMS* Cornwall *on 8 May 1941. The disguised raider sailed close on 60,000 miles and sank or captured 28 ships, including 11 whale catchers.*

the treatment we received from the soldiers of your army was always fair, friendly and chivalrous so that the days in your country appeared to us as highlights in our existence as prisoners of war, an existence which by no means was always a happy one.

The Germans were taken from South Africa to Barbados in the West Indies and then on a circuitous voyage to Britain where they spent some time in prisoner-of-war camps near Edinburgh, London and Manchester. Later they were transferred to Canada and stayed there for a few years before being sent back to Britain in the spring of 1946, and then home to Germany in November that year.

19

The sinking of *Pinguin,* or *HK 33* to use the official German name, brought to an end one of the most remarkable voyages by so-called auxiliary cruisers – the ships that were disguised as harmless merchant vessels and approached under false colours until the moment of opening fire. Unfortunately most of the raider's victims were either abandoned or overwhelmed by gunfire before they could make **RRRR** signals.

In the South Atlantic and Indian Ocean – especially the latter – these raiders became a menace and threat to the Allies' war effort. In the two years 1940 and 1941, the disguised merchant raiders accounted for 98 ships with a gross tonnage of considerably more than half a million – to be exact 593,171 tons. *Pinguin,* which logged close on 60,000 miles, made a notable contribution to these successes during the 328 days she was at sea – only 37 days less than a year and a feat exceeded only by *Atlantis.* *Pinguin* sank or captured 28 ships (including 11 whale-catchers) which was more than any other raider. In addition, one ship was sunk and another damaged as a result of her mine-laying operation off Australia. The 52,000 tons of captured shipping she sent back to Germany with prize crews was a record for both the First and Second World Wars.

The sinking of *Pinguin* on 8 May 1941 coincided with a turning point in the damage done by merchant raiders. Whereas 38 ships (190,623 tons) were sunk or captured by these raiders in the first six months of 1941, only 6 ships (35,904 tons) were lost in the second half of the year.

But the success and nuisance value of raiders cannot be evaluated

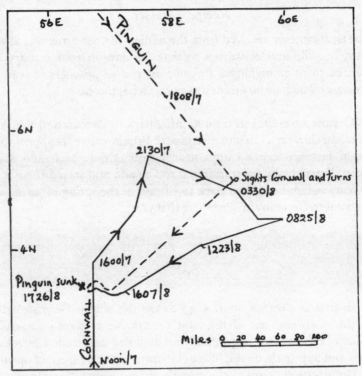

The sinking of the German raider Pinguin, *by HMS* Cornwall *on 8 May
1941. The tracks of the two ships from 7 May until the sinking late on
the afternoon of the 8th are shown, including* Pinguin's *fateful turn to
the south-west and* Cornwall's *change of course at 8.25 a.m. after her
aircraft sighted the raider.*

only in terms of the number of ships sunk or captured. As stated in the
instructions to the raiders, their chief aim was to

> divert enemy naval forces from home waters by forcing the enemy
> to form convoys and to make strong protection available for his
> overseas trade even in remote waters; by forcing the enemy to employ
> his naval forces as much as possible ... To achieve this, it is more im-
> portant to keep the enemy on the alert and occupied over a long
> period than to sink a large number of ships, which would lead to the
> shortening of the life of the auxiliary cruiser.

Measured against these considerations and in the wider context of
adding to the strain on the Allies' war effort, the merchant raiders
could claim considerable success. They caused heavy County Class
and other cruisers in the Royal Navy to sail hundreds of thousands of
miles protecting merchant shipping, escorting troopship convoys and
patrolling the oceans.

The leading contingent from HMS *Cornwall* in the march past in Durban to celebrate the sinking of the German raider *Pinguin*. Lieut-Commander J. S. Milner, who was in command of the parade, is reporting to the Commanding Officer, Captain P. C. W. Manwaring, at the entrance to the City Hall. Partly obscured by the Captain is the Mayor of Durban, Mr Rupert Ellis Brown, who took the salute. On the left is Commander J. Fair.

HMS *Cornwall* as she was in 1942.

(Left) Admiral Yamamoto, the 'gambler' who was Commander-in-Chief of the Combined Japanese Fleet. *(Right)* Admiral Sir James Somerville.

(Left) Lieutenant-Commander Mitsuo Fuchida. *(Right)* Vice-Admiral Chuichi Nagumo.

Looking back on *Cornwall*'s encounter with *Pinguin*, three points stand out. The track chart of the action shows the first two. Firstly, there was Captain Krüder's decision to make a 90-degree change of course from south-east to south-west when the 'shadow' that was *Cornwall* was sighted at 3.30 a.m. on 8 May. It was a turn of fate – the wrong turn. If, instead of altering course 90-degrees to starboard, he had changed course slightly to port and gone east, it is almost certain that the raider would have got away.

Secondly, if *Cornwall* had not had two Walrus aircraft for reconnaissance flights, she would almost certainly not have intercepted the raider. When one of *Cornwall*'s aircraft sighted *Pinguin* at 7.07 a.m. on 8 May, the cruiser was steaming away from the raider and had to make almost a 180-degree turn to get on a converging course.

The third point concerns how close *Cornwall* went to the raider – one might say how close she was lured – until she was well within the shorter range of the German guns. With hindsight it is easy to be critical, perhaps too critical. *Pinguin* was camouflaged to look like the Norwegian ship *Tamerlane*, and played her part well. When signalled by one of *Cornwall*'s aircraft at about 11.20 a.m. to identify herself, she hoisted flags giving the correct signal letters of the *Tamerlane*. And when intercepted by *Cornwall* late in the afternoon, *Pinguin* made the recognised emergency RRRR (warship raider) wireless signal as from *Tamerlane* and reported that she was being followed by a suspicious ship.

All this must have put some doubts in the mind of the Commanding Officer of *Cornwall*. He had to be certain before he could open fire that the ship was not a friendly vessel. It was a heavy responsibility. He could not take a chance and sink an Allied ship, but at the same time he would not want to let an enemy disguised raider slip away. It was already late afternoon, close to sunset. *Cornwall* did not have radar and after dark it could be difficult to keep a ship under surveillance. It would be dangerous to keep too close because that could expose the warship to a torpedo attack if the vessel being shadowed was a German raider.

With all these considerations in mind, *Cornwall*'s Captain was in an unenviable position of responsibility. The raider's Captain solved the problem when *Cornwall* was well within his range by opening fire with guns and torpedoes to get in the first blow.

In *The War At Sea* Captain S. W. Roskill writes :

The methods employed by *Cornwall* in shadowing, trying to identify and in closing the raider were the subject of some adverse Admiralty comment. The action certainly emphasised the skill with which such enemy ships disguised their identity, the serious dilemma in which the captain of a ship was placed while trying to pierce the disguise, and the danger of approaching such a ship – which must possess the tactical advantage of surprise – too closely and on bearings favourable to her gun and torpedo fire.

These difficult questions were by no means easily solved. Ultimately all Allied ships were given secret call signs and, as a further insurance, a system was introduced whereby an intercepting warship at once called the Admiralty to verify whether a suspicious ship actually was what she claimed to be. These measures succeeded largely in solving the doubt regarding identity, but they were not introduced until many months ahead; meanwhile the uncertainties from which the *Cornwall*'s captain suffered were reproduced in many other contacts between British warships and ships which sometimes turned out to be friendly merchant vessels and sometimes were discovered, much later, to have been raiders or enemy supply ships.

A few months later when *Cornwall* called at Colombo, Ceylon, the Commander-in-Chief East Indies, Vice Admiral G. S. Arbuthnot, attended Sunday church service on the quarterdeck after which he addressed the ship's company. He congratulated us on sinking the raider, but added rather bluntly that as a result of mistakes and some bad luck, it was obvious that if the raider had been a proper warship *Cornwall* would have been sunk.

20

Cornwall's call at the Seychelles to patch up action damage and put German prisoners and other survivors ashore marked the end of our association with *Pinguin*, but not with raiders and other German ships. On the morning after *Cornwall* anchored at Mahé, another cruiser, HMS *Glasgow*, arrived, fuelled and sailed again at 6 p.m. When *Cornwall* weighed anchor about an hour and a half later, it was piped that we and *Glasgow* would search for some German supply ships that were thought to be in the area and that we would arrive at Mauritius on 17 May. It was also announced that if nothing untoward happened, *Cornwall* would then probably go to Durban 'to complete action repairs'.

We set off at a fast speed, about 25 knots, and had not gone far before part of the plate covering the large hole in the ship's side was ripped open. The ship had to heave to for a few hours to enable shipwrights to go over the side and make the plate more secure. The days slipped by as we crashed through fairly heavy seas and searched without finding any ships among a group of islands north-east of Mauritius.

At this time our shortage of stores became very evident. We were reduced to having bully beef for dinner almost every day. But those in the galley deserved full marks for their ingenuity in varying the form in which the 'corned dog', as it was called, was served. At one meal it would be cold, straight from the tin, at another it would be stewed, then curried or in the form of cottage pie, and finally made up as rissoles.

Cornwall arrived at Mauritius and anchored off Port Louis. While the cruiser refuelled from a tanker, afternoon leave was given to one watch and three of us went ashore togtether to see something of the island, which was sometimes called the Ile de France. It had originally been a Dutch possession, then French from 1715 until 1814 when Britain took it over and made it a crown colony. My two fellow Ordinary Seamen companions that afternoon were Tommy Thorp, the schoolmaster who was to become a headmaster after the war, and John Jordi, who subsequently had a distinguished career as a journalist. In addition to working in South Africa and Rhodesia, he gained experience in London and Washington. In 1971 he was appointed editor of *The Star*, Johannesburg, the daily newspaper with the largest circulation in South Africa. Jordi died of a heart attack in his office in 1974 at the age of 51.

Port Louis, rather drab from what we saw of it, did not impress us and we took the advice of a French shopkeeper to go by bus to Curepipe, a town about fourteen miles inland. The bus journey was notable for two things. It was quite hair-raising because the bus was driven at a reckless speed by a Mauritian who seemed to think he owned the road and pedestrians had to scatter or be run down. Every time he overtook another vehicle or turned right, he held out a red flag which was most appropriate.

The manner in which the bus was driven was, however, offset by the joy of the lovely countryside through which we travelled. One could not wish for prettier scenery – rolling green hills, sugar cane fields, colourful trees and flowers. Long stretches of the road were bordered with attractive hedges, and in parts gorgeous trees formed a soft green roof above the highway. After passing through several villages, some of them with French names, we arrived at Curepipe, a small town with a replica of the Eiffel Tower. A young man who had chatted to us in the bus suggested that we get a taxi and drive to the nearby Trou Aux Cerfs, an old volcano overlooking the town. The crater of the extinct volcano was overgrown with vegetation; even a few banana trees were thriving at the bottom. From the top of the hill we had a lovely view of Curepipe and the surrounding country stretching to mountain ranges and the sea. The afternoon's outing was a tonic and we returned to the warship much refreshed.

Back on board we learnt that *Cornwall* was due to sail at midnight for South Africa. I did not have a night watch so got into my hammock early. When I went up on deck the next morning a sailor expressed surprise at the fact that we were sailing north-east. If we were going to South Africa we should have been travelling in the opposite direction – south-west. It seemed unbelievable. And then another sailor came along and muttered : 'Another raider report.'

It transpired that just before we were due to sail at midnight, our orders were changed. A direction-finding bearing had indicated that a German surface ship was north-east of Mauritius and *Cornwall* and *Glasgow* were ordered to search for it. We did not know at the time that the ship was the German merchant raider *Orion*, which had sailed from Germany on 6 April 1940 and operated in the Atlantic, Indian and Pacific Oceans. We also did not know how close we came to an encounter with *Orion*. The raider's seaplane reported seeing a British heavy cruiser approaching on a converging course about forty-five miles away. *Orion* changed course and sped away, but later in the day sighted smoke on the horizon, which was presumed to be from *Cornwall*.

Cornwall had raced ahead of *Glasgow* at 26 knots in fairly heavy seas and carried out a patrol near the Chagos Archipelago, but did not see any ships. We were ordered to return to Mauritius where we stayed only a few hours to refuel and then got under way to Durban.

The fact that *Cornwall*, which had sunk a German raider, was coming to Durban must have been well advertised. On the Sunday afternoon, 25 May 1941, when the cruiser arrived with her large battle ensign flying and sailed slowly up the river-like harbour, we were given a terrific welcome. Merchant ships in the crowded harbour sounded their sirens, tugs hooted and people in pleasure launches, yachts, motor-boats and rowing-boats cheered and waved. It was winter at Durban and the ship's company, wearing blue uniforms instead of tropical shorts for the first time in two months, was formed up in their parts of ship while the Royal Marine Band played popular martial music on the quarterdeck. It was a thrilling experience. Quite a crowd of people who had gathered on the quayside at Maydon Wharf, where we berthed, gave three lusty cheers as *Cornwall* came alongside. But there was something on the quayside that interested us more than the enthusiastic crowd, much as we appreciated their warm welcome. It was a large heap of mailbags – the first mail we had received in two months. Mail was always the first thing taken on board to be sorted and distributed as soon as possible. The mailbags were hoisted aboard even before the gangway was lowered.

It was obvious *Cornwall* would be in port for at least a fortnight to be repaired, so as soon as libertymen were allowed ashore at five o'clock that Sunday afternoon Tommy Thorp and I made straight for the Post Office to telephone our wives and tell them to come to Durban, his from Port Elizabeth and mine from Cape Town. The train journey from Cape Town was a particularly long, roundabout one extending over three nights and two days. Alice packed in record time and went to the station that night in the hope that she would be able to get a place in the train even though she did not have a reservation. The train was fully booked, but in those days a ten-shilling tip worked wonders and, if necessary, the guard would give up his compartment, especially if a serviceman was involved.

So Alice duly got on the train, which was due to arrive at Durban at 8 a.m. on Wednesday. I was given special leave to meet her, rose at the crack of dawn and was at the station long before the train was due. A cup of coffee and slice of toast at the station restaurant helped to fill in time and then I paced impatiently up and down the platform. Eventually the clock chimed eight o'clock and right on time the train steamed into the station. Alice was leaning out of the compartment. So was another woman who was met by an officer. I was too excited and preoccupied to remember to salute him, but I do not suppose he noticed either.

Alice and I went by taxi to Twines Hotel where I had booked accommodation for her. It was not one of the best hotels in Durban but was conveniently situated on the Esplanade overlooking the harbour, not too far from where *Cornwall* was berthed and also close to the centre of the city. Another consideration was that the woman manager of the hotel was very pleasant and particularly kind to men in the Navy, Army or Air Force. Some time later Twines was to come in useful as a code name in a cable.

During *Cornwall*'s stay at Durban a contingent of 400 members of the ship's company, led by the Royal Marine Band, marched through the city at the invitation of the Mayor, Mr Rupert Ellis Brown, whose younger son was a midshipman in the cruiser. It was quite a memorable day. A report in the Durban newspaper, the *Natal Mercury*, read:

> Durban had its first opportunity since the outbreak of war of showing its appreciation of the Royal Navy when a visiting contingent yesterday marched through the city, the Mayor, Councillor Rupert Ellis Brown, taking the salute outside the City Hall. From Albert Park, where the contingent paraded, the pavements were thickly lined with eager onlookers and as the heart of the city was approached the crowds grew more and more dense, every possible vantage point being occupied. The roar of cheering seemed at times to drown the Marines band, and by it one could easily trace the progress of the marching sailors.
>
> Great as was the reception as they marched down West Street, the sailors received the greatest cheer of all when they marched past the Mayor and the officer commanding the parade at the City Hall. Here a vast crowd had gathered, determined to make every demonstration of its knowledge of what the Navy means to Durban and, indeed, to South Africa. Durban certainly did adequate honour to its visitors.

After the parade we were the guests of the Mayor at a pleasant luncheon in the City Hall where he said: 'The last thing anyone associated with the Silent Service wishes to do is to have to make a speech or listen to one. It is not my intention to inflict either of these possibilities on you. I have to indicate, however, that the lives of the City Councillors would not have been worth living had they let go this opportunity of saying "Thank you". It is not always possible, of course, to implement one's desires and the exigencies of your service seldom allow for this. Your Captain, I know, is a man of deeds, not words, but on a recent occasion I believe he made one notable short speech which was well acclaimed by everyone. That was: "Splice the main brace." That order is only given to mark a notable occasion, and may the ship's company be fortunate enough again to be in a situation to justify it. So thank you again for what you have done, and thank you for what you are continuously doing – keeping our sea routes open.'

Thanking the City of Durban, the Commanding Officer of *Cornwall*, Captain Manwaring, said: 'This city treats us like its own sons and this city is doing as much towards the war effort – and probably more – as many other places in the Empire. Honour done by such a city is a very great honour indeed.'

While *Cornwall* was at Durban, the sinking of the German battleship *Bismarck* was announced and we were overjoyed to hear that our sister County Class cruiser, *Dorsetshire*, had played a notable part in the action by giving the Nazi warship the coup de grace with her torpedoes. The announcement was greeted with cheers.

The fortnight following the arrival of my wife was a glorious time. But all good things come to an end, and on the morning of 10 June I heard that *Cornwall* was definitely sailing at 2.15 p.m. that day. I phoned Alice at the hotel and arranged with her to come to Maydon Wharf just after noon (our dinner break was from noon to 1.15 p.m.). Permission was given for me to see her on the quayside and we spent close on an hour chatting before I had to say farewell and go on board to get ready for leaving harbour.

21

HMS *Cornwall*'s brief but eventful encounter with *Pinguin* should have served as a warning to other warships not to venture too close to ships suspected of being disguised raiders. Yet six months later the Australian light cruiser *Sydney* fell into the trap and became a victim in a ghastly action. At first it was a mystery – *Sydney* disappeared with all hands and without trace. It was only later that the grim story could be pieced together from enemy sources.

The raider *Kormoran*, which had had a lean time in the Indian Ocean, sinking only three small ships in five months, was intercepted by HMAS *Sydney* about 200 miles off the coast of Western Australia late in the afternoon of 19 November 1941. The raider was disguised as the Dutch vessel *Straat Malakka*. *Sydney*, the same class as the New Zealand cruiser *Achilles*, which had taken part in the action against the *Admiral Graf Spee* in the Battle of the River Plate, continued closing the range as she challenged *Kormoran*. The disguised German ship hoisted the signal letters of the *Straat Malakka*.

The two ships were now on parallel courses only 1,200 to 1,500 yards apart – virtually point blank range. *Sydney*'s guns and torpedo tubes were trained on *Kormoran* and the raider's concealed guns and torpedo tubes were trained on the Australian cruiser. *Sydney* signalled two of the letters of the *Straat Malakka*'s secret call sign and demanded that the other ship complete them. With this the captain of the raider, Captain Theodore Detmers, knew he could not carry on the deception and immediately gave the order to open fire. *Sydney* also opened fire within a few seconds, but the *Kormoran*'s first salvo wrecked her bridge and a torpedo put her two forward turrets out of action. *Sydney*'s second salvo scored a hit and set *Kormoran*'s fuel tanks alight.

Sydney, which was on the starboard side of the raider, was in desperate straits. She turned sharply to port, apparently in an effort to ram *Kormoran*, but passed just astern of her. The raider continued firing at point blank range, while *Sydney* replied with her after turrets and also fired four torpedoes which missed.

About half an hour after the ships opened fire, *Sydney* was moving slowly away, on fire and down by the bows. *Kormoran* had stopped with her engine-room on fire. Some hours later a glare on the horizon was thought to be the *Sydney* blowing up. There were no survivors from her crew of about 700.

Kormoran had to be abandoned late that night because the fire was approaching the mine chambers. Shortly afterwards she blew up. It had been a fight to the death for both ships. Altogether 315 of the *Kormoran*'s crew of 400 men reached Australia, some being picked up by ships, the others getting to land in boats.

Churchill described the loss of the Australian cruiser as 'a sombre sacrifice in lonely waters'.

In sharp contrast to the tragic loss of HMAS *Sydney*, the sinking of the raider *Atlantis* by the County Class cruiser HMS *Devonshire* three days later was a copybook operation. *Devonshire* intercepted *Atlantis* on 22 November, stayed out of range, checked by wireless that she was not the Dutch ship *Polyphemus* she purported to be, opened fire and that was the end of the raider.

But there was more to the story than that summary of the encounter. *Atlantis* was on her way home to Germany after being at sea for almost twenty months since setting out on 31 March 1940. In the words of Captain Bernhard Rogge, the Commanding Officer, 'the tension on board was nerve-racking' because the crew 'hoped to be in a German-held harbour by Christmas'. On her way north in the South Atlantic the raider had to rendezvous with a U-boat, *U-126*, to provide it with fuel and other supplies.

On 21 November one of the aircraft used by *Atlantis* for reconnaissance capsized when landing in a heavy swell and was lost. The ship's second plane could not be assembled in time for dawn reconnaissance the next day so early that morning when she met the U-boat about four degrees south of the equator, Captain Rogge did not know that not too far beyond the horizon was the British cruiser *Devonshire*.

A Walrus seaplane catapulted from *Devonshire* very early reported on its return at 7.10 a.m. that it had sighted a suspicious ship. The Commanding Officer of *Devonshire*, Captain R. D. Oliver, immediately increased speed to 25 knots and altered course towards the ship.

Meantime there was a cordial gathering on board *Atlantis* of Rogge and the captain of the U-boat, Bauer, and some of his crew while the submarine was taken in tow by the raider. Rogge had arranged a special breakfast for Bauer – 'white table-cloth, airy cabin, peacetime ham and eggs and waiter dressed in the best Nord-deutscher Lloyd tradition', as Rogge wrote later in an article published in the South African Defence Force magazine *Commando*. 'The joy of meeting a comrade in arms in the middle of the Atlantic Ocean lent a special atmosphere to the occasion.'

But Bauer not only missed the special breakfast; he also missed the boat in the sense that he could not get back on board his U-boat before it had to do an emergency dive.

Hardly had we enjoyed the first cup of coffee when the voice of the look-out came to our ears : 'Two masts ahead' [wrote Rogge]. The *Atlantis* lay stopped with the U-boat in tow; a motor-launch chug-chugged to and fro taking material and provisions to *U-126*; our mechanics were busy changing a faulty piston in one of our main diesels (a job that takes at least four hours, even with well-trained mechanics like ours).

From the bridge I saw three funnels between thin masts . . . a cruiser of the London Class, perhaps the *Dorsetshire* on which I had been a frequent guest in 1936 when the German cruiser *Karlsruhe* was visiting Hong Kong.

The U-boat had to take emergency action and dive without her captain and at least one of the officers, who were stranded on board *Atlantis*. But there was enough evidence for the *Devonshire*'s aircraft, which had been catapulted off again and flew round the raider in wide circles, to report the presence of a submarine. It had also been noted that the suspicious ship's main structure resembled that of *Atlantis*, which was designated *Raider C* by the Royal Navy.

At 8.37 a.m. *Devonshire* fired 'two salvoes spread to right and left, intended to provoke a return fire and establish the stranger's identity . . . or to induce her to abandon ship and avoid unnecessary bloodshed, especially as she probably had a number of British prisoners on board'.

Atlantis immediately made a raider wireless signal purporting to come from the ship *Polyphemus*. The Commanding Officer of *Devonshire* thereupon sent a signal to the Commander-in-Chief South Atlantic asking whether *Polyphemus* could be in that area. All the time *Devonshire* kept out of range of the raider's guns and avoided being in a position that would expose her to a torpedo attack from the U-boat.

At 9.34 a.m. *Devonshire* received a reply, 'No', to her query about the *Polyphemus*, which was in New York harbour. She immediately opened fire at a range of 17,000 yards.

Then the destruction of our auxiliary cruiser began [wrote Rogge]. Salvo after salvo crashed into the water around us, and soon shell after shell hit the ship. After the first salvo I turned hard before the wind and laid a smoke-screen with both generators on the bow and stern; then I lay, stopped in the smoke, and allowed the ship to drift with engines at slow ... most of the crew were sent to the boats ... the impact of the 20,3-centimetre [8-inch] shells wrought fearful destruction; the whole ship forward was ablaze ... The inadequate range of our guns and the destruction of our torpedo installations did not allow of any reply.

I did not fire at the enemy aircraft as I wanted to give the impression of being a defenceless merchant vessel : the enemy might then conclude that he had sunk nothing more than an unarmed German supply ship, and might continue his defence measures by keeping naval forces in the South Atlantic after our destruction.

After eight more heavy shells had struck my ship, I decided to destroy her, rapidly and finally, by setting off our demolition charges ... Almost simultaneously with the explosion of the demolition charge aft, the forward magazine was blown up by an enemy shell.

Rogge managed to get off his ship just before she sank. Casualties included seven of the crew who were killed or died of wounds. The U-boat took on board 55 men, including the wounded, and put 52 others on deck wearing lifebelts. The remaining 201 survivors were put in two motor-launches and four cutters which were taken in tow towards South America. Naval Headquarters in Germany responded to a signal asking for help by arranging for the supply ship *Python* to rendezvous two days later on 24 November to replenish the U-boat and take over the survivors from *Atlantis*.

In accordance with previous arrangements *Python* then met two U-boats south of St Helena to give them oil fuel, torpedoes and provisions. While the replenishing operation was still in progress on 1 December, *Dorsetshire* arrived as a result of her Walrus aircraft sighting the masts of a ship. When *Dorsetshire* fired two warning shots at long range, *Python* was abandoned and scuttled, capsizing and sinking after fire and explosions had been observed by *Dorsetshire*. The cruiser made off because of the presence of U-boats.

Altogether 414 men, including survivors from *Atlantis*, were accommodated in the two U-boats, a motor-launch, ten lifeboats and seven rubber dinghies, the larger boats being taken in tow by the submarines. German Naval Headquarters ordered two other U-boats to go to the assistance of the survivors. They arrived on 3 and 5 December and all the survivors travelled in crowded U-boats for more than 2,500 miles until they were transferred to four Italian submarines near the Cape Verde Islands off the bulge of West Africa. They all reached the French port of St Nazaire safely between 23 and 29 December – quite a remarkable achievement.

So ended the saga of *Atlantis*, like *Pinguin* a former Hansa Line vessel, which was at sea for the record time of 602 days, sailed 102,000 miles and sank or captured 22 ships totalling 145,698 tons. The survivors were given a heroes' welcome on their arrival in Berlin from France in a special train.

It was also a time for justifiable jubilation by the Royal Navy. Three of the most successful disguised merchant ship raiders, *Pinguin* (8 May), *Kormoran* (19 November) and *Atlantis* (22 November), had been eliminated in addition to several supply ships.

PART THREE

The Monsters

I

HMS *Cornwall's* association with the monsters began when she left Durban on 10 June 1941 after completing action repairs. As indicated by the name 'monsters', they were big – very big. There were six of them but they did not all move around in the sea together. When *Cornwall* sailed out of Durban harbour, past the Bluff into the open sea, three of the monsters were waiting for her.

Monsters was the name given to large troop-carrying liners which were luxury ships in peace-time but were now, under British control, making a huge contribution to the war effort by transporting troops rapidly over long distances. Four of the monsters were British ships of the Cunard-White Star fleet – the largest ship in the world, *Queen Elizabeth* (83,675 tons), *Queen Mary* (81,235 tons), *Aquitania* (44,786 tons) and *Mauretania* (35,739 tons). The other two were the French ship *Ile de France* (43,450 tons), which had been requisitioned in 1940, and *Nieuw Amsterdam* (36,287 tons), which was on charter from the Dutch.

The youngest of the monsters was also the largest, *Queen Elizabeth*, which was nearing completion when the Second World War broke out. Her maiden voyage was crossing the Atlantic in March 1940 to dock at New York where she stayed until November that year when she went to Singapore to be fitted out for transporting troops. *Queen Mary* made her maiden voyage in 1936 and was on her way to New York when war broke out in 1939. She stayed at New York until March the next year when she was sent to Sydney to be converted for carrying troops.

Queen Elizabeth and *Queen Mary* were originally fitted to carry 6,000 troops each, but the number was increased until they could each accommodate as many as 15,000. They frequently sailed without escorts, relying on their speed of $28\frac{1}{2}$ knots and astute routing for their safety. *Aquitania* could carry up to 8,000 troops and *Mauretania* 7,600. *Ile de France* and *Nieuw Amsterdam* could each carry at least as many as *Mauretania*, so between them the six monsters could transport more than 60,000 troops.

In May 1943 Britain's Prime Minister, Mr Winston Churchill, and several top service chiefs and other officials travelled to the United States in *Queen Mary* to attend an important meeting with President Roosevelt and his leaders. Among the passengers in *Queen Mary* were about 5,000 German prisoners, Churchill brushing aside a suggestion that for security reeasons they should be transferred to another ship. Clever precautions had been taken to conceal the fact that the Prime Minister and other VIPs were to be passengers in *Queen Mary* when she sailed from the Clyde. One of them was the posting of notices in Dutch 'to suggest that Queen Wilhelmina and her suite were travelling to America in the ship'. Churchill records that 'so effective were the cover plans that even some members of the Cabinet Office staff, who had embarked in the *Queen Mary* for the Hot Springs Food Conference, were dumbfounded to see us board the ship'.

Two days before *Queen Mary* arrived at New York she was met and escorted by United States warships. The next day Churchill, with his typical sense of humour, sent this signal to Roosevelt : 'Since yesterday we have been surrounded by the United States Navy, and we all greatly appreciate the high value you evidently set on our continued survival.'

When *Cornwall* sailed from Durban the three monsters waiting to be escorted by her were *Mauretania*, *Ile de France* and *Nieuw Amsterdam*. The thousands of troops they had on board and bound for the Middle East included the 2nd (South African) Division, which was to join the Allied forces in the North African desert.

As soon as *Cornwall* was clear of the harbour, we closed up at action stations to test communications and other circuits and ensure that everything was working efficiently after the spell of just over a fortnight in port. We headed north with the three big ships astern of us and soon were steaming at 20½ knots, the regular speed when in convoy with these monsters. It was a treat after the large, slow convoy we escorted to the Red Sea a couple of months earlier. The speed gave a welcome breeze that tempered the uncomfortable heat and humidity.

One thing *Cornwall* really excelled at was rolling. What with being a long, narrow ship with three funnels, high freeboard – about thirty feet from the water-line to the deck – and a large hangar abaft, she was a bit top-heavy which was conducive to excessive rolling. In the afternoon six days after leaving Durban we encountered a particularly heavy ground swell off Cape Guardafui at the horn of Africa, just before entering the Gulf of Aden. The cruiser rolled so much that lockers toppled over and crockery was broken. At the time I was having a doze stretched out on a table in the recreation space. I was rudely awakened when the table keeled over and deposited me unceremoniously on top of another matelot who was sleeping on a bench next to it.

2

After we had seen the three monsters safely into the Red Sea and spent a couple of days sweating at Aden, *Cornwall* called at the Seychelles on her way south. While at anchor one evening, a group of sailors on the foc's'le started discussing the shell-fire in the recent action against the German raider *Pinguin*. This prompted one of the older hands to recall that he had taken part in the evacuation of British troops at Dunkirk. He had been in a small boat and experienced plenty of bombing by the Nazi planes. He mentioned that the raider action was the first time he had been under shell-fire.

'Which do you prefer, bombing from the air or shelling in a surface action?' a youngster asked him.

'To be perfectly frank, neither,' he replied. 'I'm not one of the death or glory boys.'

'Sorry,' said the youngster, 'I put that rather clumsily. What I mean is, which do you consider is worse?'

'Well, if I had a choice,' said the old hand, 'I would prefer to be bombed by aircraft. I think being shelled in a surface action is worse.'

If that old hand was still alive ten months later, I cannot help wondering if he had changed his mind about dive-bombers.

During the few days that *Cornwall* was anchored in the harbour at the picturesque island of Mahé in the Seychelles group, which consists of 191 islands and islets, I slung my hammock in the open on the upper deck at night and slept like a log in the fresh air. Indeed, I slept so soundly that I did not even wake when two members of the Royal Marine Band had an altercation within a yard or two of my hammock. I heard about it only the next day. The band had been ashore at Victoria, the capital of the Seychelles, to play at a dance. On arrival back on board *Cornwall*, the two men became involved in a rowdy argument, during which one of them became overwrought and hit out at the other. He ducked neatly so, instead of the attacker's fist hitting him, it came into very painful contact with some steel superstructure.

The next day I happened to be in the Sick Bay when the bandsman came in nursing his injured hand. His thumb was fractured and he spent some time with his hand in plaster of paris. I could not help smiling when, in reply to the doctor, he described how he had slipped and fallen on his thumb. I was in the Sick Bay because I had been put on the sick list as a result of injuring my leg in a fall while working in the motor-boat. When on the sick list, unless confined to bed, one remained in the Sick Bay during the morning. But that did not mean having no work to do. One was employed cleaning up the Sick Bay – sweeping, polishing brightwork, washing paintwork, and so on.

While *Cornwall* was carrying out a patrol in equatorial waters north of the Seychelles, I had a new experience one evening. I was 'in the rattle', which is a naval expression meaning in trouble of a fairly serious nature. If one is ticked off, it is referred to as being given 'a bottle'. But if the offence is more serious and one has to face a charge, that is being 'in the rattle'.

Able Seaman Bloggs and I were in the rattle because we did not help to darken ship, an essential precaution for blacking out when at sea. Every evening 'Darken ship' was piped and the watch on deck had to close portholes, hatches and generally see that no lights were showing. On this occasion starboard watch had to darken ship. At the time Bloggie, with whom I had become friendly as a result of being paired with him as look-out, and I were enjoying some exercise walking up and down the deck. We were chatting, the loudspeakers were blaring forth music relayed from a radio and we did not hear the pipe to darken ship.

The first we knew of it was when a rather officious young Leading Seaman told us to report on the bridge with our caps at 8 p.m. In such cases offenders were arraigned before the officer of the watch, who decided whether the case should be dismissed or go before the Commander. We duly donned our caps and made our way to the bridge at eight o'clock. We waited on the forebridge, which was below the part of the bridge known as the compass platform where the officer of the watch was on duty. The Leading Seaman was waiting for us and within a matter of seconds a Regulating Petty Officer – a sort of policeman on board – arrived. The RPO read out our names very formally : 'Ordinary Seaman Dimbleby and Able Seaman Bloggs'. This apparently satisfied him that we were present and he ordered us to go up the short ladder leading to the compass platform. We were lined up in front of the officer of the watch, ordered to take off our caps and our names were again read out, only this time the charge against us was added.

(Top left) Bill Barrett, a leading member of the Royal Marine Band, who had a key gunnery control position for *Cornwall*'s main armament. *(Bottom left)* Ken Dimbleby in the overalls he was wearing when *Cornwall* sank. *(Right)* Tommy Thorp, who became an officer after the sinking of HMS *Cornwall*.

While HMS *Dorsetshire (left)* completes a circle with her steering out of action, HMS *Cornwall* is enveloped in the smoke of bomb explosions during the attack by Japanese dive-bombers on Easter Sunday, 1942. Both ships were sunk in less than 20 minutes.

HMS *Cornwall* lists to port and is down by the head, with part of the foc's'le already under water, shortly before she sank bows first after the Japanese dive-bombing attack on 5 April 1942.

Bloggie and I explained the circumstances in which we had not heard the pipe to darken ship and, after hearing the evidence, the officer of the watch was satisfied that we had not deliberately neglected our duty.

'Case dismissed,' he declared.

'On caps,' ordered the RPO. 'Right turn, double march.'

So off trotted Bloggie and I, none the worse for being in the rattle and not a little amused.

Bloggie, who was twenty-six – a couple of months younger than I – had been in the Navy since the age of sixteen. He was a quietly spoken, clean living and very genuine person whose friendship meant a lot to me while serving in *Cornwall*. He was engaged to a young woman whom he had known since childhood and had arranged to marry her the next time the ship got to England. At all the ports where he was able to go ashore his main concern was to buy articles for his fiancée's trousseau. Everyone knew him as Bloggie. It was not until forty years later when I saw a copy of the official 'Missing presumed killed' list in *The Fleet* that I discovered his name was Frederick W. Bloggs. It just did not sound right for him, neither Frederick nor Fred. I always remember him as Bloggie and I am sure that is what he would prefer.

3

The day after I was in the rattle was a memorable one for those of us who had joined *Cornwall* at Simonstown four months earlier. On 1 July it was announced that the ship had been at sea for 100 days since leaving Simonstown on 28 February 1941, and during that time had travelled 32,254 miles. The next day we crossed the equator for the fourteenth time. We were still on a rather boring patrol, steaming at only 12 knots, but a pleasant surprise was in store for us a day later. We met the *Nieuw Amsterdam,* increased speed and set off to escort her at 20½ knots to Durban. After patrolling close to the equator at a slow speed for a week, it was a breath of fresh air to be speeding along ahead of the handsome Dutch ship.

But on the lower deck we wondered why we had to escort the *Nieuw Amsterdam* because we heard the other two monsters we had convoyed north, *Ile de France* and *Mauretania*, had returned to Durban on their own. Our curiosity was satisfied a few days later when we learnt that the Greek royal family and Cabinet Ministers from Greece were on board the *Nieuw Amsterdam*. They had been evacuated when the

Germans overran their country. When *Cornwall* arrived at Durban and sailed into the harbour, the Greek flag flew from her mainmast and the white ensign from the foremast. Before we docked King George of Greece sent a signal thanking us for escorting him and wishing us the best of luck. A copy of the signal was posted on the notice board.

One did not have to be a fortune-teller to know what our next trip would be. Durban was teeming with British soldiers, the *Nieuw Amsterdam* had arrived with *Cornwall*, and waiting in the harbour were the *Mauretania* and *Ile de France*. In fact, it was the same again for the next couple of months – a week in convoy with the three monsters up to the Red Sea and then a couple of days in Aden for *Cornwall*.

On one of these fast convoy runs to the north we had on board fifty members of the British South Africa Police from Rhodesia who said they were bound for Abyssinia to help round up armed Italian levies who were still roaming the country. We had hardly left Durban harbour when the swells took their toll of some of the policemen. This led to an amusing incident concerning a bucket, which was a sailor's precious possession. Most matelots had a bucket in which they washed and did their laundry. A regular practice after washing was to tip the bucket of water over one's head to have an improvised shower as there were only wash basins in the bathroom.

One policeman who was finding the effects of the cruiser's motion in the swells a bit too much asked a sailor if he could borrow a bucket that was standing nearby. The sailor thought the member of the BSAP wanted to use it for washing in and replied : 'Dig out' (a naval expression meaning 'carry on' or 'help yourself'). The policeman hardly had time to say 'Thanks' before grabbing the bucket and 'bringing up his heart' in it, much to the amusement of all except the owner of the bucket.

The BSAP contingent got on very well with the sailors. On the first morning after leaving Durban we were amused to find that they had been made to lend a hand at scrubbing decks. They did not mind and thought it quite a joke. They were a cheerful lot and also turned out for our PT sessions in the afternoons. In a tug-of-war contest they beat the Royal Navy. But they were not always popular. During the night, when watches were changed, sailors coming off or going on watch knew their routes so well on the mess decks that even in the dim light they did not bump any of the many hammocks in which their shipmates were sleeping. But the policemen could not judge their heights and often bumped hammocks – to the accompaniment of naval curses from those in them.

While a couple of us were busy painting the square box-like hangar one morning, the ship's Chaplain, the Reverend J. M. Bird, one of the most popular men in the warship, came up and started chatting to us. He mentioned that he had recently received a letter from an old maiden aunt to whom he had sent a photograph of the ship. She had mistaken the rather prominent hangar for a chapel and remarked on how lovely his 'big chapel' was with its stained glass windows. What she thought were stained-glass windows were Carley floats suspended on the sides of the hangar. The time was to come when those Carley floats really were life-savers, but unfortunately the Chaplain was not one of those able to make use of them.

It was during this voyage that I peeled more potatoes at one session than ever before – or since – in my life. It has not been claimed as a record in the Royal Navy, but no one has ever disputed my claim to its being a record in my family. In the Navy potatoes were always referred to as spuds. Every day after dinner one heard the pipe : 'Spuds are now being issued at the foremost spud locker.' Only once did I hear a bosun's mate pipe : 'Potatoes are now being issued . . . ' And everyone roared with laughter because it sounded so incongruous.

One of the duties of the cooks in a mess was to peel the daily issue of spuds and take them to the galley. We took turns at being cooks, two doing duty each day. Calling the duty men cooks was a naval misnomer because they did not have anything to do with the actual cooking. Apart from peeling spuds, their job was to fetch and serve the meals and then wash up and clean the mess.

In our mess it was the practice for the cooks to peel the spuds at breakfast time. New cooks took over at dinner time at midday. It so happened that I had the forenoon watch from 8 a.m. until dinner time on the day I was one of the cooks so would not be able to give my fellow cook much assistance. To make amends I decided to peel the potatoes the previous afternoon. As luck would have it, the spuds were rather small that day so I would have to peel a large number because the English sailor had to have his full quota of spuds. Indeed, I felt the Navy would stop operating if there were not enough spuds. So I got cracking and counted each spud meticulously as I finished removing its jacket and quite a large part of its body, too. As the number mounted I became determined to reach 100. The 100th spud was peeled just in time for me to have a quick wash before going on watch.

Perhaps it was just as well that there was a more than adequate serving of spuds to fortify us for our arrival at Aden a couple of days later after leaving the three monsters in the Red Sea. When we arrived it was 10 a.m. on *Cornwall*'s clocks, but they were one hour ahead of local time at Aden so were promptly put back an hour, which meant an hour's extra work. The thought of an extra hour's work in the heat – it was particularly hot, even by Aden's standards – was not pleasing.

At Aden ships did not berth at a quay, but were moored to buoys by very thick wires. But first of all a thick rope was taken to the buoy to take the initial strain. Our rope broke under the strain just when the first wire was being taken to the buoy. The result was that the ship was gradually slewed round by the tide. 'What a picnic,' as the matelots remarked. While a tug pushed *Cornwall*, we had to heave on wires on the foc's'le. With the relentless sun burning our bare backs, we heaved and heaved until we ached.

After more than an hour the warship was eventually moored and we breathed a sigh of relief. But a few minutes later those of us working on the foc's'le just about spat blood. We were told that the ship had to be moved to another buoy. It was another 'picnic' . . . more heaving . . . the wires never seemed to end . . . and they felt heavier and heavier. The Captain would shout from the bridge : 'Stop heaving on that wire.'

'Heave,' an officer on the foc's'le would order. And then we would get hell for not knowing what we were supposed to do.

'You bloody idiot,' the Captain shouted on one occasion to the officer.

The officer, of course, passed it on to us, calling us 'a lot of bloody Girl Guides', much to our annoyance.

Noon arrived – our dinner hour – but we could not go to dinner. We were given a short break, which we spent in the shade under the foremast turret, and then had to work for another hour before we were eventually able to fall out and go down to our mess to get some much-needed sustenance.

4

Aden became the focal point in *Cornwall*'s operations even after convoying the three monsters, *Mauretania, Ile de France* and *Nieuw Amsterdam*, from Durban up north. It could hardly be welcomed as a congenial port to be calling at regularly. The first time I saw Aden and went ashore was a disappointment because I had always imagined it to be a large place with plenty of oriental glamour. Seen from the ship, everything looked so barren, the drab town lying at the foot of light brown hills devoid of vegetation. The only greenery to be seen was a small cluster of trees – reputed to be gardens – on the foreshore of the town. To the left the hills fell away to extensive flats where salt pans were made by pumping sea water on to the land.

Probably because it was so hot and thirsty in Aden, it was not necessary to look for a hotel to have a drink. When Ian Keith and I went ashore, we discovered that nearly every shop sold drinks and even provided tables and chairs for clients who were more interested in liquid refreshment than the other wares. After quenching our thirst with a cold beer in a grocery store, Ian and I visited the bazaars for which Aden was supposed to be well known, but found them unattractive. In the main street the so-called bazaars were very ordinary shops selling goods made in India, China and even Britain. The back streets were not the cleanest of places.

We teamed up with a couple of other sailors from *Cornwall* and engaged a taxi driven by a young Somali, whom we named Allie and who said he would take us to the places worth seeing. We drove first to a township aptly named Crater because it lies in the crater made by the hills behind the port of Aden. It was very dusty, dirty and, in keeping with other places near Aden, nearly every building was a shop of some description. The streets, which were merely the spaces between the rows of flat-roofed buildings, were cluttered up with children and old men smoking long and sometimes very ornate pipes. All along the sidewalks were small open-air cafés where the aged and wise sat and smoked while smelly camels mixed with the crowd just as though they were part of the family. Some of the inhabitants of Crater provided an oriental touch with their bright silken garments, but most of the people were shabbily dressed and many of the menfolk seemed intent on emulating the frugal fashion of Mahatma Gandhi. Many of the children pestered visitors incessantly for baksheesh (a tip).

Allie drove us from Crater to the not very impressive botanical gardens and then to what are known as the Tanks at the end of the gardens. They are a series of reservoirs built in steps up a narrow and very sheer ravine. There are twelve reservoirs which, when full, can hold twenty million gallons of water, but when we saw them they must have contained only about twenty. We were also told that nothing definite was known about the origin of the Tanks, but it was believed they were built in the time of the Queen of Sheba. They were discovered by the British Governor at Aden in 1854, completely overgrown with bush and had to be cleaned out. The twelve tanks, or reservoirs as I prefer to call them, are joined by channels over which are constructed stone bridges. Steps lead up from one reservoir to the next.

We were shown over the Tanks by an old Arab who looked after the botanical gardens. I refer to him as old because he was lean and had grey hair, but he wore black and white checked trousers and a green striped pyjama-like coat. Actually he was only forty. I was amazed at how well he spoke English and commented on it. He proudly informed me that there were English as well as Arab-medium schools in Crater, where one could take the London matriculation examination.

'Did you write the matriculation examination?' I asked him.

'No,' he replied, 'but I am going to.'

'When?' I asked, rather surprised. He was forty years old and he still intended taking the examination.

'When the war is over,' he said in his quiet way. 'I am studying for it now. All great men are old, so it is never too late.'

The smiling Allie drove us back to Aden via the Royal Air Force base and what is known as Arab town, a filthy village teeming with people, camels, sheep, dogs and cats in dusty streets. Altogether we drove twenty-five to thirty miles and Allie charged us nine shillings each, which we thought reasonable. Later we discovered that he had charged just about double the regulation fare for the trip.

5

The time had come for *Cornwall* to meet the two great monsters, *Queen Elizabeth* and *Queen Mary*. We were operating on the East Indies Station and, after the three trips from Durban to the Red Sea with the smaller monsters, *Mauretania, Ile de France* and *Nieuw Amsterdam*, interspersed between dreary patrolling and escorting slow individual ships, we arrived at Colombo at the end of August. We were greeted by the huge sign :

CEYLON

FOR GOOD

TEA

In peace-time the sign was illuminated at night and visible from way out at sea. Now, with the war coming to the end of its second year and eyes being turned anxiously to the east where a new danger threatened from Japan, it was blacked out at night and could be seen only in the daytime.

As we were to be at Colombo for about ten days to have one or two of our 8-inch guns changed, arrangements had been made for the starboard and port watches to go on leave in turn for four days. We were to be sent to hosts all over Ceylon. About 350 of us went off in the starboard watch and, as the ship was moored to a buoy in the harbour, we had to go ashore by boat. After breakfast at 5.30 a.m. we trooped down the gangway on to a tug that took us to the landing jetty. Some of the crew went by bus to their hosts, but a large batch of us were taken to the station to travel inland by train. It was an interesting journey through picturesque country with magnificent scenery, the train meandering through the lowlands with flowering trees, coconut and banana trees, bamboos and palms, among many others, past rice lands, canals, rivers and lakes and into jungles. As the train climbed into the higher country, we came to the tea plantations that play such an important part in the country's economy.

There were gay scenes at the many stations and sidings where the train stopped, men and youngsters enticing the sailors to buy beer, buns and bananas among other fruit and sweetmeats. At almost every station a few sailors alighted to go to their hosts. I had been instructed to get off with several others at Nanuoya, about 100 miles from Colombo, where the train arrived in the early afternoon. Most of the chaps had paired off but, as my friend Bloggie had been changed to port watch, I was on my own. When an elderly woman, who seemed to be in charge of organising things, bustled along, I asked if anyone was taking only one sailor. A man in his early thirties who was with her said : 'Yes, I am. Come along with me.'

Thus I found myself on a tea estate with the Bond family, a charming couple with two sons aged four and two. The few days I spent with them were a delightful interlude. Every bedroom in what they called their bungalow had its own bathroom. After six months living on the mess deck of a warship, it was a joy to revel in such home comforts. But I must confess to being surprised when the Indian servant brought in early morning 'tea' the next day. Quotation marks are used with the word tea because it consisted of a pot of real Ceylon tea, a large slice of papaw and two bananas – and breakfast was to be served less than a hour later.

During my stay I was shown over the Bonds' 300-acre estate, which was 5,000 feet above sea level, encompassed the sides of three hills and a small valley and required a staff of 500. A large number of them were women who did the picking of leaves in the tea plantations. (It is almost misleading to use the word plantation because one thinks in terms of trees, whereas the tea bushes were only eighteen inches to two feet high.) I was surprised to learn that the leaves could be used to make tea within twenty-four hours of being picked. The estate had its own factory where the tea leaves were dried, sifted, sorted, tasted and graded. Tasting was, of course, done without milk. One took a sip of the black tea, swilled it around one's mouth and then spat it into a bucket. There was no limit to the amount of noise the taster could make, so this tasting time as a very audible operation.

One of a tea planter's problems was dealing with those of his big staff. Bond had to set aside a fixed hour every day when his employees could unburden themselves of their troubles and worries. While I was at Maha Eluja, the name of the estate, one of the Tamils said he could not stay in his room because it was haunted. This meant one of the men who specialised in such spiritual problems would have to be called in to 'de-haunt' the room.

Although in the bracing air of the mountains about 100 miles from the harbour at Colombo, I was not altogether away from the Navy. But for the fact that tea planters were regarded as key men, Bond would have joined the Royal Navy when war broke out. He was so keen on the Navy that his hobby was making models of warships, which he kept in a special cabinet in his lounge.

When the starboard watch arrived back in Colombo on the fourth day of leave, *Cornwall* was in dry dock and infested with workmen running around like a lot of cockroaches and stealing just about everything they could lay their hands on. I dumped my locked suitcase next to my locker and made my way to a large chestnut tree that stood beside the dry dock. When a warship was in the dock a canteen was opened next to the tree and it was the custom for sailors to take their supper under the tree and wash it down with a bottle of beer. Fortunately *Cornwall* left the dry dock the next day when the port watch went on leave and was moored again in the harbour.

The day after the port watch returned from leave, we sailed from Colombo to Trincomalee, a large natural harbour on the east side of Ceylon. While based at 'Trinco', we spent some days and nights carrying out gunnery trials, firing at targets towed first by a tug and then an auxiliary fleet vessel.

Early on the Monday morning (15 September) the two *Queens* arrived, accompanied by a cruiser and laden with troops bound for the Middle East. *Queen Mary* anchored quite close to *Cornwall* in the harbour, but *Queen Elizabeth* 'dropped hook' just outside the entrance. The next morning *Cornwall* weighed anchor and sailed out to spend some time on an anti-aircraft practice shoot. At about midday *Queen Elizabeth* and *Queen Mary* hove in sight and we set off with them, both living up to the majesty of their names – royal blood among the world's leading liners. They made a stately sight as they cut through the sea astern of us, as steady as rocks at 24-knots while *Cornwall* pitched and tossed, with water coming over the foc's'le and washing down the upper deck. At 20½-knots with the smaller monsters the decks were dry, but at 24 we were wet.

Soon after we got under way, the announcement was made that we were convoying the two monsters to the Red Sea and would arrive at Aden on 21 September. It was hardly necessary to pipe where we were going. It was obvious that the two *Queens*, full of troops, could be going only one way from Ceylon at that stage of the war and that was to the Middle East. After Germany had attacked the USSR three months earlier on 22 June, the Russians were reeling back almost to the gates of Moscow. The Mediterranean was closed to British convoys and the position of the British and Commonwealth forces in the North African desert was fraught with difficulties.

This was a very special convoy. All convoys were a big responsibility for the warships escorting them, but having to escort the two largest liners in the world, filled with several thousand troops, necessitated taking extra precautions to ensure their safety. During the middle watch on our first night at sea with the two *Queens*, *Cornwall* nearly collided with another ship. Visibility was poor and the ship suddenly loomed up directly ahead of us. The wheel was put hard over to starboard and we swung away just in time.

Soon after breakfast the next morning it was piped that a suspicious vessel had been sighted. No chances were being taken. 'Action stations' was sounded and from our elevated position, those of us on the air defence platform had a good view of the suspicious ship. It was a small merchantman. One of the ratings commented : 'I'm willing to bet it's British. They almost always seem to make a mess of answering signals when challenged.'

Sure enough, after being closed up at action stations for about fifteen minutes, the secure was sounded and it was piped that the ship had been identified as British. We changed course to rejoin the *Queen Elizabeth* and *Queen Mary*, which had gone off in the opposite direction.

As we sped across the Indian Ocean it was fascinating during the daytime just watching the two supermonsters, graceful despite their huge size, seemingly imperturbable and the embodiment of such immense power. Strangely, the *Queen Mary* always looked larger although she was 2,440 tons less than her 83,675-ton elder sister, *Queen Elizabeth*. No doubt it was because of her extra funnel. She had three and the *Queen Elizabeth* two.

After what was reported to be the fastest crossing of the Indian Ocean ever made by a warship, we entered the Red Sea at night only a few hours more than four days after leaving Trincomalee. We escorted the *Queens* about 150 miles up the Red Sea and then, early the next morning, left them to continue on their own to Suez. It was a case of au revoir, not goodbye, because we were destined to meet again.

The heat was stifling in the Red Sea and, if anything, worse when *Cornwall* arrived at Aden in the early evening.

'They call Aden the Gateway to the East,' lamented a Scottish rating more accustomed to snow than sweat. 'To me it's the gateway to hell, if not hell itself.'

6

While *Cornwall* was anchored in the bay at Aden – we had left the harbour that morning – I had a most unexpected experience. Indeed, I think it could justifiably be described as a rare experience. Our old friend *Mauretania* had arrived the previous day and was moored some distance away in the harbour. After dinner I went up on deck for a breather and was enjoying what little sea breeze there was to get some relief from the heat and humidity. While relaxing on the upper deck a young signalman came up and said the Chief Yeoman had a signal for me from *Mauretania*. I was quite taken aback. A signal for me, an Ordinary Seaman, from *Mauretania* . . . it did not make sense. Anyway I went up to the bridge and reported myself to Sam Langford, the Chief Yeoman.

'I was told you have a signal for me,' I said with some diffidence.

'Yes, here it is,' replied the Chief Yeoman and handed me the signal which I still have among my mementoes.

It was addressed to K. G. Dimbleby (incorrectly added A.B. because I was still an Ordinary Seaman) and was from 'Third Officer Jones and Clarke'. The signal had been flashed by lamp from *Mauretania* and read : 'Saw Desmond three weeks ago in Durban. He sends regards.'

Desmond is my younger brother and I was grateful to Jones and Clarke for the message that brought some cheer into an otherwise cheerless day. It brought back happy memories – and an amusing one. After being selected to go on an officers' course in the South African Army, Des was stationed for a time at Sonderwater, a camp about thirty miles from Pretoria. The man in charge of training the young officers was a Permanent Force captain, an outstanding soldier who had been sent to Britain on a special course. The story is told that one bitterly cold winter's night, the captain sat at the dinner table in the mess wearing his greatcoat with the collar turned up over his ears and generally looking miserable. The president of the mess, an Active Citizen Force colonel, remarked on how cold the captain looked and asked him : 'How did you fare when you were in England during winter?'

All eyes were on the captain as the officers, young and not so young, waited for his polite reply. Looking out from the shelter of his greatcoat, the captain replied in his heavy Afrikaans accent : 'I fokkin' near died.'

On arrival at the battlefront in North Africa, Des was seconded to a British regiment, the King's Own Yorkshire Light Infantry (KOYLI). He was wounded by a mine during the invasion of Sicily and this led to his having an unexpected naval experience.

My evacuation, lying as a spectator on a stretcher, was funny [he wrote from a hospital in Tripoli]. Together with the other wounded, we were being transported to a hospital ship when a cruiser intercepted us to say that the hospital ship had been sunk. We were taken aboard the cruiser and spent the night and most of the next day on board. There was quite a to-do, what with enemy aircraft bombing us and our ships bombarding the coast. However, in the end we were transferred to another hospital ship, and after she had hung about for a day or two, we were brought here.

Des rejoined the KOYLI regiment in Italy after being discharged from hospital, and in 1944 was awarded the Military Cross 'for gallant and distinguished services'.

7

When *Cornwall* left Aden we knew we were not going to Durban. A Commodore who had taken passage in the cruiser from Trincomalee and was bound for Durban had transferred from *Cornwall* to *Maure-tania*, which was obviously returning to Durban to continue her shuttle service with troops for the Middle East. Also, we were not alone when we got under way at 14 knots, which seemed like crawling after convoying the two *Queens* at 24. We had as company two ships and it was piped that they were 'special ships' which we would escort 'to the vicinity of Ceylon'.

The reason for this vague announcement became apparent six days later when we arrived at Addu Atoll in the Maldive group of islands. The group comprises about 2,000 small coral islands which form a north-south chain 475 miles long and 80 miles wide. The total land area is only 115 square miles. None of the islands covers more than five square miles. Most of them are smaller than that and are like platforms about six feet above sea level. Features of the islands are lagoons with incredibly clear water, white sand beaches, grass, low-growing tropical plants, coconut palms and fruit trees.

The Maldive Islands are grouped in twelve clusters called atolls. Barrier coral reefs around the atolls help to protect them from the sea. Addu Atoll is situated at the southern end of the Maldives, the islands and coral reefs in the group forming a harbour large enough to shelter a whole fleet of warships. (At one time later it accommodated a fleet of five battleships, two aircraft-carriers, cruisers, destroyers and supply ships.) An air base was established on Gan, one of the islands in Addu Atoll. Almost hidden among the trees were the huts in which the islanders lived. The Maldives were a British Protectorate from 1887 to 1965 when they became an independent republic.

When *Cornwall* arrived at Addu Atoll, 600 miles south-west of Ceylon, on 30 September 1941, the atoll was code-named Port T and was being developed as a secret naval base – a well-kept secret that fortunately did not become known to the Japanese because Port T was to play an important part during a critical time. It was evident that the two 'special ships' *Cornwall* had escorted there had a special cargo for the base.

Being almost on the equator, Port T was very hot and the humidity was awful. When Admiral Sir James Somerville first visited the secret base some months later, he declared: 'This beats the band for an abomination of heat and desolation.' *Cornwall*'s ship's company baked and sweated there for eight days, keeping watches day and night the same as when at sea. Work parties were sent ashore to help get the base established. The discomfort was to some extent offset by the fact that a ship arrived with the first mail we had received for two months.

Because I was a journalist in peace-time and could write shorthand, I was detailed on several occasions to record and type the evidence at inquiries. While at Port T, I had to attend an inquiry one day followed the next by a Disciplinary Court which was held in a fleet auxiliary ship. The court sat all day and then I had to get busy transcribing my shorthand record and typing copies of the evidence. It was heavy going and during the night a very pleasant Paymaster Lieutenant-Commander came in and asked if I would care for a whisky. When I told him I was not partial to spirits, he explained very apologetically that there was no beer on board. I had been given a mattress and blanket and stretched out on the upper deck of the auxiliary ship when I decided to adjourn at 1.30 a.m. The raucous voice of a burly Petty Officer awakened me in time to be back at the typewriter before 7 a.m. The job was eventually completed at noon and I returned to *Cornwall* a whole guinea richer for my labours.

8

As *Cornwall* sailed from Port T in a southerly direction, we were informed that our orders were to rendezvous with another cruiser, HMS *Enterprise*, and carry out a patrol off Madagascar in an effort to intercept a Vichy French convoy that would probably be escorted by warships. All sorts of stories circulated about the probable strength of the Vichy warships and some of the ratings became quite morbid. The reason was that during our stay at Colombo, one of them had visited a fortune-teller who informed him that the ship would be in action soon and a number of his friends would be killed. We duly carried out a patrol in company with *Enterprise*, a ship that was later to earn our eternal gratitude, but did not meet the convoy. The fortune-teller had either used a stock story for sailors – or perhaps he was seeing events further ahead.

The patrol was, however, not without incident. One night *Cornwall*'s whole electric system broke down. The Captain was furious. I was on watch as a look-out on the bridge at the time and heard it all. He sent for the Engineer Commander and the Torpedo Officer and told them to hold an immediate inquiry. The defect was soon rectified, but the Captain nevertheless insisted on a full inquiry without delay.

'I want to know who is responsible,' he said. 'Here we are liable to meet the enemy at any moment and the ship is helpless just because some idiot does not know his job.'

He paused for a moment, then exploded again.

'I'll have a court martial,' he thundered.

It was during this patrol that I struck up a friendship with Bill Barrett that ended tragically a few months later. Musician Barrett, to give him his official rank, was a member of the Royal Marine Band. He joined the Navy when he was fourteen and even at that tender age was an accomplished musician. He could have been a bandmaster at the age of twenty-two, but was upset by something and told the Captain of the ship he was serving in then that he did not want the promotion. Now thirty-five, he had recently received the long service medal from *Cornwall*'s Captain. After reading Bill's service papers, the Captain said : 'I am always pleased to do anything for a man with your fine record.'

Bill was a cut above most men on the lower deck. He was well read, a thinker and a man of sterling character. During peacetime service, mostly in flagships in the Mediterranean and Far East, he had some exceptionally interesting experiences, including playing at the coronation of the Emperor of Japan. He played a few instruments, his favourite being the viola – an accomplishment that led to his receiving an open invitation to join the Cape Town Municipal Orchestra after the war. He had become privately engaged to a young woman at the Cape and looked forward to settling there as soon as he could get his discharge from the Navy.

He was also a keen sportsman – a leading water polo player, good cricketer and, in his youth, a champion boxer. It was a mutual interest in playing cricket that started our friendship. As a result of a chat he had with our new Gunnery Officer, Lieutenant C. E. J. Streatfield, cricket was revived and we had enjoyable games in Colombo, Aden and Bombay.

Our first game was against HMS *Exeter*, the cruiser renowned for the fight she put up against the German pocket battleship in the River Plate action early in the war. She was so badly damaged in that engagement that it had been suggested she should be laid up at the Falkland Islands for the rest of the war. Churchill did not agree and, at his insistence, she was sailed back to Britain and repaired for further service, which unfortunately was to end so sadly in the east. *Exeter* was at Colombo when *Cornwall* arrived there after the Madagascar patrol and challenged us to a game of cricket. It was a battle fought peacefully on a picturesque field – a battle the famous ship did not win.

It was early in November 1941, after carrying out exercises and a practice shoot with *Exeter*, that *Cornwall* was sent half way to Australia to take over escorting the *Queen Elizabeth* and *Queen Mary* from the Australian cruiser *Canberra*. We did a fast run to Trincomalee, calling there only long enough to refuel, and then across to the Red Sea where we said farewell to the two great monsters.

Our fast trips in convoy with the *Queens* were enjoyable but not without an incident. It happened one night when *Cornwall* was leading the two monsters into the Red Sea and there was nearly a collision with the *Queen Mary*. Fortunately for us the ships did not collide because it could have been a major disaster. Almost a year later there was a collision between the *Queen Mary* and smaller cruiser, HMS *Curacoa*, which had been converted to an anti-aircraft ship. Soon after the Western Approaches escort had joined the *Queen Mary*, which was coming from America to Britain and sailing north of Ireland, *Curacoa* was steaming ahead with the liner zig-zagging astern of her. The 81,235-ton *Queen Mary* rammed the 4,190-ton cruiser cutting her in half. Altogether 338 lives were lost in the terrifying accident. Protracted legal action on the question of responsibility was eventually taken on appeal to the House of Lords, which ruled that the Admiralty was two-thirds to blame and the Cunard-White Star Company one-third.

This was the only mishap in the two *Queens'* war service, of inestimable value, during which they transported 1,243,538 troops. It was a thrilling experience just to be in their company at sea.

The *Queen Elizabeth* and *Queen Mary* were both reconditioned after the war and resumed commercial service. But with ever-increasing passenger traffic by air, the days of giant liners were numbered. It is sad to reflect on the fate of the *Queen Elizabeth*. She was sold in 1968 for use as an exhibition and convention centre at Fort Lauderdale, about twenty-five miles north of Miami on the east coast of the United States. Two years later she was sold to Orient Overseas Line, renamed *Seawise University* and refitted at Hong Kong for service as a floating educational institution. A few days before she was due to sail for trials in this new tertiary educational capacity, fire broke out in the ship and she capsized and sank in Hong Kong harbour. It was an undignified end for the famous ship.

The *Queen Mary* was sold in 1967 to the City of Long Beach, California, where she was converted to remain at anchor as a floating Museum of the Sea.

PART FOUR

The Gambler

I

Sadakichi Takano, a schoolmaster in a Japanese village, was fifty-six years old when his seventh child, a son, was born on 4 April 1884. He had five other sons and did not know what name to give the new one. When his wife, Mineko, pressed him to think of one, he solved the problem quite simply. The latest child was born when he was fifty-six so call him Fifty-Six which, in Japanese characters, is Isoroku.

Isoroku was fifteen when he applied to enter the Naval Academy on the island of Etajima, near Hiroshima which was one of the two cities in Japan to be devastated by atomic bombs to terminate the Second World War. The next year he came second when he wrote the entrance examination, and then embarked on a rigorous four-year course at the Academy where cadets were not allowed to drink, smoke, eat sweets or go out with girls.

Young Isoroku Takano was destined to become a famous admiral, but not as Admiral Takano. At the age of thirty, a year after his father and mother died, he was adopted in accordance with Japanese custom by a prominent and wealthy family named Yamamoto. He renounced his surname of Takano and took the name of Yamamoto. So it was as Admiral Yamamoto that he became Commander-in-Chief of the Combined Japanese Fleet and played such a fateful part in the Second World War.

Yamamoto's adoption in 1914, when he was a Lieutenant-Commander, coincided with the outbreak of the First World War in which Japan sided with Britain and the Allies. In 1917 Japan helped the Allies by providing escorts for convoys in the Mediterranean and the Indian Ocean.

Some years after the war Japan became set on an expansionist policy aimed at obtaining a footing in China and acquiring her own sources of oil and other strategic raw materials. In 1931 she occupied Manchuria, an area larger than France and Germany combined. At that time Yamamoto, who had spent a few years in the United States – at

Harvard University during the war and as naval attaché to the Japanese
Embassy in Washington 1925–27 – had reached the rank of Rear-
Admiral. He had been promoted to Vice-Admiral when he represented
Japan at the naval conference in London in 1934. On his return from
the conference he was appointed Navy Vice-Minister. It was in 1934
that Japan denounced the naval treaties that limited the size of her
fleet compared with those of Britain and the United States.

Japan thereupon embarked on a secret programme of building warships, including the huge battleship *Yamato* (72,000 tons), the biggest
warship ever built, which was completed in 1941 and became Yamamoto's flagship. Yamamoto made a notable contribution in planning
the expansion of the Japanese Navy. He had long foreseen that the
whole concept of naval warfare would change with aircraft-carriers and
aircraft the deciding factors. At his insistence, Japan built more carriers
and developed some of the best aircraft in the world, notably the Zero
fighter and dive-bombers that played such a crucial part in the sea
battles in the Second World War.

Naval airmen were trained to a high pitch of fanatical efficiency.
Although not a career aviation officer himself, Yamamoto had learnt to
fly and had held several important air posts. He was described by
Captain Mitsuo Fuchida and Commander Masatake Okumiya as 'one
of the foremost promoters of naval aviation'.

But while he applied himself with the utmost vigour to the building
of a powerful, ultra-modern and highly efficient navy, ready for any
eventuality, he was not in favour of rushing into war. His outspoken
assertions that Japan could not win a war with Britain and the United
States made him many enemies, particularly among the extreme
nationalists. They branded him as pro-American, a traitor and threatened to assassinate him. He refused to have a bodyguard, but by the
middle of 1939, when the international situation had deteriorated, the
Navy Minister, Admiral Yonai, ordered him to have a special police
guard.

A couple of months later Admiral Yonai decided that the only way to
preserve Yamamoto from danger as a result of his outspoken anti-war
stand was to remove him from the political sphere. Accordingly, in mid-
August he was appointed Commander-in-Chief of the Combined Fleet
with the rank of full Admiral.

'It was the only way to save his life – to send him off to sea,' said
Admiral Yonai.

A fortnight after Yamamoto was appointed, Germany invaded
Poland and the Second World War started.

Headed by the Army, those in Japan who favoured an aggressive expansionist policy had asserted themselves some years earlier. The Anti-Comintern Pact with Germany was signed in November 1936. War with China was started the next year and on 23 September 1940 the Japanese moved into the northern provinces of French Indo-China. Four days later Japan signed the Tripartite Pact with Germany and Italy. She was now firmly aligned with the Axis powers. By July 1941 she had gained control of the whole of Indo-China which gave her an important strategic base for further aggression.

America reacted strongly to these moves and, with the support of Britain and the Netherlands East Indies, imposed severe sanctions on Japan, including an oil embargo. The alternative was, among other conditions, to withdraw from Indo-China and China. These conditions were unacceptable to Japan and, while the façade of diplomatic negotiations continued, the drift to war was inevitable – on a date that had already been secretly set by Japan.

2

When Admiral Yamamoto went aboard his flagship, *Nagato*, after being appointed Commander-in-Chief Combined Fleet in 1939, he laid down the following fleet policy: firstly, priority must be given to air training; secondly, if war breaks out, the American fleet in Hawaii must be brought to decisive battle at the earliest opportunity. This fitted in well with the policy for war agreed upon in 1941 by the army and navy and approved at an Imperial Conference. Japan's aim was to get access to oil by capturing the rich oil-producing areas of South-East Asia as quickly as possible.

To achieve this, it would be necessary to deal a crippling blow to the United States Pacific Fleet to prevent it from intervening during the first few months of hostilities. It would also be essential to drive the British and Americans out of Singapore and the Philippines respectively to eliminate bases from which counter-attacks could be launched, and to safeguard lines of communication. The capture of Singapore, an important British base at the southern end of the Malay Peninsula, was one of the main objectives because it was regarded as the key to victory in the south.

It was Yamamoto who, in January 1941 conceived the idea of a surprise air attack from carriers on the American Fleet in Pearl Harbor at Hawaii in the east at the same time as the invasion of the areas of South-East Asia. He was a realist in his approach to war with the United States. Taking into account Japan's naval strength and national resources, he warned that the fleet could not fight successfully for more than a year or two. He knew that if it came to a prolonged war, Japan could not hope to defeat America with her vast resources, which would become more and more the deciding factor. So, if possible, a quick knock-out blow was a priority, even if it meant not keeping to the rules.

Yamamoto was by no means alone in being basically opposed to Japan 'plunging into war'. According to Fuchida and Okumiya, most of the navy's leaders 'were disposed towards peace. Pacifist sentiment was particularly strong among the older admirals who cautioned against blind belief in Japan's invincibility'.

As the diplomatic negotiations between Japan and America dragged on with apparently no hope of agreement being reached, the pro-war faction in the Navy argued that a clash with the United States was inevitable if the disastrous, strangulating effects of the oil embargo were to be avoided. Generally speaking, wrote Fuchida and Okumiya, most naval officers 'stood aloof from the long and bitter controversy over the issue of war or peace. Leaving this fateful question to be de-cided at the highest level of the national political leadership, they went on pouring all their energies into augmenting the combat efficiency and readiness of the fleet'.

The Pearl Harbor plan was not accepted without opposition. The more conservative Naval General Staff under Admiral Nagano pressed for the acceptance of a more orthodox offensive to capture the oil-producing areas with a concentration of naval strength, including air-craft-carriers, and then engage the American fleet if it intervened. This was in accordance with the old defensive doctrine that had dominated Japan's naval strategy for several years.

The Naval General Staff's opposition to the Pearl Harbor plan included the argument that it was too much of a gamble. Paradoxical as it may seem, the gambling element was in keeping with Yamamoto's temperament. He enjoyed games of chance and was a very capable and venturesome player of bridge and poker – especially poker. He was described as having the gambler's all-or-nothing spirit. So his being a realist did not really conflict with the gambler in his make-up. He realised that huge risks had to be taken and the Japanese fleet had to embark on a gigantic – but meticulously planned – gamble to deal a decisive blow at the United States Pacific Fleet.

In Shakespeare's play *Henry VI*, the king says: 'Thrice is he arm'd that hath his quarrel just.'

No doubt Yamamoto and the Japanese war lords preferred the line that Henry Wheeler Shaw added to Shakespeare: 'But four times he who gets his blow in fust.'

Yamamoto referred his bold Pearl Harbor plan to Admiral Onishi, then Chief of Staff of the Eleventh Air Fleet, to study its practicability. Onishi, who was later to become organiser of the first kamikaze (suicide) air units, in turn referred the plan to Commander Genda, who shared his belief in the key role of naval air power. Genda, who had been a daring fighter pilot, was also an outstanding air tactician. His report stipulated that one of the essential conditions to ensure success in the proposed attack on Pearl Harbor was that all six of the fleet's large aircraft-carriers take part.

This report convinced Yamamoto that his idea of a carrier-borne attack on the American naval base was sound. A forceful leader, he was the navy's dominant figure who could take bold, imaginative decisions. He had opposed Japan going to war, but once that decision was taken, he would be responsible for the successful prosecution of the war at sea. He would not yield to the opposition to his plan and even threatened to resign as Commander-in-Chief Combined Fleet if it was not adopted.

Surprisingly, one of those who opposed the plan at first was Vice-Admiral Nagumo, who later led the carrier force on several successful operations. He was concerned about the vulnerability of the carriers, but his views were not shared by all of his subordinate commanders in the First Air Fleet. Yamamoto declared that he was prepared to take personal command of the carrier striking force at Pearl Harbor if Nagumo remained half-hearted. Nagumo thereupon agreed to command the carrier force in the operation.

'The defensive concepts of pre-war days were dead and buried,' wrote Fuchida and Okumiya. 'The new watchword was "Attack!"'

The final plan for war with the United States, the British Commonwealth and the Netherlands East Indies was agreed upon by the Army and Navy on 20 October 1941. At an Imperial Conference on 5 November it was decided that the armed forces should be ready for war by 1 December, and that Japan would resort to war if the diplomatic negotiations failed to achieve a settlement by the end of November. Two days later, on 7 November, the forces were warned that the tentative date for the start of hostilities was Sunday, 7 December (Pearl Harbor time). Sunday was chosen because it was a day when the United States Pacific Fleet would normally be in harbour.

General Tojo, Prime Minister and Minister of War, announced at an Imperial Conference on 1 December the final decision to go to war, and the next day it was confirmed to naval and army commanders that hostilities would begin on 7 December.

Meanwhile the Navy and Army had started moving to get into position for the offensive actions. Nagumo's First Air Fleet, comprising six aircraft-carriers protected by two fast battleships, cruisers and destroyers, was already at sea. It had sailed on 26 November on a 3,000-mile circuitous route to avoid detection and arrived shortly before 6 a.m. on 7 December at the position set for flying off aircraft to attack Pearl Harbor. The first wave of forty torpedo-bombers, fifty high-level bombers and forty dive-bombers escorted by fighters was launched immediately. Altogether 353 aircraft were flown off by 7.15 a.m. Protected by a layer of cloud, the planes approached Hawaii at a height of 9,000 feet and the first bombs were dropped on Pearl Harbor at 7.55 a.m. – right on the planned time for the onslaught.

By 9.45 a.m., an hour and fifty minutes after the first bombs had been dropped, the attack ended. In that short time, it had taken a terrible toll. All eight battleships in the harbour were put out of action (three sunk, one capsized, four damaged), two cruisers and three destroyers were damaged, one auxiliary ship sunk, one capsized and two damaged. Altogether 188 aircraft were destroyed and 30 naval aircraft damaged. Casualties included 2,403 servicemen and civilians killed and 1,178 wounded.

The incredibly low price the Japanese paid for this catastrophic blow was 29 aircraft (55 crewmen) and five midget submarines.

Churchill deplored the 'treacherous blow taken before any declaration of war' and referred to the 'ruthless efficiency of the Japanese airmen'.

Roosevelt said of 7 December 1941 that it was 'a date which will live in infamy'.

It is ironical that while the Pearl Harbor operation was a great achievement by the Japanese, and in that sense an outstanding success, it was fundamentally a failure. It achieved an object of dealing a crippling blow to the United States Pacific Fleet, but the American aircraft-carriers, which were to be the main target, were not in harbour. The Japanese believed four carriers were based on Pearl Harbor and expected them to be sitting targets, but actually there were only two and they were both safely at sea when the base was attacked. A third carrier, which was on the American west coast, was due to join the Pacific Fleet shortly.

Another aspect of the failure was that the Japanese concentrated on putting ships and aircraft out of action and did not destroy the vital installations at the naval base, which was the only base in the Pacific for the American fleet.

The fact that Japan's entry into the war brought the United States in on the side of the British Commonwealth was a source of great relief to Churchill. He now regarded eventual victory as certain and wrote that after hearing of the attack on Pearl Harbor, 'being saturated and satiated with emotion and sensation, I went to bed and slept the sleep of the saved and thankful'.

If he could have foreseen some of the events that were to follow – events that were to cause him more anxiety than even the desperate days of Dunkirk – his sleep that night might well have been disturbed by nightmares.

3

As recounted earlier, HMS *Cornwall* was in the Mozambique Channel, bound for Durban, when the news of Pearl Harbor broke and it was announced that orders had been received to commence hostilities with Japan. After escorting the *Queen Elizabeth* and *Queen Mary* into the Red Sea in November and topping up with fuel at Aden, the cruiser had sailed with orders to carry out a patrol south to the Seychelle Islands. It became obvious later that this was to fill in time because our old friends *Mauretania* and *Ile de France*, packed with troops, would be waiting at Durban to be escorted north again.

In any event, we never got to the Seychelles. Two days after leaving Aden, *Cornwall* intercepted the *Surcouf*, a filthy little Vichy French ship of about 900 tons, and sent across a boarding party to take her to Aden. *Cornwall* had to return to Aden to await the arrival of the *Surcouf*. Lieutenant-Commander Milner and his boarding party came aboard the cruiser looking very grubby after the few days in the French ship.

And so *Cornwall* set off south again on 1 December, the ship's company elated by the announcement that we were due to arrive at Durban on 11 December. The day before our arrival was a day of disasters. First, there was the comparatively minor disaster when one of *Cornwall*'s Walrus seaplanes was lost. A float was torn off as it was landing in the sea alongside the cruiser. It heeled over and the pilot and observer had to jump into the water. A boat was quickly lowered and the airmen were rescued. They had no sooner been helped from the water than a large shark glided lazily past. The damaged plane drifted along the length of the ship and sank.

Later came the shattering news that *Prince of Wales* and *Repulse* had been sunk by the Japanese off the coast of Malaya north of Singapore. The 35,000-ton *Prince of Wales*, one of Britain's newest and most powerful battleships, a pride of the Royal Navy, and the 32,000-ton battle-cruiser *Repulse*, sunk within eight days of arriving at Singapore and only three days after Pearl Harbor – it seemed unbelievable that such a disaster could have happened.

With the danger of Japan entering the war increasing in mid-1941, Churchill had become more and more anxious and did everything possible to deter or delay such a move. In August 1941 he raised the question of forming an Eastern Fleet. Later, as a forerunner to forming the fleet, it was decided to send *Prince of Wales*, *Repulse* and four destroyers to Singapore. It had been intended to send the aircraft-carrier *Indomitable* with these ships but she was disabled in an accident. Admiral Sir Tom Phillips, who had been Vice-Chief of the Naval Staff, was appointed Commander-in-Chief of this embryo Eastern Fleet with his flag hoisted in *Prince of Wales*.

Churchill was convinced that sending *Prince of Wales* out east would be 'the best possible deterrent' to Japan. In one of his moments of undue exuberance, he told Stalin in a message : 'With the object of keeping Japan quiet we are sending our latest battleship, *Prince of Wales*, which can catch and kill any Japanese ship, into the Indian Ocean, and are building up a powerful battle squadron there.' He, and other Allied leaders, had yet to learn that the battleship was no longer the major component in naval warfare, and that the vital factor in defence and attack was now air power – an advantage the Japanese were using with great effect.

When Phillips reached Cape Town in *Prince of Wales* on 16 November on the way to Singapore, he flew to Pretoria to see Field-Marshal Smuts, Prime Minister of South Africa. Churchill had suggested to Smuts that he should meet the admiral. Smuts, a worldly wise man, was an international statesman whose views and advice were respected by Churchill and other Western leaders. Field Marshal Sir Alan Brooke, Chief of the Imperial General Staff, noted in his diary :

Smuts I look upon as one of the biggest of nature's gentlemen that I have ever seen. A wonderful clear grasp of all things, coupled with the most exceptional charm. Interested in all matters, and gifted with the most marvellous judgment . . . I was a tremendous admirer of his, and any word he spoke carried immense weight with me.

After the meeting in Pretoria, Phillips told his Chief of Staff that Smuts agreed with the policy of sending the two capital ships to Singapore as a deterrent against further Japanese aggression. But on 18 November Smuts sent a cable to Churchill in which he expressed 'serious concern' at the division of Allied strength between Singapore and Pearl Harbor. 'If the Japanese are really nippy, there is here an opening for a first-class disaster,' he said.

Disasters had followed quickly – first Pearl Harbor on 7 December and then the sinking of *Prince of Wales* and *Repulse* three days later. Almost simultaneously with the attack on Pearl Harbor, the Japanese invasion of Malaya to capture Singapore had started. News had been received of a large Japanese seaborne expedition in the Gulf of Siam to the north of Singapore and Admiral Phillips decided to go into action against it. He sailed from Singapore at 5.35 p.m. on 8 December with *Prince of Wales*, *Repulse* and four destroyers, *Electra*, *Express*, *Tenedos* and *Vampire*. It was ironical that these warships should be designated Force Z, a letter that almost seemed to herald the fate of the two capital ships.

Shortly before sailing, Phillips was informed by the Air Force that it was doubtful if fighter protection could be provided where he wanted it in the Gulf of Siam on 10 December. Some hours later, at 1.25 a.m. on 9 December, he received a signal stating definitely that fighter protection so far north would not be possible. The signal also warned that the Japanese had large bomber forces in southern Indo-China and possibly also in Siam, which adjoined Malaya.

Early in the afternoon of the 9th Force Z was sighted by a Japanese submarine which reported its position, course and speed. When three enemy aircraft were seen by *Prince of Wales* that evening, Phillips realised that the element of surprise, on which he had banked, had gone so he turned Force Z south and set a course for Singapore. Late that night, however, he received a signal reporting a Japanese landing at Kuantan, about 200 miles north of Singapore. He decided that he could make a surprise attack on the invading forces at Kuantan and that the risk was justified, so altered course accordingly.

Meanwhile a large force of eighty-five Japanese aircraft (thirty-four high level and fifty-one torpedo bombers), whose pilots had been specially trained and were the pick of the Naval Air Arm, took off from near Saigon in Indo-China just before dawn on 10 December. The British warships had been sighted on their southerly course by another Japanese submarine at 2.10 a.m. that day and the bombers were directed to the ships by a reconnaissance plane.

A determined and well co-ordinated attack on the *Prince of Wales* and *Repulse* by the high level and torpedo bombers started shortly after 11 a.m. During the onslaught, which lasted for almost two hours, the battleship and battle-cruiser were each hit by five torpedoes. *Repulse*, which was hit by a bomb amidships that did not explode and had some nearer misses, rolled over and sank at 12.33 a.m. The *Prince of Wales*, which suffered two direct bomb hits in addition to the torpedoes, capsized and sank at 1.20 p.m.

The Operations Room at Singapore was not aware of the attack on *Prince of Wales* and *Repulse* until a signal, 'Enemy aircraft bombing', which was made at 11.50 a.m. by the Commanding Officer of *Repulse*, Captain W. G. Tennant, was received at 12.19 p.m. Curiously, Admiral Phillips never signalled Singapore although the warships were then within range for fighter protection. Eleven Buffalo fighter aircraft took off within seven minutes of *Repulse*'s signal being received, but they arrived over the scene of the attack just in time to see *Prince of Wales* sink.

The 2,081 survivors from the two ships were picked up by three destroyers (the fourth destroyer, *Tenedos*, had been detached on the evening of the 9th to go on ahead to Singapore). Altogether 840 men, including Admiral Phillips and the Commanding Officer of *Prince of Wales*, Captain J. C. Leach, perished on this day of disaster that sent shock waves through the whole of the Royal Navy.

In *The War Against Japan*, the conduct of the crews of the warships is described as 'one ray of light from the darkness of the tragedy'. The pilot of one of the Buffalo aircraft that arrived on the scene just as *Prince of Wales* sank, wrote in his report :

It was obvious that the three destroyers were going to take hours to pick up those hundreds of men clinging to bits of wreckage and swimming around in the filthy, oily water. Above all this the threat of another bombing and machine-gun attack was imminent. Every one of those men must have realised that. Yet as I flew round, every man waved and put up his thumb as I flew over him. After an hour, lack of petrol forced me to leave, but during that hour I had seen many men in dire danger waving, cheering and joking, as if they were holiday-makers at Brighton waving at a low-flying aircraft. It shook me, for here was something above human nature.

The Japanese had good cause to rejoice. Not only had they accounted for two British capital ships so soon after Pearl Harbor, their naval air-

craft had achieved this success operating 400 miles from their base –
at that time a unique feat – for the loss of only three of their planes.
Churchill commented: 'The efficiency of the Japanese in air warfare
was at this time greatly underestimated by both ourselves and by the
Americans.'

This was, if anything, an understatement. Before Pearl Harbor, and
even afterwards, it was not uncommon to hear men in the Royal Navy
decry the Japanese as airmen and the quality of their aircraft. One
heard such derogatory remarks, laced liberally with adjectives, as:
'The Japs are no good as airmen; they suffer from air sickness,' and:
'Their planes are made of rice paper and bamboo shoots.' The sinking
of *Prince of Wales* and *Repulse* was the Royal Navy's first experience
of Japanese air attacks. It was an unpleasant eye-opener and painful
lesson.

Captain Augustus Agar, Commanding Officer of HMS *Dorsetshire*,
wrote later:

> Admiralty Intelligence officers were confident that the Japanese dis-
> liked aviation and were not air-minded. It was not until after Pearl
> Harbor that we learnt how they took the greatest care not to show
> to our naval attaches their carriers or methods of training their naval
> pilots.

Churchill recounted with unconcealed emotion how he heard about the
sinking of *Prince of Wales* and *Repulse*. While he was still in bed reading official papers on the morning of 10 December, he was telephoned
by Admiral of the Fleet Sir Dudley Pound, First Sea Lord and Chief of
Naval Staff, who reported the grim news and added: 'Tom Phillips is
drowned.'

'Are you sure it's true?' asked Churchill.

'There is no doubt at all,' replied Pound.

> So I put the telephone down [wrote Churchill]. I was thankful to
> be alone. In all the war I never received a more direct shock. The
> reader of these pages [*The Second World War* Vol III] will realise
> how many efforts, hopes and plans foundered with these two ships.
> As I turned over and twisted in bed, the full horror of the news sank
> in upon me. There were no British or American capital ships in the
> Indian Ocean or the Pacific except the American survivors of Pearl
> Harbor, who were hastening back to California. Over all this vast

expanse of waters Japan was supreme, and we everywhere were weak and naked.

Vice-Admiral Sir James Somerville, who was in command of Force H in the Western Mediterranean and distinguished himself with his daring operations, was 'shocked and dismayed' at the news of the sinkings. But, says his biographer, Somerville was hardly surprised because he had misgivings when Sir Tom Phillips was appointed Commander-in-Chief of the Eastern Fleet. He regarded Phillips as 'inexperienced in the practicalities of modern war at sea . . . an advocate of "pushing on regardless of cost" and ignorant of the effect of well-handled air power on naval operations'.

Somerville wrote :

I should think it was very doubtful indeed if we could provide shore-based fighter support to those two ships. I personally would not have dreamt of taking up two battleships like that without adequate air or surface support . . . Altogether a deplorable and tragic business . . . I don't agree with what W.C. [Churchill] said, that the operation was a proper one to be carried out even if it entailed certain risks. To my mind it was out of the question to expose two battleships to heavy air attack unless they were well covered by our shore-based fighters, and this does not appear to have been the case.

By one of the strange turns of fate, five days after the loss of *Prince of Wales* and *Repulse*, Somerville received a signal from the Admiralty telling him that he would be required to become Commander-in-Chief of the Eastern Fleet. Vice-Admiral Sir Geoffrey Layton, who had been in command of the China Station and shore establishments at Singapore, had already embarked in a passenger liner to return to Britain when the two capital ships were lost. He was at once recalled, disembarked and was ordered by the Admiralty to assume temporary command of the Eastern Fleet until Somerville arrived in the east.

4

Christmas, 1941 . . . HMS *Cornwall* was back at Aden after a fast trip from Durban escorting *Mauretania* and *Ile de France* to the entrance of the Red Sea. If one had a choice, Aden was not the sort of place where one would want to spend Christmas Day. But it is surprising how the Navy can generate the cheerful spirit of Christmas, even in a cheerless place more akin to Hades. Someone had even found some genuine greenery to decorate the masts, which was quite an achievement at Aden.

Being in port – any port – instead of on the high seas at Christmas time had advantages. There was always the chance of receiving mail. We had not received any for several weeks, so the pile of letters and parcels on the mess table on the morning of 24 December – the ship had arrived the previous night – was a very welcome present even though the letters dated back a couple of months. My mail included a much battered, but still edible, long-lasting fruit cake that my wife had posted for my birthday (23 October).

Another advantage of being in port was that on Christmas Day we did not have dawn action stations and could enjoy a 'lie in' to the extent of being roused to lash up and stow at 6.30 instead of 6 a.m.

The festivities started on Christmas Eve with an enjoyable concert on the quarterdeck, the programme consisting of two short plays and musical items. One of the plays, with a cast from the lower deck, had a serious theme, while the other, produced by the officers, was humorous. The musical items were shared by the Royal Marine Band and a jazz group composed of ratings, thus catering for all tastes. A rendering of 'Poet and Peasant' by the Royal Marine Band would be followed by 'Where's That Tiger?' by the jazz fiends.

The first part of Christmas morning was a busy time. After cleaning up, special festive supplies had to be obtained from the victualling department and the messes decorated. The long mess tables were made surprisingly attractive, 'Merry Christmas' being spelt out with sweets, nuts and oranges, and liberal use being made of the different wares to display the well-known 'V' for victory sign.

After church service on the quarterdeck came 'Captain's rounds', the skipper visiting every mess. He was accompanied by the officers and preceded by the Royal Marine Band which played an appropriate tune on each mess deck – for example, 'Keep the Home Fires Burning' for the stokers. The tune chosen for the seamen's mess deck was the South African song, 'Sarie Marais'. This was not merely for the benefit of the many South Africans serving in the cruiser. It was also very popular among the British ratings and was one of Captain Manwaring's favourite tunes. Whenever he had a dinner party, he insisted on the Royal Marine Band playing it.

Because of wartime conditions, the Captain had issued an instruction forbidding officers to indulge in their custom of treating men to drinks, but he himself was guilty of contravening it. He was particularly fond of the Royal Marine Band and ordered his steward to give every member a beer.

'I'll break my rule for no one but you,' he told the members of the band.

When the Captain had completed his rounds, we sat down to this dinner, which included a bottle of cold beer :

> *Cream of tomato soup*
> *Roast turkey and ham*
> *Cabbage, green peas, roast potatoes*
> *Christmas pudding and custard sauce*
> *Mixed nuts, sweets and fruit*

At tea-time in the afternoon we had Christmas cake, and the bakery staff deserved full marks for their efforts. They had been busy for some weeks making about 100 cakes, each one adorned with a decoration such as Santa Claus, Christmas trees, bells and so on. One cake was particularly outstanding. It bore an icing model of a battleship escorted by a couple of destroyers.

Cornwall did full justice to her last Christmas Day. The next day we sailed and escorted a ship south to the equator where we took over a convoy from the battleship HMS *Royal Sovereign*, which we accompanied to Bombay. Ironically, one of the liners in this convoy was the British ship named *Empress of Japan*.

The landing-stage for liberty boats from ships anchored in the harbour at Bombay was the Gateway of India, the magnificent ornate building with a high majestic archway that was erected to commemorate the visit of King George V and Queen Mary. The splendour of the entrance to this city of many attractive buildings was besmirched by the inevitable touts for brothels who pestered sailors the moment they stepped ashore. The well-dressed agent who accosted me and held out his 'visiting card' was not deterred by my telling him I was not interested. He persisted in following me until I threatened to kick him where it would hurt most.

Blatant touting for prostitutes was encountered in most places the ship visited – Mauritius, Mombasa, Aden, Colombo and even the lovely island of Mahé in the Seychelles. One night in Bombay, after we had followed up a game of cricket in the afternoon with dinner at a restaurant, Bill said to Tommy and me : 'Come on, I'll show you one of the sights of Bombay that will shake you.' We got into a gharry and Bill told the driver : 'Grant Road'.

Grant Road was not a back street but a fairly prominent thoroughfare through which trams ran. Yet it was nothing more than a hive of low brothels. It was absolutely revolting. The black prostitutes sat on stools behind iron bars like animals in cages, while others thrust their heads out of upstairs windows and beckoned invitingly to any male in sight.

It certainly was an experience just to see Grant Road – and a relief to get away from such degradation. The driver of the gharry apparently did not understand English. To every directive we gave him, he merely said what sounded like 'he, he' or 'hair, hair' and gave the horse another clout with the whip. We had to get the assistance of local passers-by to let him know that we wanted to get back to the landing-stage at the Gateway of India. When we eventually arrived there and asked how much was the fare, he merely shrugged as though to indicate that he did not understand what we were saying. So Bill, who had visited Bombay several times, decided upon what he regarded as a reasonable amount. When we gave the money to the driver, he revealed that he was not altogether unacquainted with the English language. 'You bloody bastards,' he said, and we left him cursing alternately in English and his native tongue which, fortunately, we did not understand.

Bombay seemed to abound with brothels of various grades and, with so much temptation, it was inevitable that No 1 mess – a mess on board reserved for venereal disease cases – was fairly full when *Cornwall* left on 17 January after a few days' visit. One case being treated was a teenage youngster who was reduced to tears by the result of his 'adventure' ashore. He dreaded having to face his mother when he got home. Then came news that his brother had been killed in the Western Desert. His cup of remorse overflowed. But he never got home to face his mother. Not long afterwards Japanese bombs solved his problem.

5

The tidal wave of Japanese conquests was sweeping irresistibly south-west and south, engulfing Siam and British, Dutch and American possessions. Within hours of the attack on Pearl Harbor on 7 December, the Japanese overran Siam, attacked Hong Kong and Malaya and made some landings on the Philippines. After only a week they started the main invasion of the Philippines and landed on British Borneo. Hong Kong surrendered on Christmas night. In the Philippines, Manila was occupied on 3 January and only Bataan was holding out. The invasion of Burma started on 15 January. Four days later the Governor of British Borneo surrendered and the adjacent East Indies island, Celebes, was occupied. It was a grim start to 1942 for the Allies in the East, defeat following defeat after the catastrophes of Pearl Harbor and the *Prince of Wales* and *Repulse.*

February brought no respite. The day after *Cornwall* left Bombay in mid-January, the Captain told us after Sunday church parade on the quarterdeck that we had narrowly missed having to take a convoy to Singapore and, as far as he could make out, we had a couple of months of hard work ahead.

The cruiser did a quick dash across the Arabian Sea to Aden to escort a convoy of eight ships bound for Colombo. The day before arriving at Ceylon we heard that a ship had been torpedoed close to Colombo. That evening it was piped that everyone had to wear lifebelts all the time, and extra lookouts were detailed for duty during the morning watch (4 to 8 a.m.). Shortly after dawn a Catalina flying boat and a couple of Swordfish aircraft arrived on the scene from Ceylon to give the convoy aerial escort as a precaution against a submarine attack during the last few hours before reaching Colombo on 2 February.

As we sailed into the harbour, loud laughter greeted the announcement by the bosun's mate : 'Mae Wests may now be taken off.' Our lifebelts were called Mae Wests, but they were tubes of modest size that were tied around one's chest and certainly did not do justice to the dimensions of the famous actress after whom they were named.

The next day we were at sea again, this time heading south-east with a convoy of eight ships, some bound for Singapore and some for the East Indies. Cornwall had orders to escort them to the Sunda Strait, between Sumatra and Java, where they were to be taken over by another cruiser. This time we had an anti-submarine escort of destroyers and corvettes, which was comforting because within a short time of leaving Colombo a signal was intercepted from a tanker that had sailed an hour or so before our convoy reporting that she had been attacked by a submarine. The anti-submarine escorts stayed with us until we were well clear of Ceylon. One of the corvettes got a 'ping' on its asdic and dropped a few depth charges, but there were no positive results to indicate whether it had been a submarine.

It was a slow, eight-knot convoy which made things more tense. As we were approaching the Sunda Strait, there was an alarm at about 4.30 in the morning when a darkened ship was sighted. We went to action stations and *Cornwall* positioned herself between the convoy and the 'enemy'. As the other ship drew nearer in the moonlight, it was seen to be a large warship with its guns trained on us. Our guns were trained on it, all ready to open fire. The climax came when *Cornwall*'s signal-man flashed the challenge. The other warship replied and all was well. It was a Dutch cruiser. The 'secure' was sounded and, with a sigh of relief, we fell out from action stations.

An Australian cruiser, HMAS *Hobart*, met us near the Sunda Strait and took over the convoy which, we heard, was the last one to get to Singapore before that important base surrendered on 15 February. An Able Seaman looked at the Australian cruiser and remarked that she was the best ship in the Royal Navy. He was asked how he could possibly consider *Hobart* the best ship. She was a fairly old 6-inch cruiser with a strange appearance because her two funnels were wide apart with a crane between them.

'Any ship that takes this convoy from us is the finest ship in the Navy,' replied the AB.

Cornwall did a quick return trip to Colombo, which was now the main base for the Royal Navy's operations in the east. We arrived on Friday, 13 February, to find another convoy waiting for us. We only had time to top up with fuel and were off again the next day. *Cornwall* headed for the Bay of Bengal and set a north-easterly course with the convoy, which was bound for Rangoon with sorely needed supplies for the troops defending Burma. Again we had anti-submarine escorts and also a sloop until well into the Bay of Bengal, after which we carried on with the sloop and a corvette.

During this trip, while reading some mail that had been brought aboard at Colombo, I came across an article on Singapore in an English periodical that dated back a couple of months. It was written by a retired naval officer who extolled the defences of the base in Malaya. He declared very emphatically that Singapore was 'an impregnable fortress' that could never be captured. It made ironic reading because Singapore had surrendered a few days earlier, and the next day the Japanese had also occupied southern Sumatra.

A week after we had set out with the Burma-bound convoy – the last to reach Rangoon – *Cornwall* left it when sixty-five miles from the port to carry on with the two smaller escorts. We returned quickly to Colombo where we arrived on 24 February flying the yellow flag because we had a case of smallpox on board, so there was no shore leave.

It was a few weeks since we had been able to stretch our legs on land and many a jaundiced eye was cast at the yellow flag.

When *Cornwall* sailed into Colombo harbour that day, there were several passenger ships crammed with Australian troops bound for their home country because of the threat from advancing Japanese forces. One of these liners was directly astern of *Cornwall* as we made fast to buoys. The Aussies on deck greeted us with such remarks as 'Where was the Navy at Singapore? . . . What are you doing in port? . . . Why aren't you at sea?'

The sailors were quick to retort with some verbal salvoes about Malaya and fully held their own in the exchanges of banter. They were not lacking when it came to repartee and humour, and laughter floated across the harbour as one side and then the other scored a point.

To crown it all, our next task was to escort the convoy of Australian troops to Fremantle. We were due to sail on the evening of 28 February. The wires to the buoys had been slipped and *Cornwall*'s screws were already churning the dirty water in the harbour as a tug eased her bows round. The Aussies in the liner nearby crowded the rails on deck to watch the warship leave harbour, when suddenly there was a change of orders. *Cornwall*'s engines stopped and we started making fast to the buoys again.

'Wot's up, scared?' shouted some of the Aussies on the deck of the liner.

They had the last laugh and we shared it with them. The next morning we were all buddies when *Cornwall* sailed out to escort them back home to Australia. The escorts during the first few days included the battleship HMS *Royal Sovereign*, an Armed Merchant Cruiser, destroyers and corvettes.

The interlude with the Aussies in Colombo harbour provided some light relief, but there was nothing one could be cheerful about in the war news. While *Cornwall* was escorting the convoy bound for Rangoon, the Japanese landed in southern Sumatra on 16 February. Three days' later, Port Darwin, the Allies' strategic base in the north of Australia, was considerably damaged in a surprise attack. It was carried out by aircraft from four of Admiral Nagumo's carriers, which had taken part in the assault on Pearl Harbor, supplemented by shore-based aircraft from the Celebes. Twelve ships were sunk in the harbour at Port Darwin and shore installations were so badly damaged that the base was out of action for some months.

And then while *Cornwall* was waiting at Colombo to undertake the long-range convoy duty to Australia, the tragedy of the Battle of the

Java Sea was taking place. It started on 26 February with the desperate but vain attempt by the remaining naval units in those waters to prevent the Japanese sea-borne invasion forces from landing on the large Dutch East Indies island of Java. The warships – British, Dutch and American, some of them damaged – were operating under considerable strain from steaming and fighting for almost three months. In the Java Sea battle, which was spread over three days, they were handicapped also by lack of air reconnaissance and support.

The battle was full of heroism, with warships fighting until there were no more shells in their magazines. It marked the sad end of the famous cruiser HMS *Exeter*, which had made an amazing comeback after the terrible damage suffered early the war in the fight against the German pocket battleship *Admiral Graf Spee* in the Battle of the River Plate. After being seriously damaged in the Java Sea when hit in the boiler-room by an 8-inch shell, she and two destroyers, HMS *Encounter* and the United States warship *Pope*, ran into a superior Japanese force of four cruisers and several destroyers when making for the Sunda Strait. *Exeter* and *Encounter* were sunk by shellfire and *Pope* by dive-bombers.

The Allied losses in the Battle of the Java Sea included five cruisers, eight destroyers and one sloop.

'Rarely can so much have been won for so small a cost as was accomplished by Japan between December 1941, and March 1942,' wrote Captain Roskill. 'The way all these operations had been conducted left no room for doubt regarding the skill, power and efficiency of the Japanese Navy.'

The Japanese landed on Java on 1 March. A week later Rangoon and Java surrendered, and the invaders landed on northern Sumatra and New Guinea. The conquest of the rich southern area, which was Japan's prime objective in going to war, was completed. Because of the conquests bordering the Indian Ocean, the convoy *Cornwall* was escorting to Australia had to go on a circuitous route to give Java a wide berth, and the much lengthened voyage to Fremantle took two weeks. The trip on our own back to Colombo lasted only eight days.

6

Sir James Somerville, now promoted to the rank of full Admiral, had no illusions about the strength of the Eastern Fleet he was to command, or the unenviable task involved in defending the Indian Ocean against the Japanese. The Indian Ocean had become a crucial area in the war. With the Mediterannean closed, it provided the only sea supply route round South Africa for the Allied armies in the Middle East and for material support through Persia to help the Russians in their desperate defence against the invading German forces. The Indian Ocean was also the supply route to India and Burma, and gave access to the oil from the Persian Gulf. It might also have been needed to defend Australia and New Zealand if the Japanese decided to push their invasion farther south.

At a cost of what were acknowledged to be 'almost trivial' losses, the Japanese stood astride Malaya and the Dutch East Indies on the eastern border of the Indian Ocean and controlled the strategic accesses through the Straits of Malacca between Malaya and northern Sumatra, and Sunda between northern Sumatra and Java. The Indian Ocean was wide open to invasion from the east so it had become an absolute priority to build up Britain's Eastern Fleet to defend the area or at least deter the Japanese from advancing farther west. Early in March the First Sea Lord, Admiral Pound, sent Churchill a warning that Ceylon was now threatened and its loss would 'undermine our whole strategic position in the Middle East as well as the Far East'.

It had been planned originally to establish a strong fleet, including some of the Royal Navy's most modern capital ships. But the speed of Japan's conquests had taken everyone by surprise, and the toll of losses of Britain's capital ships in addition to cruisers and destroyers had brought the Royal Navy to a parlous state. Apart from losses in the defence of the South-East Asian area, including the capital ships *Prince of Wales* and *Repulse*, serious blows had been suffered in the Mediterranean. U-boats had sunk the battleship *Barham*, and aircraft-carrier *Ark Royal* in November 1941, and Italian frogmen, using under-water time bombs, had damaged and put out of action the battleships *Queen Elizabeth* and *Valiant* in Alexandria harbour in December. As a result, at the start of 1942 the Commander-in-Chief Mediterranean, Sir Andrew Cunningham, did not have in commission a single battleship and his fleet had been reduced to cruisers and destroyers.

There was still the Battle of the Atlantic and capital ships had to be kept in the Home Fleet to deal with any of the powerful German warships that might break out. It was therefore a case of scraping the bottom of the barrel when it came to allocating ships to serve in Admiral Somerville's Eastern Fleet. His flagship was to be HMS *Warspite*, the 27-year-old First World War battleship that had been modernised and was bound for Ceylon after spending some time in the United States where damage suffered at Crete was repaired. The other capital ships in the fleet were the four old, slow, outdated R-class battleships, *Resolution*, *Ramillies*, *Royal Sovereign* and *Revenge*. They were also built during the First World War but had not been modernised. Churchill branded them as 'floating coffins' which 'are easy prey to the modern Japanese vessels, and can neither fight nor run'.

So when Somerville took passage in the aircraft-carrier *Formidable*, which sailed from the Clyde in the early hours of 17 February 1942, he had some big problems on his mind. The Admiral wrote almost daily to his wife and his very outspoken letters, together with official communications, give a good insight into his thinking and plans. Soon after *Formidable* arrived at Cape Town on 10 March, Vice-Admiral Algernon Willis, whom Somerville had chosen to be his second-in-command, arrived in HMS *Resolution*. The two Admirals got together and, in response to the Admiralty's outdated ideas on how a couple of the old R-class battleships could be used to defend Ceylon, they drafted a signal which was followed by a letter from Somerville setting out the policy they intended to pursue. It included the following points:

The loss of Ceylon would be a most serious matter, but if the Japanese attempted the capture with practically the whole of their Fleet, we should obviously be uunable to deal with this scale of attack. . . . If they attempt a lesser scale of attack on Ceylon, the best deterrent, and the best counter too, is to keep our Eastern Fleet 'in being' and avoid losses by attrition. This can best be achieved by keeping the Fleet at sea as much as possible with feints east of Ceylon from time to time. I feel that we must avoid having our Fleet destroyed in penny numbers by undertaking operations which do not give reasonable prospects of success.

If the Japanese get Ceylon, it will be extremely difficult but not necessarily impossible to maintain our communications to the Middle East. But if the Japanese capture Ceylon *and* destroy the greater part of the Eastern Fleet, then I admit the situation becomes really desperate.

The crux of this policy was to keep the fleet 'in being'. It was felt that as long as the Eastern Fleet was in existence, it would be a deterrent because the Japanese would have to use a large force operating a long way from its home base to embark on a major commitment in the Indian Ocean. In this regard, Somerville was heartened by the views of Field Marshal Smuts, whom he and Willis visited while in Cape Town.

> I was most impressed by him and his marvellous clear vision [wrote Somerville]. Willis and I had a confab before we met him and found that our ideas concerning the naval strategy to be pursued in the East coincided, though they did not agree with those expressed by T.L. [Their Lordships of the Admiralty]. Smuts agreed with us and that makes me think that probably we are on the right lines. . . . The defence of Ceylon is our obvious preoccupation at this moment, but I am convinced it is not good policy to take excessive chances with the Eastern Fleet for the sake of Ceylon. . . . I don't intend to throw away the Eastern Fleet.

Referring to the voyage in *Formidable*, Somerville's biographer remarks that he 'had a greater knowledge of the operation and tactical use of aircraft than any other senior officer of the ship, and of most admirals of his time'. Somerville himself wrote : 'They view with great dislike the fact that I know too much about operating aircraft to accept blindly any stuff they like to hand out.' He repeatedly took to the air as an observer while exercises were in progress and put pressure on training and improving air crews.

Somerville was also well aware that 'the meagre air defences allotted to Ceylon were no bar to a repetition of Pearl Harbor at Colombo or Trincomalee'.

As *Formidable* approached Ceylon, Somerville expedited his arrival at Colombo by being flown the last ninety miles in one of the carrier's aircraft. The fact that the Commander-in-Chief arrived by air gave rise to a story which resulted in his exclaiming good-humouredly, 'That's a bloody lie !', some months later when I had to submit for his approval an article on the Eastern Fleet and the Ceylon crisis.

7

The Japanese were so much ahead of their time-table for conquests that they had a problem. Singapore had been captured in 69 days, 31 less than the 100 allowed in the time-table, Java and Sumatra in 90 and 94 days respectively instead of 150 each. In the Philippines, except for isolated pockets of resistance like Bataan peninsula (122 days) and the island of Corregidor (149 days), the invasion was well ahead of the schedule of 50 days. Manila, the capital, was occupied in 26 days.

So Japan was confronted with the question of what to do next? Should she go on the defensive and consolidate what had been conquered, or should she continue a vigorous offensive in an effort to break the resistance of the Allies? If the latter, there was the further question of which way to strike – whether to go westward into the Indian Ocean against Britain or eastward against the United States?

Consideration of these questions of strategy led to protracted discussions during March and April. In the meantime, the gambler, Admiral Yamamoto, decided to try to knock out the British Eastern Fleet. On 9 March Vice-Admiral Kondo, Commander-in-Chief 2nd Fleet, was ordered to plan the interim operations in the west. These included raids on Colombo and Trincomalee, the two naval bases in Ceylon, and attacks on shipping in the Bay of Bengal.

One purpose of the operations was to ensure the safety of convoys taking supplies and reinforcements for the Japanese army in Burma. As Rangoon had been evacuated by the Allies, it was now possible for the Japanese to use the sea instead of the long and difficult land route to supply the army still fighting in the north of Burma. The operations were also designed as a show of strength to India and to help stir trouble in that country where the delicate political relations with Britain were a source of concern for the Allies.

Vice-Admiral Nagumo, who had led the raid on Pearl Harbor with his First Air Fleet, was given command of the attacks on Ceylon. Vice-Admiral Ozawa's Malaya Force, consisting of the light fleet carrier, *Ryujo* (31 aircraft), seven cruisers and destroyers, which supported the occupation of the Andaman and Nicobar Islands on 23 March, was ordered to carry out the attacks on shipping in the Bay of Bengal. He was to synchronise his offensive with Nagumo's assault on Ceylon.

Nagumo's orders were to knock out the Royal Navy's Eastern Fleet which, it was hoped, he would find in harbour at Colombo or Trincomalee, or divided between the two bases. If he did not find the fleet, he was to concentrate on other shipping in the harbours, dockyards and airfields. He hoped for another Pearl Harbor when his First Air Fleet sailed from Kendari in the Celebes on Thursday, 26 March.

The same day *Cornwall* arrived back at Colombo from Australia.

PART FIVE

Japanese Easter Eggs

I

Our thoughts were very much on the Eastern Fleet when *Cornwall* sailed into Colombo harbour. Stories had been current in the lower deck about the formation of a fleet to resist Japanese encroachment in the Indian Ocean and an attack on Ceylon. During the voyage back from Australia, the chances of *Cornwall* being included in the fleet were a keen topic of conversation. On arrival at Colombo we noted that the shipping cramming the harbour included an assortment of warships – a big aircraft-carrier, *Formidable*, our old friend and fellow County Class cruiser *Dorsetshire*, a couple of lighter cruisers and a number of destroyers, sloops and corvettes.

We had hardly finished making fast to buoys before word got around that Admiral Sir James Somerville, who had arrived at Colombo two days earlier on Tuesday, 24 March, was to be Commander-in-Chief of the Eastern Fleet. The effect of this information was exhilarating. In fact, the atmosphere among naval personnel became quite electric. After all the news of depressing defeats at the hands of the Japanese, it was a tonic to have in command of the fleet a man who had distinguished himself as the daring Flag Officer commanding Force H in the Western Mediterranean. The London newspaper *The Times* referred to Somerville as 'the inspiring leader, skilful commander and fighting admiral'.

Soon after Somerville arrived at Colombo, he went on board one of the cruisers to address the ship's company and, as he wrote, he 'was greeted with rousing cheers in spite of the fact that all I could promise them was the hell of a time'. There was much excitement in *Cornwall* when a notice appeared announcing that the Commander-in-Chief would come on board on Saturday to address the ship's company. We looked forward to his visit very keenly, but unfortunately circumstances forced him to send a signal regretting that he had to cancel the visit.

Somerville was one of the outstanding characters in the Royal Navy. He had an acute, razor-sharp mind and revelled in humour and lighthearted moments even in the most serious situations. His biographer describes him as 'a forceful personality' and refers to his 'mischievous spirit, sparkling repartee and uninhibited wit'. But although daring when the occasion demanded, he was no foolhardy daredevil. Perhaps he summed himself up well when he wrote to his wife after an action while commanding Force H in the Western Mediterranean:

> I have no ambition, as you know, and, unlike Nelson, I don't crave for glory. All I want to do is the best I can to help the country as I see it. I have an urge to throw caution to the winds and take a chance on things, but I stifle it when I feel that to do so would not be the right or best service I can do the country. I don't suggest that my judgment is infallible, but where the judgment leads me I go and don't think of personal consequences.

Somerville was knighted twice, first in 1939 when he was appointed to the Knighthood of the Order of the Bath, and again in 1941 while serving in the Mediterranean when he was appointed Knight Commander of the Order of the British Empire. Being knighted a second time put him at the receiving end of the wit of his friend Admiral Sir Andrew Cunningham, Commander-in-Chief of the Mediterranean, whose congratulatory signal read: 'What, twice a knight at your age?'

I had first-hand experience of Somerville's good humour some months after the Ceylon crisis when serving as an assistant to the Staff Officer (Intelligence), Lieutenant-Commander J. M. F. (Michael) Phillimore, at Naval Headquarters in Durban. It so happened that Somerville arrived in his flagship the day after I had written an article on the Eastern Fleet and the Japanese incursion into the India Ocean. It had to be submitted to the Commander-in-Chief and I was instructed to take it to his flagship. As a recently commissioned junior officer, I was distinctly nervous when I went aboard the battleship and on to the quarterdeck where I handed the article to the Admiral's secretary, Paymaster Captain Alan Laybourne. He read it and then said he was taking it down below to the Admiral.

I wondered with some apprehension what Admiral Somerville's reaction would be. Within a few minutes his secretary returned and said 'the Admiral' wanted to see me. I followed him below to the Admiral's cabin like a lamb going to the slaughter. I had not bargained on seeing Somerville himself. Why did he want to see me? Had anything I had written annoyed him? Was I in for a blast? Until recently an

Able Seaman and then a mere Sub-Lieutenant, I wondered how I should greet him.

But my apprehension was soon dispelled. It was one of Durban's hot, humid days. Admiral Somerville, who detested tropical heat and humidity, was sitting behind his desk and looked flushed by the heat. He had discarded the tunic of his white uniform, and all he wore above the waist was a vest and pair of braces. He got up, greeted me jovially, then waved to a chair and said : 'Anchor your arse !'

It could hardly have been less formal and, had I not been so tense as a result of unexpectedly being summoned to see the Admiral himself, I should have burst out laughing at the unconventional invitation to sit down. Anyway, I anchored my arse on the chair while he read the article. Everything seemed to be going fine, without any queries, until suddenly Admiral Somerville exclaimed : 'That's a bloody lie !'

'What, sir?' I asked.

The Admiral referred me to the section of the article in which I wrote that he flew out from Britain to assume command of the Eastern Fleet.

I said 'Sorry', and explained that my information was limited to what I heard on the lower deck. It was only much later that I learnt that while he did not fly out from Britain, he did arrive at Colombo by air in one of the aircraft from the carrier *Formidable*. This had led to the story being circulated that he travelled by air from Britain.

There were no other queries about the article and the Commander-in-Chief cheerfully agreed to a newspaper's request to photograph him on the quarterdeck the next day.

2

Vice-Admiral Sir Geoffrey Layton, who had been given temporary command of the Eastern Fleet pending the arrival of Somerville, had moved his headquarters to Batavia after the fall of Singapore and then, in mid-January, to Ceylon. Roskill records that on arrival in Ceylon, Layton found 'the same atmosphere of inertia and complacent optimism which had contributed to the débâcle in Malaya'. He impressed on the British Government the need for a single all-powerful central authority. This was strongly supported by the Chief of the Imperial General Staff, Field Marshal Sir Alan Brooke. To Layton's surprise, he was appointed supreme Commander-in-Chief Ceylon on 5 March with the acting rank of full Admiral and wide powers over the naval, military, air force and civilian authorities on the island, including the Governor, Sir Andrew Caldecot. A forceful personality, Layton set about improving all aspects of the defence of Ceylon. His appointment was a decision that was more than justified. It pleased Somerville who, on arrival at Colombo, found Layton presiding at a meeting and was much impressed.

> There was little doubt as to who was master in that house [he wrote]. He's very drastic, but that's what is needed here. . . . He takes complete charge of Ceylon and stands no nonsense from anyone. He pulls all the Minister's legs . . . and they work for him all the harder.

Somerville brushed aside complaints from the naval Commander-in-Chief East Indies, Vice-Admiral G. S. Arbuthnot, about Layton's ruthless control.

> I told him that in my opinion Geoffrey Layton was saving Ceylon from itself [he wrote]. He's roaring up the Ministers, Editors of papers and harbour authorities and is doing wonders. . . . He and I work absolutely hand in hand and call each other the most frightful names.

Colombo was all agog with reports about the danger threatening from the east. Many British women and children had been evacuated, some to South Africa, including Mrs Bond on whose husband's tea plantation I had spent a few days of leave. The army had been reinforced and efforts made to bolster the air defences.

On Friday, 27 March, the day after *Cornwall* arrived at Colombo, Somerville formally took over as Commander-in-Chief of the Eastern Fleet. At noon his flagship, the battleship *Warspite*, sailed into the harbour. It was reported that as soon as *Warspite* was sighted, the Commander-in-Chief hurried to the landing jetty and paced up and down, impatient to get aboard. The warship was barely through the entrance to the harbour when he set off in his launch. Almost before the ship had completed making fast to buoys, he was aboard and his flag hoisted. He was no stranger to *Warspite*. In the Mediterranean in 1927 he had been Commanding Officer of the ship.

Immediately after the flagship arrived, all shore leave was cancelled. Within a matter of hours of Somerville hoisting his flag, an Intelligence report was received on the Saturday morning about an impending attack by the Japanese that was expected on 1 April. According to the report, the attack was expected to be made by a force consisting of two or more aircraft-carriers, several cruisers and destroyers possibly supported by battleships.

We heard on Saturday morning that *Cornwall* would sail at 2 p.m. with the other units of the Eastern Fleet at Colombo. After dinner I went up to relax on the deck at about 1 p.m. It was a typically hot, enervating day in the tropics, and I sat gazing lazily at *Warspite* moored nearby. Suddenly a bugle call rang out from the loudspeakers. What's that? I reflected leisurely. The 'Cable party' call had been sounded a few minutes earlier and I had noted that the men concerned were preparing to weigh anchor. Was it the 'Special sea-duty men' call? No . . . then the penny dropped and I jumped up. It was 'Repel aircraft' – an air-raid alarm. The sirens could now be heard wailing ashore. I sprinted to my action station. Within a few minutes Royal Air Force planes had taken off and could be seen climbing above Colombo.

Our departure was expedited and *Cornwall* was out of the harbour well before the expected sailing time of 2 p.m. All the warships sailed in a hurry but no enemy aircraft appeared. As soon as we were all out at sea, the 'all clear' was sounded. The alarm savoured of a move to get everyone on their toes and perhaps also to distract attention ashore from the warship's departure. Somerville wanted to get busy training his fleet as soon as possible – as he put it, 'to collect all my scattered and untrained boys to see what I can do about it'.

The warships that sailed from Colombo on the Saturday afternoon were only about a third of the Eastern Fleet. The four R-Class battle-ships, fleet aircraft-carrier *Indomitable*, and eight destroyers had been exercising under Vice-Admiral Willis, Somerville's second-in-command, from the secret base, Port T, at Addu Atoll in the Maldive Islands, 600 miles south-west of Ceylon. The third group, including the carrier *Hermes*, the first Royal Navy ship to be specifically designed as an aircraft-carrier, was coming from Trincomalee. The rendezvous of the three groups was to be south of Ceylon. Meanwhile *Warspite*, *Formidable*, cruisers and destroyers from Colombo were put through their paces and we soon had experience of Somerville's sharp eye and humorous signals even when handing out a raspberry. When one of the cruisers did not turn sharply enough and had to increase speed to catch up, he signalled: 'Run, rabbit, run.' On another occasion a cruiser started turning the wrong way but quickly corrected the error. 'T-U-T' read the signal flashed from the flagship.

Somerville had a reputation for being very frank with the men serving under him. That first night at sea under his command, he signalled all ships that we were out 'to search for and engage Japanese units that may attempt to attack Ceylon'.

The meeting of the forces comprising the Eastern Fleet was a memorable occasion, especially for those of us who had never sailed in a fleet. The tropical sea was calm and a rich blue, creased white by the bow waves and wakes of the warships. On the horizon appeared small black dots. They became bigger . . . more black dots . . . gradually they all took shape . . . battleships, aircraft-carriers, cruisers and destroyers. Signals were flashed from the flagship. The forces merged and manoeuvred into position. Cruisers wheeled while destroyers, the terriers of the seas, sped to take up their stations. The battleships formed up in line ahead with the flagship, *Warspite*, a stately leader of the fleet. It was an imposing inspiring sight, a fleet of five battleships, three aircraft-carriers, seven cruisers and fourteen destroyers – twenty-nine warships, the biggest fleet assembled in the Indian Ocean.

When the fleet was sailing in formation, Somerville, with a typical light touch, had this signal flashed to all ships: 'I am delighted to have you all in company. Some of us are not as young as we used to be, but there's many a good tune played on an old fiddle.'

Numerically the fleet was very impressive, especially to those of us who were not aware of its limitations.

'My old battle-boats are in various states of disrepair,' Somerville had written earlier, 'and there is not a ship at present that approaches what I should call a proper standard of fighting efficiency.'

The four R-Class battleships were slow, outdated, unsuitable for service in the tropics and, in common with most other ships in the fleet, unfit for the modern naval air warfare at which the Japanese showed themselves so efficient.

Dorsetshire had interrupted a refit to join the fleet, while *Cornwall* was sorely in need of one. She was booked to go to Simonstown for a refit as soon as she could be spared. Four of the other cruisers were laid down during the First World War, and most of the destroyers were overdue for refits.

Although lacking fleet experience, the ships had endured vigorous service in the war. Between them, *Cornwall* and *Dorsetshire* had travelled about half a million miles since the outbreak of war. Men in the R-Class battleships, which had been built for service in the cold waters of the north, had to suffer acutely uncomfortable conditions in the heat of the tropics.

Hermes was a small, old aircraft-carrier. *Indomitable* and *Formidable* were modern fleet carriers but had aircraft that were for the most part obsolescent and, as was to become apparent, were no match for the more modern Japanese planes with much better performance and better trained pilots. The air crews in the two British carriers lacked training and experience, the main reason being lack of time and opportunity because both ships had been laid up for repairs. *Formidable* had been damaged in action and *Indomitable* in an accident.

So Somerville had to make do with what was available to him and wasted no time in exercising the fleet and the airmen in the carriers. He had the planes flying day and night, practising and on reconnaissance flights.

The trouble is that the fleet I now have is much bigger than anything anyone has had to handle before during this war [he wrote]. Everyone is naturally very rusty about doing their fleet stuff – most ships have hardly been in company with another ship during the war ... I must say that, as a result of these days at sea together, the boys are beginning to shape up nicely and, given the chance to continue these exercises, I hope to have them in some sort of trim before very long. Have handed out a good many raspberries, I must admit, but I believe it's essential to force the pace like blazes if you want to get a real move on.

The Commander-in-Chief divided the fleet as follows into fast (Force A) and slow (Force B) divisions :

Force A: The battleship *Warspite* (Fleet Flagship), two aircraft-carriers, *Indomitable* and *Formidable*, four cruisers, *Cornwall, Dorsetshire, Enterprise* and *Emerald*, and six destroyers, *Napier, Nestor, Paladin, Panther, Hotspur* and *Foxhound*.

Force B: Four battleships, *Resolution, Ramillies, Royal Sovereign* and *Revenge*, one aircraft-carrier, *Hermes*, three cruisers, *Caledon, Dragon* and *Heemskerk* (Royal Netherlands Navy), and eight destroyers, *Griffin, Norman, Arrow, Decoy, Fortune, Scout, Vampire* (Royal Australian Navy) and *Isaac Sweers* (Royal Netherlands Navy).

Fresh intelligence on Tuesday, 31 March, seemed to confirm the expectation that the Japanese attack would come soon, though no sign of the enemy fleet had been seen during the air patrols by long-range Catalinas based on Ceylon. On that day Somerville positioned the Eastern Fleet about eighty miles south of Dondra Head, the most southern point of Ceylon, and patrolled an area extending to the south-east of the island. He manoeuvred the fleet so as to keep clear of the area Japanese reconnaissance planes would be likely to search during the day, but to be at a convenient distance from the enemy's flying-off position to launch torpedo attacks at night. He expected that the Japanese would come from the south-east via the Sunda Strait and that their attack on Ceylon would be timed for dawn.

Somerville could not risk a day action. It must be remembered that he did not know the exact strength of the expected Japanese force. The only information he had was the intelligence report that it was believed to consist of two or more aircraft-carriers, several cruisers and destroyers and possibly supported by battleships. It may have been stronger. Before sailing from Colombo he had received a personal secret signal from the First Sea Lord, Admiral Sir Dudley Pound, strongly advising him not to allow his Eastern Fleet to become engaged with anything except inferior forces until it could be reinforced. It will be recalled that Somerville realised the best policy was to keep the fleet 'in being'. But an unnecessarily passive role was not one he would relish and he still hoped to be able to deliver a night attack on the Japanese force. There was an air of expectancy in the fleet as we patrolled on Tuesday, Wednesday and Thursday (31 March, 1 and 2 April) but no sighting reports were received from reconnaissance aircraft.

Somerville was faced with problems when he reviewed the situation on the Thursday evening. Had the intelligence reports of an impending attack by the Japanese been wrong, or had the enemy become aware of the concentration of the Eastern Fleet and postponed their plan? He decided that the alternative must be the case.

'I fear they have taken fright, which is a pity because if I could have given them a good crack now, it would have been very timely,' he wrote.

Another problem was that the four R-Class battleships had, as Somerville put it, 'confessed with salt tears running down their sides that they must return to harbour very quickly as they were running out of water'. There was also the question of some of the other ships needing to refuel.

At nine o'clock that Thursday night he called off the operation south of Ceylon. He could not risk the possibility of a Pearl Harbor by taking the fleet to the nearest base, which was Colombo, and set course for Port T to replenish the warships during the apparent lull. *Hermes* and *Vampire* were sent to Trincomalee to prepare for an operation they were to take part in at Madagascar, and on Good Friday morning *Cornwall* and *Dorsetshire* were detached from the fleet and ordered to go to Colombo. *Dorsetshire* was to resume her interrupted refit, and

HMS Cornwall's motor-boat (right) filled inside with wounded survivors, being brought alongside HMS Enterprise by the rescuing cruiser's pinnace, which is packed with wounded sailors. The stretcher case in white on the canopy of the motor-boat is Chief Yeoman Sam Langford.

(Above) Unwounded
survivors from HMS
Cornwall muster on the
quarterdeck of HMS
Enterprise where they we
addressed by their
Commanding Officer,
Captain P. C. W.
Manwaring (in white shirt
with his back to the
camera). Some of the
Eastern Fleet ships can b
seen on the horizon.

(Left) Wounded survivors
are lowered on pallets by
crane into barges at Port
to be taken to the hospita
ship, *Vita*. Their eyes wer
bandaged as protection
against the sun as Port T
on the equator.

Cornwall was to escort an Australian troop convoy due to arrive on 8 April.

Somerville's statement about the Japanese taking fright must have caused him to blush a couple of days later.

3

When *Cornwall* and *Dorsetshire* arrived at Colombo on Easter Saturday morning, 4 April, it was a bit of an anti-climax after the expectation of action while at sea with the Eastern Fleet. It seemed that the crisis was over and things had reverted to normal. All-night leave was granted to the port watch and a large number of men caught the first liberty boat soon after dinner. Bill and I decided to wait for the 4.30 p.m. liberty boat, but shortly after two o'clock there was an air raid alarm and the starboard watch plus those in the port watch who had not already gone ashore closed up at action stations. The Captain whiled away the time on the bridge playing a game similar to draughts with the Navigating Officer.

No enemy aircraft appeared and eventually the all clear was sounded. By then it was too late to shave, bath and change from battle dress into clean tropical rig in time to catch the 4.30 liberty boat so Bill and I decided to go ashore in the next one at 6 p.m. But once again we were thwarted. Suddenly things changed from the feeling of normality that prevailed when the ship arrived in the morning. At 5.30 we were standing next to the gangway with the other libertymen waiting to be fallen in and inspected – the routine before being allowed to go ashore – when Commander Fair ran along the deck and shouted : 'All leave is stopped – general recall.' He ordered the messenger on duty to tell the quartermaster to pipe the steaming watch below immediately.

'There goes our glass of cold beer,' lamented Bill as we made our way below to change again. We cursed our bad luck. We had looked forward to a walk ashore followed by some liquid refreshment and dinner.

It was obvious something big was in the wind and the atmosphere on board tensed up dramatically. The duty watch was already preparing the cruiser for sea. Boats came alongside crammed with men who had been ashore. It was surprising how quickly the libertymen were rounded up. The general recall went around Colombo in hotel lounges and bars, bazaars and places of entertainment. The order spread quickly, urgently : 'All naval personnel return to your ships.'

Bill Alcock and a fellow Engine Room Artificer went to a cinema to see the Laurel and Hardy film *Hold That Ghost*. The woman in the ticket office asked : 'Which ship are you from ?'

Feeling security-minded, Alcock said : 'What's that got to do with you ?'

'Well, if you are from the *Cornwall*, there is a general recall,' the woman replied, so they had a quick drink and hurried to the landing jetty to get a boat back to the ship.

On board *Cornwall* there was much speculation about the reason for the recall and buzzes flew fast and furious. Men who had been ashore were bombarded with questions in the hope that they had heard something, while those who had remained on board were asked : 'What do you know ?'

4

Less than forty-eight hours after arriving at Ceylon to augment the few Catalina flying-boats available to carry out long-range reconnaissance, Squadron Leader L. J. Birchell and his crew of eight took off from Koggala, a land-locked lagoon on the south-west coast, at about 6 a.m. on Saturday, 4 April. The Catalina had up to thirty hours' endurance and they were ordered to patrol an area 250 miles south-east of Ceylon. Later in the day they were told to switch the patrol farther to the south. They had reached the southernmost point of their search, about 350 miles south south-east of Ceylon, and were just about to change course to return to base when a small speck was seen on the horizon. It was late afternoon where they were flying because of the difference in time – they were east of Ceylon. They flew farther south to investigate and in the distance saw the Japanese fleet consisting of battleships, aircraft-carriers, cruisers and destroyers.

The radio operator, Sergeant F. C. Phillips, hurriedly made a signal to headquarters in Ceylon reporting the sighting of a powerful enemy force. Birchell turned northwards at maximum speed to get away, but the Catalina had been seen by the Japanese and six Zero fighters, capable of flying at almost double the 180 miles an hour of the flying boat, took off from one of the carriers. They rapidly overtook the Catalina and launched a merciless attack in an effort to prevent a

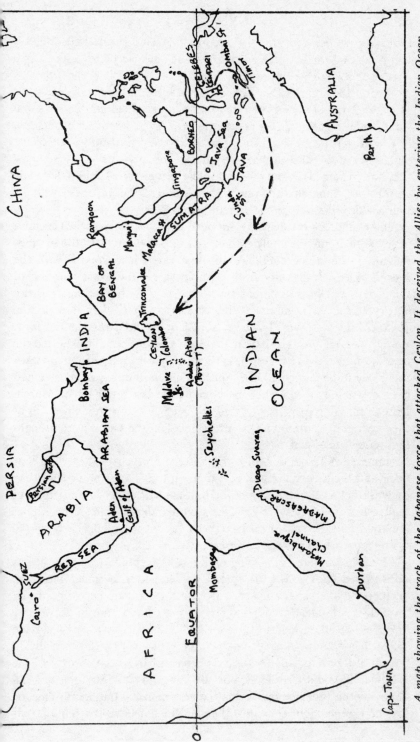

A map showing the track of the Japanese force that attacked Ceylon. It deceived the Allies by entering the Indian Ocean from much farther south than expected – through the Ombai Strait instead of the Sunda or Malacca Straits.

radio report being made. In accordance with regulations, Phillips was repeating the message when a cannon shell from one of the Zeros wrecked his wireless equipment.

Two of the crew of the Catalina were killed in the action, but even after the flying-boat had been shot down the Japanese strafed the seven survivors in the sea, killing another man. The six surviving airmen, all of whom were wounded, three seriously, were picked up by one of the destroyers in the fleet and severely beaten because the Japanese knew they had managed to send the signal. The airmen were subjected to some of the foul, inhuman treatment that branded the Japanese with an unenviable reputation in the Second World War.

The Catalina's invaluable sighting report was received in Ceylon a little garbled but essentially correct. It was passed on to all the services, including Admiral Somerville who had arrived at Port T with the Eastern Fleet. It has not been possible to get the exact wording of the signal, but it is apparent from reports that the message did not specify the exact number of aircraft-carriers and other ships in the Japanese fleet. It was, however, sufficient to indicate that the force was a powerful one and that an attack on Ceylon could be expected the next morning. As a result of the earlier intelligence report that an attack was likely to be launched on 1 April, as much shipping as possible had been cleared from Colombo harbour in the last few days of March. Now every effort was hastily made to get what ships remained out of the way at sea and the limited air defences on the island were brought to a state of readiness.

Somerville's fast Force A of the Eastern Fleet arrived at Port T at noon and the slower Force B at 3 p.m. on that Easter Saturday to top up with fuel and, in the case of the R-Class battleships in particular, to replenish supplies of water. As the Commander-in-Chief's biographer remarks, 'seldom can a fleet have been caught more hopelessly on the wrong foot . . . 600 miles from the enemy'.

Motor-boats were taking Flag Officers and Captains from the various ships to the flagship, *Warspite*, for a conference with Somerville when he received the signal that the Japanese force had been sighted by Birchell's Catalina. It said that before the composition of the enemy force could be reported, the Catalina had been shot down. So Somerville still did not know exactly how powerful the fleet was, especially in respect of tthe most important units, aircraft-carriers.

Somerville's Eastern Fleet was too far away to interfere with an attack by the Japanese on Ceylon the next morning but, in any case, he was now even more conscious that he did not have the requisite air strength to risk a daylight action. However, he still had in mind to get into a position from which he could use his carriers' aircraft to deliver torpedo attacks at night.

All the ships in his Force A could sail almost immediately except the two cruisers, *Enterprise* and *Emerald*, which could not be ready until midnight. With the two heavy cruisers, *Dorsetshire* and *Cornwall*, at Colombo, he could not sail without *Enterprise* and *Emerald*, the only other cruisers in his fast division. He therefore gave orders that Force A should sail as soon as the two cruisers were ready and left shortly after midnight. Force B was to sail as soon as it could be ready some hours later and it got under way at 7 a.m.

When the Catalina's sighting signal was received in Colombo on the Saturday afternoon, the Commanding Officers of *Dorsetshire* and *Cornwall*, Captain Agar and Captain Manwaring, were summoned to a conference in the Operations Room ashore with the Commander-in-Chief East Indies, Admiral Arbuthnot. They were given orders to sail south as soon as possible that night to rejoin the Eastern Fleet and signals were sent to the *Hermes* and *Vampire* at Trincomalee ordering them to sail to the north-east to keep them out of the way of the Japanese force.

Neither *Dorsetshire* nor *Cornwall* could be ready to sail at speed until about 10 p.m. After supper a crowd collected on the fo'c'sle of *Cornwall* and started a sing-song which evoked much laughter. Looking back, I should say it was a form of escapism from the undercurrent of tension on board while waiting for the ship to sail. It was a case of swan-songs for some of those who took part in the singing that night.

When *Cornwall* weighed anchor soon after 10 p.m. and sailed slowly out of Colombo harbour, all but two members of the ship's company were on board. It was incredible how successful the recall had been. We heard that the two who missed the ship – they were both senior men from the lower deck – had gone ashore to visit some friends and did not hear about the recall until late. They hired a bum boat in an effort to get to *Cornwall*, but when they drew near the cruiser was already under way. The only man who did not sail in *Dorsetshire* was the Gunnery Officer who was ill in hospital. Even members of the *Dorsetshire*'s crew who had gone on special leave to tea estates inland got back to the ship in time.

Some weeks earlier my cruising and action stations had been changed to the Transmitting Station (TS) which was manned almost entirely by members of the Royal Marine Band. The officer in charge was a Royal Marine Lieutenant and Bill had a key job on the plotting table which played a vital part in the control of the ship's main armament. I had to go on watch at 4 a.m. so went below to get into my hammock before the ship sailed, but the rumbling of the anchor chain coming inboard put paid to my effort to get to sleep early.

When the ship was under way I felt restless and unsettled, tossed and turned in my hammock, perspired in the muggy heat of the mess deck and could not sleep. Eventually I decided to go up top for a breath of air and smoke on the upper deck. I lit a cigarette in the recreation space because it was an offence to strike a match on the upper deck at night and stepped out into the darkness on deck. It was a particularly dark night and *Dorsetshire* could be seen as just a black smudge on our starboard side. The two cruisers were steaming at 23 knots on a course of 220 degrees (almost due south-west) which, if maintained, would have taken them straight to Port T.

While standing on the deck peering into the darkness and lost in my thoughts, a voice suddenly said : 'Give us a light, chum.' I had not seen the other sailor on deck.

'Sure,' I said snapping out of my reverie, and held out my cigarette for him to light his from it.

'Got the middle watch?' he asked.

'No, the morning,' I replied.

'What's up. Can't you sleep?' he said.

'No, my mind's too active – can't settle.'

'Same here. It's sort of eerie isn't it. Can't help feeling something is going to happen.'

We smoked and chatted. I recalled that while on patrol with the Eastern Fleet a few days earlier, the Gunnery Officer had come down to the TS and, in the course of conversation, remarked : 'If we find the Jap fleet, it will be the biggest naval action so far in this war.'

The muted pipe, 'Call the starboard watch,' was heard shortly before midnight. We continued chatting, standing all the time and gazing out into the blackness of the night. It must have been close on 1 a.m. before I went down to the mess deck and swung myself into my hammock to have some sleep before turning out to go on watch.

While *Dorsetshire* and *Cornwall* were sailing on their southerly course to join Somerville's Force A, which was heading north-easterly from Port T, the Japanese fleet was steaming steadily north-west towards Ceylon. It was the start of Easter Sunday (5 April) and the stage was set for what was destined to be an unforgettable day for the 1,546 men serving in the two County Class cruisers.

5

The Japanese had succeeded in carrying out a deception with the First Air Fleet commanded by Vice-Admiral Nagumo. The Allies expected the force to enter the Indian Ocean from the Sunda Strait between Sumatra and Java or even possibly the Malacca Strait at the northern end of Sumatra. Instead when the fleet sailed from the Celebes, it came into the Indian Ocean well south of Java through the Ombai Strait between Flores and Timor. In the Indian Ocean the fleet fuelled from tankers on its way north to Ceylon.

The Japanese had never intended carrying out the assault on Ceylon on 1 April as expected by Allied intelligence. The plan was to launch the attack on a Sunday, as at Pearl Harbor, when it was hoped to catch the Eastern Fleet in port. Easter Sunday was the day chosen for the action and when the force was sighted by the Catalina on Easter Saturday, it was very much on schedule heading for a position south of Ceylon from which it could fly off planes from its carriers shortly before dawn.

Nagumo's fleet was also more powerful than expected. It comprised five of the six aircraft-carriers he used at Pearl Harbor (the sixth, *Kaga*, had gone to Japan for repairs), four fast battleships compared with two at Pearl Harbor, three cruisers and eight destroyers. The five carriers, *Akagi* (Nagumo's flagship), *Soryu*, *Hiryu*, *Shokaku* and *Zuikaku*, each had at least sixty aircraft so Nagumo had more than 300 planes compared with about ninety inferior ones available from the three carriers in Somerville's Eastern Fleet.

Referring to Nagumo's formidable fleet, Churchill commented after the war: 'This was the antagonist for whom our fleet had waited so eagerly up till 2 April. We had narrowly escaped a disastrous fleet action.'

According to Fuchida and Okumiya, the Japanese estimated the composition of the British Eastern Fleet to be two battleships, two aircraft-carriers, three heavy cruisers, four to seven light cruisers and an unspecified number of destroyers. They considerably overestimated the shore-based air strength in the area, believing it to be about 300 planes.

Vice-Admiral Ozawa, commander of the Malaya Force, had sailed on 1 April into the Bay of Bengal with his light aircraft-carrier, six cruisers and some destroyers from Mergui, the most southern Burma

port on the Kra Isthmus. His departure was timed to enable him to
be in position to attack merchant shipping in the area off the east coast
of India at the same time as Nagumo's fleet went into action against
Ceylon on Sunday.

A Catalina that took off from Koggala in Ceylon early on the Saturday night (4 April) to carry out a reconnaissance to the south sent a
signal between midnight and 1 a.m. that it had sighted a Japanese
destroyer. Nothing more was heard from the aircraft, which was
presumed to have been shot down. Another Catalina that took off a few
hours later reported sighting battleships, cruisers and destroyers but not
aircraft carriers, which must have been to the south of these covering
ships.

Shortly before dawn on Easter Sunday, when Nagumo's fleet was
about 200 miles south of Ceylon, the carriers turned into the wind for
planes to take off. The eager airmen, their confidence boosted by
successes at and since Pearl Harbor, including their recent attack on
Port Darwin on 19 February, headed north for Colombo. In *The War
At Sea* Captain Roskill gives the number of aircraft as 91 bombers and
36 fighters, a total of 127. Fuchida and Okumiya say the force consisted
of 180 planes – 90 level bombers, 54 dive-bombers and 36 fighters.
Whatever the correct figure may be, it was a powerful air armada.
Fuchida, who led the assault by 353 planes on Pearl Harbor, was again
in command, flying as observer in one of the Kate level bombers.

'We were expecting trouble this time since an enemy flying-boat had
spotted us the preceding day and, though shot down by our combat air
patrol, had undoubtedly reported the presence of our force,' he recalled.

The roar of the aircraft in the dim light before dawn heralded a day
that prompted Churchill to write : 'Breathtaking events were now to
take place in the Bay of Bengal and in the Indian Ocean.'

6

During the night *Dorsetshire* and *Cornwall* had received orders from
Admiral Somerville to join him in a position just north of the equator
and 77 degrees 36 east at 4 p.m. on Sunday. This necessitated an
alteration of course and at 7 a.m. the two cruisers changed from 220
degrees to 185, which was almost due south and thus farther east and
closer to the enemy force.

Down in the TS during the morning watch I had noticed that the pitometer was registering our speed as 26 knots. About an hour later Captain Agar received a report in *Dorsetshire* about the early morning sighting by a Catalina of two Japanese battleships, two cruisers and destroyers. He was the senior Captain and ordered an increase in speed to $27\frac{1}{2}$ knots, *Cornwall*'s maximum, so as to join the Eastern Fleet as soon as possible.

While we were having breakfast it was piped that *Cornwall* and *Dorsetshire* were then crossing the path of a large Japanese fleet about 100 miles to the east and that everyone would close up at action stations at nine o'clock and stay closed up all day. Three decks down in the TS it was uncomfortably hot and muggy with the thermometer registering over 100 degrees. During the morning we were allowed to go up in pairs for a break of a few minutes on the upper deck to get some fresh air. It was a relief to be in the relatively cool open air. But there was a feeling of suspense and tension, with the upper deck deserted and strangely quiet except for occasional movement by men manning the four-inch and pom pom guns on the iron deck above. It was a fine sunny day, and calm blue sea with *Cornwall* and *Dorsetshire* cleaving white bow waves as they raced south.

Back in the TS the loudspeaker crackled and then the firm voice of the Chaplain, the Reverend J. M. Bird, was heard. As the normal Sunday morning church service could not be held on the quarterdeck, he broadcast a short service. It was impressive and moving as he said: 'We pray not for our personal safety, but for courage to do our duty.' It was his last prayer and it was heard all over the ship.

Soon after the service ended an RNVR doctor, Surgeon Lieutenant C. Kirby, came through tthe hatch and down the perpendicular ladder into the TS.

'Don't forget, the Sick Bay is your nearest dressing station,' he told us. We were never to see him again.

The Royal Marine officer in charge of the TS received a message from the director control tower. 'A Japanese plane has been shadowing us,' he said.

The plane had been sighted by *Cornwall* and reported to Captain Agar in *Dorsetshire*. It was about twenty miles astern and disappeared soon afterwards. Somerville said later that if a sighting report had been made, he would have considered breaking wireless silence to arrange an earlier rendezvous and give fighter aircraft cover to the two cruisers during the closing stages of their approach.

It is very doubtful if that would have saved the ships from their fate. A float plane on a reconnaissance flight from the Japanese cruiser *Tone*

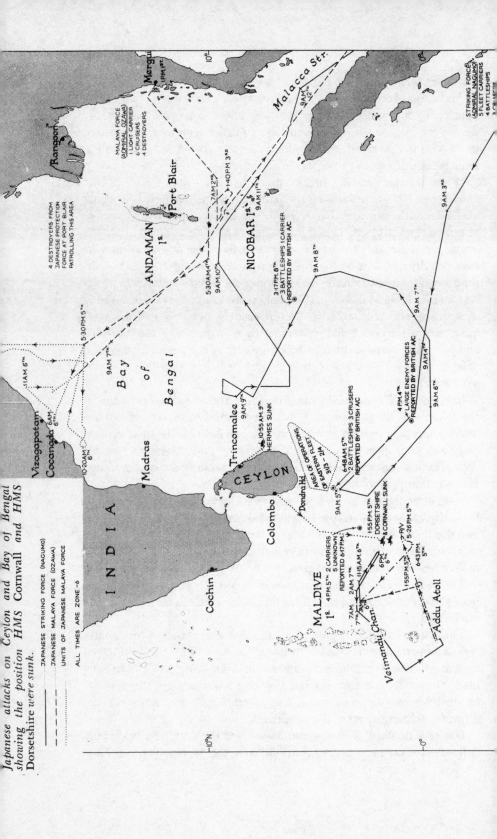

Japanese attacks on Ceylon and Bay of Bengal showing the position HMS Cornwall and HMS Dorsetshire were sunk.

JAPANESE STRIKING FORCE (NAGUMO)

JAPANESE MALAYA FORCE (OZAWA)

UNITS OF JAPANESE MALAYA FORCE

ALL TIMES ARE ZONE −6

STRIKING FORCE (ADMIRAL NAGUMO)
5 FLEET CARRIERS
4 BATTLESHIPS

MALAYA FORCE (ADMIRAL OZAWA)
1 LIGHT CARRIER
6 CRUISERS
4 DESTROYERS

4 DESTROYERS FROM JAPANESE PROTECTION FORCE AT PORT BLAIR PATROLLING THIS AREA

Rangoon

Mergui (1PM, IST)

Port Blair

ANDAMAN Is.

5.30AM 4TH
9AM 10TH
7AM 2ND
1.40PM 3RD

NICOBAR Is.
9AM 11TH

Malacca Str.

9AM 12TH

9AM 3RD

3.17PM 8TH
3 BATTLESHIPS 1 CARRIER REPORTED BY BRITISH AC

9AM 8TH

9AM 7TH

9AM 6TH

9AM 4TH
4PM 4TH
LARGE ENEMY FORCES REPORTED BY BRITISH AC

Bay of Bengal

5.30PM 5TH

9AM 7TH

11AM 6TH

Vizagapatam 6AM, 6TH
Cocanada 6AM, 6TH

10.20AM, 6TH

Madras

Cochin

I N D I A

Trincomalee
9AM 9TH

10.55AM 9TH
HERMES SUNK

CEYLON

Colombo

Dondra Hd.

AREA OF OPERATIONS OF EASTERN FLEET
3/1/3 − 2/4

9AM 5TH

6.48AM 5TH
2 BATTLESHIPS 3 CRUISERS REPORTED BY BRITISH AC

1.55PM 5TH
DORSETSHIRE
& CORNWALL SUNK

MALDIVE Is.

4PM 5TH 2 CARRIERS 5 UNKNOWN REPORTED 6.17PM

7AM, 2AM 7TH

11.45AM 6TH

6PM
6TH

1.55PM 5TH
R/V
5.26PM 5TH

6.43PM
5TH

Veimandu Chan.

Addu Atoll

10°N

0°

10°

had seen *Cornwall* and *Dorsetshire*. It signalled Nagumo in his flagship, the carrier *Akagi*, that two destroyers had been sighted steaming south-west at 25 knots. The signal was corrected to read cruisers instead of destroyers and Nagumo ordered a bombing force to take off to attack as soon as Fuchida's planes returned from Colombo. Meanwhile, the cruisers were to be shadowed. At various times during the morning a shadowing plane was seen by *Dorsetshire* and *Cornwall*.

The raid on Colombo was not the success the Japanese had hoped for when planning the sortie into the Indian Ocean. There was no Sunday Pearl Harbor because the Eastern Fleet was hundreds of miles away. After *Cornwall* and *Dorsetshire* sailed from Colombo on the Saturday night, the only naval ships in the harbour were the old destroyer *Tenedos*, which was undergoing a refit, the 11,198-ton Armed Merchant Cruiser *Hector*, and a submarine depot ship *Lucia*. *Tenedos* and *Hector* were sunk by the bombers and *Lucia* damaged. One of the few merchant ships still in the harbour was damaged and so were workshops and quays.

Reports of the number of aircraft lost vary. It would seem that in the aerial combat at least thirteen of the forty-two fighters available to defend Colombo were destroyed (nine of the thirty-six Royal Air Force Hurricanes and four of the six Fleet Air Arm Fulmars). In addition, six old Fleet Air Arm Swordfish planes that were loaded with torpedoes and sent from Trincomalee to refuel before going out to attack the Japanese ships were 'sitting ducks' for the enemy's Zero fighters and were shot down before they could land at Colombo.

The Japanese claimed to have shot down forty-one British aircraft and admitted the loss of only seven planes, but their losses must have been muh higher, according to claims by British fighter pilots.

Fuchida, sitting in a bomber over Colombo, was just about to send a signal to Nagumo that a second wave attack would not be necessary at Ceylon when he overheard the radio message from one of the float planes searching to the west that the two cruisers had been sighted. Thinking that surface units were being sent to attack the Japanese fleet, he was perturbed and ordered his planes to return to the carriers as quickly as possible. He was relieved on his return 'to learn that the two enemy cruisers had been running away, not attacking, and that no other enemy forces had been seen'. An élite force of eighty dive-bombers, led by their doyen, Lieutenant-Commander Egusa, had already taken off to attack the cruisers.

On board *Cornwall* men manning anti-aircraft guns and others in exposed positions wore tin hats or had them conveniently close at hand to be put on at a moment's notice. From midday the ship's company was sent for a quick dinner in relays so that the guns and all the other positions were always manned. A shadowing aircraft, which was sighted astern at about 1 p.m., closed to within about fourteen miles of the cruisers. It soon disappeared, but because *Dorsetshire* and *Cornwall* were then only about ninety miles from the position ordered for their rendezvous with Force A of the Eastern Fleet, Captain Agar decided to break wireless silence and make a sighting report to warn Admiral Somerville. The signal was sent via a shore radio station at Ceylon, but was received in Somerville's flagship in a mutilated form. It was not until 2 p.m. that the signal was identified as coming from *Dorsetshire*. By then it was too late.

7

The hands of clocks were just moving on to 1.40 p.m. It was a fine afternoon with some relatively low light cloud cover and the tropical sun almost directly overhead. Egusa, who was in command of the Japanese bombers, had signalled the flagship, 'Enemy in sight', as he looked down at the two cruisers in the sea far below.

On the compass platform on the bridge of *Cornwall* the aircraft were suddenly spotted. The Navigating Officer, Lieutenant J. E. R. Fearfield, dashed down from the compass platform to sound the action alarm for aircraft attack. Able Seaman Angus Sutherland, who was on duty as Captain's messenger on the bridge, heard Fearfield shout: 'There are aircraft overhead.'

Standing on the port wing of the bridge were the Gunnery Officer, Lieutenant Streatfield, and the Meteorological Officer, Lieutenant B. M. Holden. Tommy Thorp, who was on anti-submarine lookout duty nearby, heard Holden say : 'Surely not another bombing.' Holden had been drafted to serve in *Cornwall* after surviving the Japanese high-level bombing and torpedo attacks which sank the battle-cruiser *Repulse* a few days short of four months earlier.

It was another bombing, but with a difference. This time it was not high-level or torpedo attacks but dive-bombing. The assault was cleverly planned, the planes approaching at considerable height and positioning themselves to be able to dive with the sun behind them, thus making it more difficult to be seen. *Cornwall* did not have radar and *Dorsetshire* had a small screen of the earliest type that could pick up objects only at very short distances. Confused streaks had appeared on *Dorsetshire*'s radar screen and the Chief Telegraphist, Shaddick, said 'he was sure something was about'. There was a faint hope that any aircraft might be from our own Eastern Fleet as Captain Agar expected the cruisers to be under the protection of planes from the fleet's carriers by about 2 p.m. It was also not thought that the Japanese planes had sufficient range to reach *Dorsetshire* and *Cornwall.*

The range and performance of the Japanese aircraft had been sadly underestimated. They achieved almost complete surprise when they suddenly dived on *Cornwall* and *Dorsetshire* and launched their attack with disciplined efficiency and fury. They came down at a steep angle in flights of three to release their 500-lb bombs at a low altitude with remarkable accuracy.

The attacks were made from directly ahead. They thus took advantage of the ships' blind spot as their main anti-aircraft armament was in such a position that it could not be aimed straight ahead – one of the weaknesses of the County Class cruisers.

The first three planes dived on to *Cornwall* which was slightly astern of *Dorsetshire*. Within seconds another formation of three aircraft attacked *Dorsetshire*. Both warships tried to take avoiding action by turning hard a starboard, but to no avail. The first bombs aimed at *Cornwall* scored a near miss on the port side forward and a hit aft. The effect of near misses was incredibly violent. Captain Manwaring reported : 'The effect of these was very great, lifting the ship bodily by their force, causing her to whip heavily from end to end and carrying away all the w/t aerials and nearly shaking the mast down.'

The first three bombs aimed at *Dorsetshire* all hit her. They disabled the steering gear and put both wireless offices out of action, in addition to other damage. As a result of the steering breakdown, *Dorsetshire* continued steering to starboard and completed a circle. *Cornwall*'s steering gear was also disabled and, with the ship uncontrollable, her wake became a big zigzag.

Recalling the start of the attack, Wally Muller, who was then a 21-year-old Able Seaman at his action station on the port pom-pom, wrote :

A high-pitched whine intruded suddenly upon the senses, growing in the space of a second or two to an ear-shattering roar, then passed overhead and away. Almost immediately the ship shuddered violently with the sound of the muffled explosion of a near miss, but even before stunned realisation took hold, the scream of the second dive-bomber rent the air and there was the fearsome concussion as a bomb exploded in the ship.

Men were recovering from the initial shock and moving to do the things they knew had to be done. Someone shouted from the wing of the bridge, 'For God's sake get those guns going', just before the third bomber hurtled down with deafening crescendo, followed again by the sickening tremor of a direct hit. Guns were starting to fire back, flames belching from the twin muzzles of the four-inch mountings. The eight barrels of our multiple pom-pom, capable of firing a spread of graze-fused shells at the rate of 720 a minute, coughed in staccato bursts.

But the planes plummeted down in a continual stream, barely seconds apart, some raking the bridge and superstructure with machine-gun fire as they dived. A near miss on the port side sent a mass of discoloured water towering above the cruiser. It hung motionless for a moment, then came crashing down like a waterfall, drenching men at their guns.

Cornwall was already listing heavily to port and the guns on that side could not elevate sufficiently to hit back at the steeply diving attackers, but one Japanese bomber, in the process of pulling out, had veered into the field of fire of the port pom-pom, burst into flames and, I was assured, crashed into the sea astern.

Dense black smoke was pouring out of the cruiser's funnels and other openings, due to the havoc wreaked in the vicinity of the engine and boiler-rooms. Another explosion wrecked hydraulic power to the guns and in the smoke and clamour, men wrestled to switch controls from power to manual. Flying shrapnel activated the ship's siren on a funnel right behind us. It was blaring full blast and, with all the other noise, it was impossible to hear what the chap next to you was shouting.

Then came a hit on the S1 (forward starboard) 4-inch gun followed by a fearsome, 30-foot wall of flame which had everyone on the pom-pom deck scampering for dear life. Some people said that the flame was caused by an oil bomb, but I believe it was cordite when the ready-use 4-inch ammunition lockers exploded.

The large flame from what was described in an official report as an oil bomb enveloped the forward starboard anti-aircraft armament and starboard superstructure, and even reached as high as the top of the bridge. The men manning the 4-inch S1 gun, including my friend Ian Keith, were killed by this bomb. Battle-dress and anti-flash gear, worn in action by personnel in exposed positions, could not save them in that fire.

(I have tried to establish from Japanese sources whether an oil bomb was dropped on *Cornwall*. It is one of several questions I asked in a letter to Japanese Naval Headquarters in Tokyo, but did not receive a reply.)

Lieutenant-Commander Grove, who was on the air defence platform, recalled :

We watched the planes like hawks and as bombs came down, flung ourselves down on our faces. If the hit was close, you found yourself being bounced likea ball. We had three hits directly under us. From one of them – I was standing up – I got enveloped in a great sheet of flame. I thought I was dead, but actually my clothing saved me and I was unhurt.

The onslaught on the cruisers was devastating. It quickly knocked out the ships' main anti-aircraft armament and reduced them to little more than helpless targets. Both warships soon lost way, had lists and became practically stationery – sitting ducks to be bombed at will. The near miss on the port side of *Cornwall* had flooded parts of the bilges and dislocated electric power all over the ship. It was believed that all the men in the after engine-room were killed by a near miss on the starboard side. A bomb hit on the water line burst in the forward engine-room, which quickly filled with steam and smoke and had to be evacuated. Both boiler-rooms had to be abandoned as a result of damage caused by near misses. There were hits between the forward and centre funnels, between 'X' and 'Y' turrets on the after part of the ship and in the Sick Bay Flat on the starboard side.

A bomb that exploded on the starboard paravane damaged the fore part of the bridge and killed several men. The Chief Yeoman, Sam Langford, was the only survivor, but he had to pay a heavy price, eventually losing both legs. He told me :

The other men on the bridge at the time were Lieutenant Fearfield, a Midshipman, some look-outs and voicepipe crew. I was on a pedestal on the port side in the rear of the bridge. I was hit in both legs and knocked to the deck. Glancing round, I saw that the rest of the bridge crew were dead. I could not move myself, but fortunately one of my staff, Leading Signalman Norman Raynor, came up and managed to pull me clear.

Captain Manwaring, who was on his way back to the bridge from the Remote Control Office when the bomb exploded, was wounded in the right shoulder, but continued to direct operations.

The damage done to *Cornwall* in less than ten minutes since the attack started was lethal. All power had failed, both engine-rooms and both boiler-rooms were flooding rapidly. The ship was already slightly down by the head, the starboard outer propeller was breaking surface and the forward part of the port gunwhale was awash.

It was a shattering experience, made worse by the suddenness of the concentrated bombing. To many of *Cornwall*'s crew, particularly to those of us down below, an air attack was unexpected. Despite the report of shadowing aircraft during the morning, we thought in terms of a surface action with the Japanese fleet.

When the first bomb hit *Cornwall*, men in the Main Wireless Office thought we had fired a broadside – something that gave a very pronounced jolt throughout the warship. Guns' crews in turrets thought the ship had been torpedoed, while others down below thought we had been hit by a shell.

Down in the TS, after the hurried dinner snatched in relays, the crew were in various states of relaxation in the heat. Some were reading, some chatting and some resting. We knew that *Cornwall* and *Dorsetshire* were due to rejoin Somerville's Force A of the Eastern Fleet at 4 p.m. and it was already 1.40.

Suddenly, without any warning, there was a terrific crash. The concussion felt as though the ship had run into a solid wall. She shook and heeled over alarmingly to port. My first thought was that *Cornwall* had been hit by a shell from an enemy warship. (Nagumo's force included four battleships.) Other members of the TS crew, including the Royal Marine officer in charge, Lieutenant Reid, obviously thought likewise. His reaction was immediately to give the order, 'Load, load, load', to the 8-inch surface armament, but a second or two later he cancelled it.

More hits or near misses followed in quick succession. Again and again there was the awful concussion. The TS table, a large and solid structure, was shaken. The decks above and below in the confined space shook and instruments were smashed.

By now we knew it was bombs, not shells. We were told to evacuate the TS which had no part to play in anti-aircraft defence and, in any case, was out of action. Everyone looked grim and tied on his lifebelt. The only access to or exit from the TS was a small, square hatch in one corner that was normally closed from the deck above with a water-

HMS *Hermes* sinks within sight of Ceylon. The aircraft-carrier was caught defenceless without any planes by Japanese dive-bombers after the attack on Trincomalee on 9 April 1942.

The cruiser HMS *Enterprise* which rescued survivors from HMS *Cornwall*.

(Left) Ken Dimbleby with his son Keith, aged two, in 1942. He was commissioned Sub-Lieutenant when he was discharged from hospital four months after the sinking of Cornwall.

(Below) The survivors: a reunion between Sam Langford (left), Richard Tomczak from the Pinguin (centre) and Paddy Keeping.

tight cover when in action. Fortunately, as we were at action stations all day, it had not been battened down otherwise we should still be in that compartment in the ship.

There was no panic, the men nearest to the perpendicular ladder on the bulkhead leading the way in orderly haste. We hauled ourselves through the hatchway to the Marines' mess deck, which was two decks below the upper deck. No sooner had we got out of the TS than another bomb scored a direct hit or near miss and the ship shook and heeled over again. We were in semi-darkness down below because by then there was no electric power and there were only some emergency lamps. The ship heeled over so much to port that men lost their footing and slithered across the deck, some piling up against the ship's side.

Bill and I were lucky. We managed to grab hold of a ladder in the middle of the deck. When the immediate effect of the bomb explosion had worn off, we climbed the ladder quickly to get to the seamen's mess deck. Getting away from the Marines' mess deck was indeed a lucky break because shortly afterwards a fire broke out there and caused many deaths. Most of the TS crew of about thirty men were trapped by the fire and only a few survived. Some men emerged blinded by the flames and succumbed later in the water. One of those who did not survive was the Royal Marine officer.

By the time Bill and I reached the seamen's mess deck – one below the upper deck – it was fairly crowded with men who had come up from other positions down below and had the same thing in mind: to get up top from where one would at least be able to leave the ship before she sank. Just then another bomb made the ship heel over again. We grabbed hold of the iron leg of a mess table to stop slipping across the deck and into the hatch from which we had just managed to climb.

We had not spoken a word since the leaving the TS. There was the horrible feeling of suspense in the short time between the fall of bombs. Nerves were taut, with not knowing where the next hit would be or how much longer the ship could remain afloat under such a barrage from dive-bombers. There was no time for words – the individual had to think and act for himself. It is difficult to imagine anyone not trying to get to the upper deck in such circumstances, yet I heard a story later about a seaman in the *Dorsetshire* who would not leave the mess deck because he could not swim. He had a lifebelt but, instead of going up top and jumping into the water, he calmly said cheerio to his shipmates, lit a cigarette and sat on a mess table to wait for the ship to go down.

The quickest way to the upper deck from the seamen's mess deck was up the ladder opposite where Bill and I were standing. An alternative route was to go through the open door into the adjacent Sick Bay Flat and up a ladder that led to the Galley Flat, which opened on to part of the upper deck that was protected overhead by a gun deck. This route had the advantage of more safety up top and I intended going that way – until another bomb hit the ship. It crashed into the Sick Bay Flat about fifteen yards away. There were screams, shouts and a hissing noise that sounded like steam escaping. It was this bomb that killed the Chaplain, who had conducted his last service that morning, and the doctor who had visited the TS immediately afterwards to remind us that the Sick Bay was our nearest dressing station.

That bomb eliminated the alternative route via the Sick Bay Flat to the upper deck. A number of us dashed up the nearest ladder and into a corridor that led through the Heads Flat on the starboard side to the upper deck just astern of 'A' turret on the foc's'le. Bill was immediately in front of me, and it was with a feeling of some relief that one entered the semi-dark corridor knowing that the goal of the upper deck lay ahead.

But those few yards were by no means the end of our troubles. Suddenly the corridor was transformed from a sort of haven into an inferno. There was a crash, a hissing sound and fire swept through the corridor. Men cried out as there was the searing pain of flame on flesh. It must have been only a few seconds, but it seemed much longer before the flames passed and we surged on through foul-smelling smoke and fumes and out into the sunlight on the upper deck.

Ken Collier, a member of the gun's crew who evacuated 'A' turret, recalled seeing a man stagger out of the Heads Flat on to the fo'c'sle deck, his overalls tattered and smoking. He clung to the guard-rail for a while before collapsing and dying. There were many ugly and distressing scenes on the upper deck.

Those of us who had just arrived up top with burn wounds were in a state of shock and felt mentally numbed. I glanced instinctively across the ocean to see how *Dorsetshire* was faring on our starboard side. She was slightly astern of us and listing acutely to port. *Dorsetshire* had taken a terrible pounding, direct hits blasting her in quick succession. One of them caused an explosion in a magazine. Smoke and steam were billowing from the big cruiser as she heeled over farther on to her side and sank stern first, her bows almost vertical as she slid down to her ocean grave. In only about eight minutes since the first bomber dived on her, *Dorsetshire* had disappeared, taking with her more than 200 of her ship's company.

Watching the last moments of *Dorsetshire* was a forcible reminder that *Cornwall* was also in dire straits and could not escape the same fate. But there was not much time to think about it because the Japanese dive-bombers had not yet finished with Cornwall.

'Look out, here they come again,' shouted someone as more aircraft screamed down. There was a rush for cover under 'A' turret, even if it meant getting only one's head sheltered under the overhanging gun-house.

Although they were prime targets for the Japanese airmen, the ratings manning *Cornwall*'s machine-guns gallantly continued to hit back as best they could on their own after the main anti-aircraft armament was put out of action. One of them, Able Seaman Maurice (Bungy) Williams, paid the supreme sacrifice for his defiance with a Lewis gun on the bridge. He was machine-gunned by the diving aircraft and his upper body was 'shot to pieces', but he managed to get to a float after the ship was abandoned. He told a friend next to him that he was dying but not in any way down-hearted. Soon he was dead.

A brave act of defiance also came from Able Seaman Pickering with his Vickers point-fives on the top of the hangar. He opened up at close range on a line of Japanese planes that had come down low to have a close look at *Cornwall*.

When Lieutenant-Commander Milner had to abandon his action station in the after control tower on the hangar top, he found one of the ratings dying beside his machine-gun which had jammed. He gave Milner his wallet containing money and family photographs and said: 'Please try to get these to my wife.' The wallet and contents were sent to the Admiralty and duly delivered to the widow.

Meanwhile there was drama up forward at 'B' turret. When the guns' crews evacuated the turret, shrapnel from a bomb ripped into some of them. Leading Seaman Freddie Grimster, who was captain of the left gun, was wounded in the chest and knocked out. The shrapnel also punctured his lifebelt so his friend, Able Seaman Johnny Muller, trainer in the turret, took off his Mae West, tied it on Freddie and put him over the side into the sea. Another member of the turret's crew, Able Seaman Alby Shore, had a fatal chest wound. Johnny Muller stayed on deck with Alby until he died before going over the side himself. It was more than twenty-four hours later before Johnny and Freddie discovered that they had both survived.

Another youngster, Paddy Keeping, then sixteen years old and rated a Boy, was lying on the deck among some casualties. After getting out of 'B' turret he had been drenched by a near miss and then wounded in the back and head. While he was lying on the deck, some ratings came along to help wounded men. In his semi-conscious state, Paddy heard one of them say : 'Come on, they're all dead. Leave them.' But another, Leading Stoker George (Bella) Bright, replied : 'Paddy's not. I'm taking him.' He lifted Paddy up and, holding him in his arms, stepped off the deck into the water.

'By this time my eyes were playing up and I thought it was the oil fuel in the water,' recalled Paddy. 'But my eyesight gradually got worse until finish – total darkness. I was blind.'

A lighter moment in retrospect was when an officer got stuck in the hatch while getting out of 'B' turret and thus delayed some other members of the crew from leaving it. The delay might well have saved those still in the turret from being wounded or even killed by shrapnel from the bomb that burst nearby.

Farther aft a bomb that failed to explode slashed the edge of the iron deck amidships. Two sailors, Wally Muller and Tubby Townsend, who were sheltering under a motor-boat only a few yards away, 'gaped blankly at the jagged metal where the bomb had hit'.

The last bombs had been dropped by 1.51 p.m. – eleven minutes after the start of the attack – and efforts were made in vain to correct *Cornwall*'s list to port. The Captain gave orders to abandon the ship and made his way aft with the remaining bridge personnel to see to the launching of boats, floats, rafts and anything else that would float. Officers and ratings helped to get the dead and wounded over the side, put out fires and pushed hot ammunition that was rolling around on the upper deck through the guard-rails into the sea.

Lieutenant-Commander Milner got down from his station on the top of the hangar by sliding down one of the stays of the mainmast. He checked that the depth charges on the stern of the cruiser had been set to 'safe' – an essential precaution otherwise they would have exploded when the ship sank.

Most of the boats had been smashed by the bombing, including the big pinnace that would have been invaluable for survivors. Some men tried to launch a cutter. They got aboard and the slips were knocked off, but the lower gear had been shot away and the boat dropped like a stone. It hit the blister of the ship, which was then out of the water, bounced once and overturned on top of the men in it.

During all the activity in preparation for abandoning the ship, two telegraphist ratings, Glyn Gardner and Ivor Midlane, volunteered to go down to the Main Wireless Office, which had been put out of action and abandoned, to fetch the weighted confidential books so that they could be thrown overboard. With hindsight, it was unnecessary because the ship was obviously going to sink, but the two telegraphists were imbued with the spirit of duty and, according to regulations, code books should be thrown overboard in a time of crisis to prevent their falling into enemy hands.

The books were kept in two heavy steel chests. The youngsters did not have much difficulty in carrying the first chest to the upper deck where the Chief Petty Officer telegraphist dumped it overboard. But when they went down below again and got the second chest, the ship had developed a more acute list and gave a violent lurch. They were thrown to the deck, became separated and lost the chest, their torch and each other in the darkness. Their situation had become quite desperate because they knew the time to get out of the ship was limited.

Midlane found himself against the bulkhead in the Gunnery Office, opposite the Wireless Office, and up to his chest in water and fuel oil. He managed to pull himself out of the Gunnery Office into the sloping corridor. The way to the upper deck was along the corridor to a doorway which led to the Fore-cabin Flat in the centre of which was a steel ladder. Midlane made his way along the corridor, slipping and sliding on oily feet and grabbing whatever he could on the bulkhead for support.

The ladder, which provided access to the upper deck, was a few yards from the doorway. His oily feet could not get a grip on the sloping deck in the Fore-cabin Flat so he worked his way along the bulkhead on the starboard side of the flat until he reached a point opposite the ladder. Then he let go, slithered down the sloping deck and grabbed the ladder, which was normally vertical but by then not far off horizontal because of the ship's list to port. He scrambled up the ladder, through the hatchway on to the upper deck and went off the starboard side of the ship into the water.

Gardner was also thrown against a bulkhead. He called out Midlane's name but there was no reply and he despaired of seeing his friend again. In his struggle to make his way along the corridor, he grabbed at some rifles in brackets on the bulkhead but they came tumbling all over him. He got to the doorway leading to the ladder, which was about ten feet away, sprang to grab it but missed and slipped down the sloping deck into a pool of foul-smelling oil that had welled up from a storage tank below. He was up to his neck in it but managed to crawl out and struggle back to the doorway.

'This time I knew I had to make it,' he said. 'It was now or never. In my loneliness I prayed very hard for strength. With all my might I sprang towards the ladder and grabbed at a steel rung. I just made the distance – only just. My prayer had been answered. I paused a little to regain my breath, then hoisted myself up. I reached the top and instead of finding dry deck as I had left it, I stepped right into the Indian Ocean. The water was already lapping the raised steel edge around the hatchway, ready to pour into the ship.'

Within a couple of minutes the sea was flooding the area from which the two young telegraphists had so narrowly escaped. Other men down below did not manage to get out in time.

Among others who did escape and survive was Able Seaman Harry Stone. His action station was at the main electrical switchboard three decks down amidships. Fortunately a damage control party had opened the water-tight hatches so he and others were able to start going up the three flights of ladders to the upper deck. But when Stone was starting up the last ladder a bomb hit caused a beam to fall on him. He lay on his back on the deck, trapped with the beam pinning him down and no one near to help him. For some minutes he tried to move the beam, but in vain. After a tense struggle, however, he freed himself, got to the upper deck and off the cruiser before she sank.

How many other dramatic moments there must have been as hundreds of men, many in extremely hazardous positions, struggled frantically to get from below to the upper deck to escape from the sinking warship. Their desperation and anxiety must have built up terrible tension – and what a terrific relief for those who did make it.

The final order to abandon ship was given at 1.55 p.m. Most men left *Cornwall* from both sides amidships or farther aft, jumping or stepping into the water or on to floats, many supporting or carrying wounded comrades. The few of us still on the foc's'le did not hear any-one give the order: 'Abandon ship. Every man for himself', but it was hardly necessary. The port side was already under water and the sea was creeping irresistibly across the deck. Yet momentarily I – and, I suppose, others too – experienced a strange reluctance to leave the ship. *Cornwall* was still something solid in a seemingly limitless expanse of sea, even if she was in her death throes and sinking. She had been a home in time of war.

But the time to leave her had come. I know I was not alone in thinking: 'If I don't abandon the ship now, she is soon going to abandon me.' So I gave my lifebelt an extra blow, ensured that the valve was screwed tight, took off my sandals, put them neatly on the edge of the deck on the starboard side near the tip of the foc's'le and flopped into the water. Normally it was about thirty feet from the deck to the water, but now that the ship was well down by the head and sinking, it was only about three feet. Bearing in mind the need to avoid the suction of a sinking ship, most of the survivors were swimming or paddling to get away.

Suddenly a figure in white tropical rig, his shirt splotched red with blood, was seen clutching the guard-rail on the quarterdeck. Several voices took up the cry: 'There's the skipper!' In true naval tradition, Captain Manwaring was leaving his ship only just before the end. By that time the ship's list to port was acute. As the Captain let go of the starboard guard-rail, he slid and rolled down the ship's side into the water amid cheers from the men. It was rather a cruel touch of fate that he had to abandon his ship only a few days before his fiftieth birthday.

The end came shortly afterwards – about four minutes after the final order to abandon ship and less than twenty minutes since the start of the dive-bombing attack. Survivors watched with awe as *Cornwall*'s stern lifted higher and higher, one of her propellers that had turned millions of times revolving slowly. Then, with colours still flying, she slid bows first into the Indian Ocean. It was a poignant yet spectacular end, a sight imprinted indelibly on one's memory. Hundreds of men, who had just left her and were now splashing in the water, cheered as she took her final plunge at an angle of about thirty degrees.

It is almost too frightful even to think about the suffering of the men who went down in the ship – close on two hundred of them, some mercifully dead after being mutilated by bomb explosions, burnt, drowned in sea water or fuel oil; some wounded and dying, perhaps praying for a quick end; some, in many ways the worst off, alive but trapped in the ship, unable to escape and knowing that they had only a minute or two, or even only seconds, to live.

It must have been terrifying chaos with the inside of the huge ship in a turmoil as her stern lifted and she went down into the depths of the ocean. The agonising suffering, both mental and physical, endured by those men who are listed as 'Missing, presumed killed' in the casualty list published in the official journal *The Fleet*, is a nightmare that even the passing of the years fails to obliterate. Their names are printed in alphabetical order in the September, 1942, issue of *The Fleet* under the heading:

WAR SERVICE LOSSES
'We will remember them'

One of those mortally wounded, trapped and waiting for death – or did he mercifully lose consciousness before *Cornwall* went down? – was a youngster not yet out of his teens. His name is 108th in the official casualty list : 'Read, Alfred R., Ord.Sea.'

His full name was Alfred Rupert Read and his parents lived in Kent. He had turned eighteen, which gained him promotion in rating from a Boy to an Ordinary Seaman.

Young Alfred Read was at his action station in the telephone switchboard compartment during the bombing of *Cornwall*. He rang the officer in charge of communications and, in a calm voice, asked : 'What shall I do, sir? The compartment is flooding.'

'You had better leave at once,' the officer ordered.

'I can't, sir,' replied Read, 'both my legs are off.'

The story of Ordinary Seaman Read is known. There are so many that will never be known. One can only wonder at the drama of courage, tragedy, anguish and fear – yes, fear for which no one need be ashamed – that was entombed in the battered warship as she sank. We can but pay homage to the anonymous, unsung heroes among those who were killed, wounded or trapped alive in the doomed ship.

Within twenty minutes, two large cruisers totalling more than 20,000 tons and carrying 1,546 men, had been sunk. *Cornwall* and *Dorsetshire*, comrades in arms, had died together – the first major British naval vessels to be sunk by dive-bombers operating from carriers.

Fuchida, the Japanese air commander, wrote :

The dive-bombers scored hits with close to ninety per cent of their bombs – an enviable rate of accuracy, even considering the windless conditions. But rather than feeling exultation over the proficiency of Egusa's bombardiers, I could only feel pity for these surface ships assailed from the air at odds of forty to one.

After studying the reports, Churchill commented :

In the Gulf of Siam two of our first-class capital ships had been sunk in a few minutes by torpedo aircraft. Now two important cruisers had also perished by a totally different method of air attack – the dive-bomber. Nothing like this had been seen in the Mediterranean in all our conflicts with the German and Italian Air Forces.

8

After *Cornwall* sank, the Japanese aircraft formed up in sub-flights and flew over the men in the sea. Some survivors reported that machine-gun bullets came uncomfortably close. But generally it would appear that there was no organised machine-gunning of men in the water, perhaps just a little over-exuberance by one or two airmen giving a victory burst. In the case of *Dorsetshire*, Captain Agar reported that just before the cruiser sank one plane 'flew low down over the ship, firing his machine-gun indiscriminately in a triumphant burst into the men on the decks and in the water'.

Considering the severity of the bombing attack, a surprisingly large number of men survived. *Cornwall* went down with singularly little disturbance and left more than 550 of her ship's company alive in the sea, many of them wounded, some so seriously that death was not far off. They were spread over a large area, swimming, bobbing, clambering on to tthe six Carley floats that were launched and some rafts, or clinging to all manner of planks and other flotsam, including two large piling fenders and a portion of the mainmast that had snapped off. It was a motley collection but something of a haven for the survivors as they gathered together. Only two boats were available – a whaler (rowing boat) that had been launched and a motor-boat (defuelled) that floated off as the ship went down and fortunately remained upright.

A particularly unpleasant problem was the oil – thick, black, slippery and pungent smelling – which came welling up from the sunken ship in large quantities. It covered men's heads, faces, bodies and clothing and made everything slimy and difficult to handle.

A couple of miles away survivors from *Dorsetshire* were in a similar predicament with two leaking whalers and a skiff.

For a moment it all seemed so unreal, a bad dream. Less than half an hour earlier two cruisers had been racing through the sea at 27.5 knots – large ships more than two hundreds yards long. Now they had both gone, leaving two groups of survivors totalling more than 1,100 men in the sea about three hundred miles from land. Less than half an hour earlier their feet had been on the solid decks of the ships, feeling the steady throb of their engines as they gave every ounce of energy in response to the order for full speed. Now their feet were treading water or kicking to help them swim in search of something to give more support than just a Mae West lifebelt.

It was only too real. The sadness of the scene was wiped away by the shock of reality. I continued swimming and saw the motor-boat so struck out for it. Having left the ship from the fo'c'sle, I was some distance from the main body of survivors and luckily clear of the oil. At least the water was clean as well as warm. Another survivor advised me to take off my overalls.

'They will get heavy and weigh you down,' he said.

'Yes,' I replied, trying to sound grateful for the advice and continued swimming. I knew we were in shark-infested sea but was trying hard not to think about such things. So I had no intention of stopping, untying my lifebelt, struggling out of my overalls in the water and then putting on my lifebelt again before swimming to the motor-boat. I was quite happy with the progress made while wearing the overalls and was no doubt spurred on by the thought of sharks.

When I arrived at the motor-boat, which had floated a surprisingly long way from *Cornwall*, whom should I see standing near the stern ready to give me a helping hand to clamber aboard but Tommy Thorp. When I was given a seat on the bench inside, I was glad to find myself next to Bill. But what a transformation he had undergone. We had been together in the flames in the corridor on the way to the upper deck and were burnt in the same places – head, arms and feet. But he was in front of me and the doctor said later that he must have suffered some lung damage. Normally a strong, healthy man, he now looked drawn, haggard and just sat hunched up, speaking very little in his hoarse voice.

The motor-boat became the focal point of survivors and as more wounded arrived, Tommy and others left to make room for them. He and Ken Collier, both strong swimmers, went off to collect a wooden ladder floating a couple of hundred yards away. Collier thought he was doing another good turn when he took off his overalls and went on a fairly long swim to retrieve what appeared to be a Red Cross box. It turned out to be a parcel of signal pads. By the time Collier returned, his overalls had been torn up to provide head coverings for men in the water and he spent the rest of the time clad only in his belt and almost up to his neck in water while balancing on a submerged Carley float. Although poignant, it was an amusing sight to see men apparently sitting in water. The floats were so overloaded that they were submerged and could not be seen.

When *Cornwall* sank, Leading Signalman Raynor helped Chief Yeoman Sam Langford in the water and got him to hold on to a griping spar. Lieutenant-Commander Grove found Langford 'cheerful as a cricket' in spite of his serious wounds. Grove and Lieutenant Streatfield saw a float a long distance away and swam to get it.

Swimming in oil is not a pleasant pastime [wrote Grove]. We paddled the float back to the Chief Yeoman, got him on board and then started picking up others, including Commander Fair. We soon filled the float and starting building rafts with oddments that we collected.

Captain Manwaring was picked up and Lieutenant-Commander Milner 'also joined up on a grating, paddling along quite unperturbed'.

Later it took four of them two hours to pull the raft a quarter of a mile to the motor-boat to get the wounded to a doctor.

'The wounded cursed us for "clumsy bastards" when we had to get them out of the low-lying float into the boat,' Grove recalled. 'It is difficult when the wounded, you and float and boat are slippery with oil fuel.'

Sam Langford was placed on the canopy of the motor-boat and covered with the ship's cinema screen. He was in a bad way with his wounded legs.

Fortunately two of *Cornwall*'s doctors survived the bombing, both of them Royal Naval Volunteer Reserve men: the Senior Medical Officer, Surgeon Lieutenant-Commander H. Glyn Rees, and Surgeon Lieutenant F. W. Isaac. When the bombing started Rees was making his way from the Sick Bay to the after dressing station. He turned to go back to the Sick Bay but was prevented from doing so by a bomb explosion ahead of him. In his report he said the ship's list,

together with the absence of lights between decks and the violent concussion of rapidly consecutive explosions, made useful action almost impossible. However, a Sick Berth Attendant returned to the flooded after dressing station against a stream of escaping men and managed to retrieve a two-ounce bottle of morphia, a hypodermic syringe and a small case of surgical instruments...

The survivors were scattered over an area of about one square mile and they included many injured. Morphia injections were given to those within swimming distance. The floating motor-boat was reserved for the badly wounded, and bit by bit the floats and rafts were brought alongside it and the worst cases transferred. Those wounded who were able to sit or remain propped up were placed in the motor-boat's engine-room and after cabin. The remainder, most of them unconscious, were laid out in the forepeak and on the canopy.

The number of persons in the motor-boat was maintained at about forty wounded, three medical staff, three men at the pump and three others baling. The boat's gunwhale was within a few inches of the water, but fortunately the sea was calm and, with care, it was possible to keep the boat afloat and on an even keel.

Men with simple fractures were left on the Carley floats, and although lying in twelve inches of water they were surrounded and supported by uninjured men, and were thus less liable to further injury than they would have been in the motor-boat.

Surgeon Lieutenant Isaac attended to the wounded in the after part of the motor-boat, and Glyn Rees and a Leading Sick Berth Attendant looked after those in the fore part.

The bombing and sinking had been a traumatic experience. Gradually the survivors settled down, resigned to their plight in mid-ocean. There was nothing to do but wait and hope that the fleet would soon be able to come to our rescue.

Some of the bedraggled men started singing and were soon joined by others, cheering themselves with wartime songs like 'Roll out the Barrel'. But Commander Fair quickly put an end to the sing-song. He clambered on to the motor-boat, his white shirt and shorts blackened with fuel oil, and addressed what remained of the ship's company. He told the survivors to be of good cheer but to keep quiet to conserve their strength as there might be a long wait before being rescued. Singing would also aggravate their thirst.

Commander Fair announced that Captain Manwaring, although wounded, had survived. He said the two cruisers would soon be missed by the fleet and air searches launched from the carriers. He urged the men on floats and in the water to converge and keep together in one large body to make it easier to be seen from the air.

Hopes were raised later in the afternoon when a Fleet Air Arm Albacore plane was sighted and then another, a Fulmar, circled over the survivors and the message, 'Help is coming', was flashed with its Aldis lamp. This encouraged a tendency to euphoria among some of the survivors and the feeling that it was only a matter of hours before we would be picked up.

But the hours passed, the sun sank lower and lower and still no sign of any rescue ships. At about sunset an aircraft, considered to be Japanese, was sighted flying very high. It could not have seen us and disappeared in the gathering gloom. The stars came out and the night closed in – probably the longest night in the lives of the hundreds of survivors.

Some of them were not to see the next day. The condition of many of the wounded had deteriorated. Throats were parched and some of them cried out for water. But food and water were very limited, only some emergency rations in the motor-boat and on some of the floats being available. They had to be doled out very sparingly. In the motor-boat supper was an issue of water – about two teaspoonsful served in a tin cigarette box – and there was to be no more until the morning.

Some of the wounded became delirious and died. A man would slump on the seat in the motor-boat. The doctor would check his pulse, then the body would be put over the side. His funeral was a soft splash and ripple as the body was 'committed to the sea', to use the euphemistic phrase. The dead had to make room for other wounded.

The night seemed to be interminable as the hours went by slowly. Wounds became more painful. The craving for water became almost desperate, but there were several hours to wait before the next issue would be made in the morning.

Men in the sea tried to get some rest 'strap-hanging' on the temporary rafts made from wreckage and supported by their lifebelts. On the floats they huddled closer together as it became surprisingly chilly. A few managed to have a smoke, having salvaged sodden cigarettes and matches by sticking them into their hair during the afternoon to dry in the sun. Those who had oil in their eyes suffered painful burning and irritation. Some found that when they closed their eyes, it felt as though they were on fire. Others complained that they could not open their eyes.

Hopes of being rescued were raised when someone shouted : 'There's a light on the horizon. It must be a destroyer.' A Very pistol was found in the motor-boat and lights were fired. No response. The light on the horizon was just another star rising.

Then there was a flickering light. We flashed a reply. It was the *Dorsetshire* survivors who had been attracted by our Very lights.

And so it went on. Stars rising and coloured shooting stars (a feature of the tropics) caused hopes to be raised falsely, and then bitter disappointment.

The night wore on without sleep. Surely it must be early morning, about 4 a.m.

'What's the time ?' someone asked.

'Ten past eleven,' was the shattering reply. It was not yet midnight – still Easter Sunday.

In the words of a senior officer : 'The night was quite bloody.'

We yearned for dawn and the sun to give some warmth. But we were only one hundred miles north of the equator and after sunrise we soon cursed the tropical heat, which made life even more uncomfortable.

The Senior Medical Officer reported : 'Men in the water passed their clothing into the motor-boat to be used as covering for the wounded who were kept cool by repeatedly soaking the clothing in sea water. On the whole those in the water and on the floats were much cooler and more comfortable than those in the motor-boat.'

A ration of water was issued all round at 9 a.m. – three drachms which were the equivalent of slightly less than a level tablespoonful or a modest mouthful. The emergency stores, which were stowed in boats or lashed to Carley floats, consisted of tinned corned (bully) beef, canned fruit, some unsweetened condensed milk and some containers of fresh water. A meal would be at most a small piece of bully beef, half a canned apricot and a sip of the juice or condensed milk.

In the motor-boat a teaspoonful of bully beef was 'served' but most throats were too parched to swallow it. So it was chewed and then had to be spat out. Some men rubbed the bully beef on their lips, the fat easing the dryness and cracking from which they were suffering. When a pumpkin came floating along and was retrieved from the water, it was broken up and we were allowed to chew a piece, but not swallow it, to help keep our mouths moist. If nothing else, it gave one a different taste.

With the thick oil dispersing and leaving clear water, the new day brought something disturbing into view – sharks, some easily discernible light-grey and white shapes gliding effortlessly, others deeper and ghost-like in the water. No doubt the explosions and eruptions of fuel oil helped to keep them away the previous day. Now they were around in force, the Senior Medical Officer counting twenty-five at one time, 'including two whoppers'. Lieutenant-Commander Grove recalled that some of the sailors, with typical humour even in adversity, started giving them names. But, as recorded in a report, the sharks 'seemed content to wait for the corpses that were from time to time committed to the sea and made no attempt to molest anyone living'.

During the morning Bill's condition worsened and when the doctor poured some water into his mouth, it just ran out. He was too weak to swallow. A little later, in a rather dazed state – I was sitting opposite him in the motor-boat at the time – I saw the doctor feel his wrist to check whether there was any pulse, then pull off his shirt and pass his body over the side into the sea. Another wounded survivor was taken on board in his place.

So three of my friends did not survive. Bloggie did not make it from a shell room deep down in the ship below a turret, Ian Keith was one of the 4-inch gun's crew killed by a bomb and now Bill. There were lots of tragic little dramas among the survivors. For instance, when Angus Sutherland got off the sinking ship he came across his close friend, Able Seaman Hedley Beswetherick, horribly and mortally wounded. A few months earlier Hedley's wife had given birth to their only child – a son he never saw.

There was the other side of the coin, too – those who blessed their extra share of luck, like Engine Room Artificer Bill Alcock. When he was sent to have a quick dinner on the Sunday, he was instructed not to return to the after engine-room but to take over his relief's action station in the forward compressor room. His relief was among those in the engine-room who were killed in the bombing soon afterwards. Although he suffered burns while getting to the upper deck from the compressor room, Alcock was able to get off the ship and survive.

The Meteorological Officer, Lieutenant Holden, who had joined *Cornwall* after surviving the sinking of HMS *Repulse*, survived again.

But now, as Easter Monday dragged on and there was no sign of a rescue ship, all the survivors had to face up to the question whether they would in fact be rescued. Surgeon Lieutenant Isaac, who had been coping with the wounded in the after part of the motor-boat, collapsed from exhaustion in the early afternoon. He was propped up against the legs of his patients and made as comfortable as possible until he recovered about half an hour later and was able to carry on with his good work.

Shouts were heard in the distance at about 2 p.m. and a couple of men were seen swimming in the sea. When they were picked up by the whaler, it was discovered that they had swum from a few miles away where there were thirty-three more survivors, including wounded, on a home-made raft with the ship's dentist, Lieutenant W. P. McEldowney, in charge. The whaler collected them and then set off to fetch some more who were reported to be even farther away.

Spirits began to sag as the sun got lower and lower. Then suddenly in the late afternoon there was excitement when a Fleet Air Arm plane flew over the survivors and flashed a message : 'Help coming. Hold on.'

The aircraft disappeared and one wondered if it was going to be a repetition of the previous day's false hope when a similar signal was flashed by an aircraft, but nothing came of it. We settled down again to wait ... and hope.

9

Inadequate and at times misleading reports received by Admiral Somerville after the raid on Colombo on Easter Sunday left him in considerable doubt regarding the position of the Japanese fleet. While still unaware of the fate of *Cornwall* and *Dorsetshire*, he continued steaming eastwards towards the rendezvous position. When one of his fleet's aircraft reported shortly before 4 p.m. that wreckage and survivors had been sighted in the position where *Cornwall* and *Dorsetshire* would have been, a destroyer was detached and ordered to investigate. An hour later, however, it had to be recalled when an aircraft reported five unknown ships only thirty miles from the wreckage and steering south-west.

Somerville changed the course of Force A (one battleship, two carriers, two cruisers and destroyers) to southerly to keep in position for a night torpedo attack. But at 6.17 p.m. he received a report that a force of two carriers and three other vessels was about 140 miles away and steering north-west. He accordingly changed the course of Force A to north-west and air searches to northward were carried out during the night, but nothing was seen.

Unknown to Somerville, the Japanese ships reported to be sailing north-west were probably in the process of changing course, and Nagumo's fleet in fact sailed almost due south and then changed to south-east. So with Somerville's Force A steaming north-west and Nagumo south-east, the two fleets were sailing directly away from each other.

Meanwhile the slower Force B (the four R-Class battleships with cruisers and destroyers), which had left Port T seven hours after Force A, had been diverted to the north late in the afternoon and joined Force A at 7 a.m. on Easter Monday. Somerville had in mind that the Japanese might make for Port T to see if his Eastern Fleet was there and attack the base by air or wait for the return of the fleet. He did not know that the Japanese were not aware of the existence of the secret base at Addu Atoll in the Maldives.

He therefore decided to keep clear during the day and took the fleet on a south-easterly course, which would put it in a position for a night action if the Japanese ships returned from the vicinity of Port T. The course also took him towards the position where *Cornwall* and *Dorsetshire* had been sunk the previous afternoon. Disregarding the objections of his staff because the whereabouts of the Japanese fleet was not known, Somerville decided to go to the aid of the men who survived the sinkings. So at 1 p.m. he sent the cruiser *Enterprise*, and two destroyers *Paladin* and *Panther*, on ahead to find the survivors. Their approximate position was known, but it was not easy to pinpoint a group of men in mid-ocean and see them from a ship.

*

Ten minutes – only six hundred seconds – lay between rescue or possibly a fate too horrible to think about for the more than eleven hundred survivors. Many of them supported only by their lifebelts and flotsam, were beginning to find just keeping their faces out of the water a trial.

The aircraft that had signalled, 'Help coming. Hold on', had gone and the long, hot and weary day was drawing to a close. Among the survivors hope started to ebb again at the thought of another night in the sea. Many of the wounded would not survive. In any case, what hope would there be even for the men who would still be alive the next day?

On board *Enterprise* and the destroyers officers and look-outs scanned the sea with glasses, but there was no sign of the survivors. The warships had already gone beyond the position given for them to search and had received orders to turn back and rejoin the fleet. The signal to turn was still flying from *Enterprise* when the Navigating Officer asked the Commanding Officer, Captain J. C. Annesley, to go on 'for ten minutes more' in case an error about the position had been made in the flagship. The Captain agreed to the request.

'It was this "ten minutes" which saved us since it would have been dark at 6.30 p.m.,' wrote Captain Agar some years later in a letter. He had received a letter from the Navigating Officer telling him about the extra few minutes' search.

It was a moment of tremendous relief for the survivors when smoke was sighted on the horizon . . . then masts . . . a cruiser . . . two more ships, destroyers. In the excitement even some of *Cornwall*'s wounded stood up to see the warships and the overloaded motor-boat nearly capsized. After twenty-eight hours in the open with very little to eat, the men immediately celebrated by opening the remaining emergency rations of tins of canned fruit.

The warships raced up with every available boat already swung outboard for lowering. *Enterprise* went to *Cornwall*'s survivors and

Paladin and *Panther* to *Dorsetshire*'s. The rescue operation was carried out smartly and quickly, with daylight beginning to fade. Captain Agar, who was picked up by *Paladin*, recalled that some of the destroyer's Australian crew dived overboard to help survivors up the gangway and rope ladders. *Cornwall* and *Dorsetshire*'s boats that had remained afloat were brought alongside the gangways, and survivors who had been on rafts, floats or just clinging to wreckage were picked up by the rescuing boats or swam to the warships.

Lieutenant Streatfield had taken over *Cornwall*'s whaler with a crew who pulled it a long way on another trip to collect some survivors on a small float. Those men were so far from the main body of survivors that they could easily have missed being rescued by the warships. As the whaler was being pulled the last few yards to *Enterprise*, Streatfield said to his tired and bedraggled crew of seamen : 'Come on, let's do it in true Navy style and toss oars as we come alongside.' So the men, some of them two to an oar, did their best to toss oars (raise them to an upright position in salute).

In the destroyers where space was very limited, the wardroom and officers' quarters had to be used to help accommodate *Dorsetshire*'s wounded. Everything possible was done on board *Enterprise* to cope with the sudden influx of more than five hundred *Cornwall* men, all of them exhausted and suffering from lack of water and food, and many of them wounded. The men were taken care of individually, helped to clean themselves and given tea, food and cigarettes. The Navy does not fail when it comes to giving a helping hand.

Doctors, including those who had just been rescued, got busy immediately attending to the wounded. One of the first patients carried in for an operation was Chief Yeoman Sam Langford, who had to have a leg amputated. During the night and the next day the medical staff was assisted by non-medical officers and other ranks from among the survivors who helped selflessly to care for the wounded, although themselves desperately in need of rest.

An amusing incident was recalled by Lieutenant-Commander Grove. 'Being more or less in one piece,' he said, 'I was helping our wounded in the Sick Bay when a senior tiffy (Sick Berth Attendant) thought I was one and gave me a lot of orders which I meekly tried to carry out, much to the amusement of our chaps.'

The morning after being rescued, Lieutenant Streatfield, Chief Petty Officer Reuter and Tommy Thorp were active as a Sick Bay team to help get the wounded organised. The recreation space and Chief Petty Officers' and Petty Officers' messes were used for lying and sitting cases.

Before these spaces were properly organised [said Thorp], the sea-men's mess deck assumed a queer appearance. Two bodies were laid out on each mess table with a *Cornwall* rating – often a pal of one of the wounded men – watching over them. But soon the degrees of injuries were assessed and the seamen's mess deck was cleared.

There was a shock during the day when suddenly the anti-aircraft action stations bugle call was sounded over the loudspeakers. (It was a 'tune' that matched the words: 'There's a bomber overhead.') An-other air attack was what the survivors did not need, and I know many of the wounded thought: 'Will I be able to swim this time?'

'I cannot recall anything more shattering in its effect on the mess I was in when it sounded off,' said Thorp.

It was only at the end of the bugle call alarm, which was always repeated two or three times, that the bosun's mate announced, 'For exercise', which meant it was not a real alarm.

Captain Agar summed up the rescue of *Cornwall* and *Dorsetshire* survivors by reporting that the skill and seamanship displayed by *Enterprise*, *Paladin* and *Panther* could best be described by the bare statement that more than eleven hundred men in the water, 'for the most part exhausted and with a large number wounded, were brought on board within the space of an hour without the loss of a single life'.

When the ships rejoined the Eastern Fleet, Admiral Somerville signalled *Enterprise*: 'You and the destroyers have done a magnificent job.'

The Commander-in-Chief also reported that the spirit, fortitude and discipline of the officers and men of *Dorsetshire* and *Cornwall* during the action and throughout the subsequent ordeal in the sea were 'beyond all praise'.

10

On Easter Sunday the Japanese missed two opportunities of locating the Eastern Fleet which, after all, was the main object of their incursion into the Indian Ocean. The first was in the morning when their recon-naissance plane sighted *Dorsetshire* and *Cornwall* on their way to rejoin the fleet and reported that the warships were 'running away'. The Japanese became so preoccupied with shadowing the two cruisers until their bombers could deal with them that they did not consider some vital questions.

If the ships were running away, why were they on a course that took then perilously close to the known area of operation of Nagumo's force? If they wanted to run away, the obvious course would have been to the west or north-west. So why were they sailing almost due south? What was ahead of them that they were in an obvious hurry to reach?

The shadowing reconnaissance plane kept astern of the cruisers and turned back without searching ahead of them. It had the range to search well beyond *Dorsetshire* and *Cornwall* and, if it had done so, it would have made the much more exciting discovery of Somerville's Force A.

Fuchida and Okumiya point to over-emphasis on attack resulting in inadequate attention being paid to air search and reconnaissance in the training and organisation of Japanese naval aviators. They mention that while looking for the Eastern Fleet, planes had often lost their way in the Indian Ocean and the carriers had to send out radio signals on which they could home. This could alert the enemy to their position and, as a result, there was a reluctance on the part of Nagumo to send off search planes if it could be avoided.

The second missed opportunity came in the afternoon of Easter Sunday when Nagumo changed the course of his fleet from southerly to south-east. It was another fateful turn. If he had continued on the southerly course, his fleet must surely have come into contact with Somerville's Force A. It would seem Nagumo mistakenly believed the Eastern Fleet, which had not provided another Pearl Harbor for him at Colombo, was somewhere to the south-east. While his fleet swept round well south of Ceylon, his reconnaissance planes searching in vain for the British Eastern Fleet in the south-eastern area, it had moved farther west, Somerville thinking the Japanese might be making for Port T.

During the following two days Nagumo kept his fleet on a semi-circular course to the east outside a five hundred mile radius from the southern end of Ceylon. He altered course again on Wednesday, 8 April, to take his carriers to a position from which their planes could launch an attack on the naval base at Trincomalee the next morning.

The fateful turns – the wrong turns – by the Japanese on Easter Sunday were lucky breaks for Somerville's Eastern Fleet. If it had been sighted by Nagumo's much stronger force, the result could only have been a major disaster for the Allies. Somerville's force could not have coped with an attack by the Japanese planes which were far superior in numbers and performance, and were flown by better trained and more experienced airmen.

Although he did not know the exact composition of the Japanese force, Somerville realised by now that it was very much more powerful than his fleet, particularly in respect of the number of aircraft-carriers and planes, which had become the deciding factor in naval warfare.

While sailing south-east on the Monday afternoon, Somerville received a signal from Admiral Layton, Commander-in-Chief, Ceylon, reporting his belief that a strong Japanese fleet was still between Port T and Colombo. He therefore decided to keep clear of the Port T area until after daylight on Tuesday, 7 April, and just before sunset reversed his course (from south-east to north-west). The next day he turned west and then south-west to take the fleet through the Veimandu Channel in the Maldive Islands to make an unexpected approach to Port T from the west. After his aircraft had searched the area, he took the fleet into Port T at 11 a.m. on the Wednesday, 8 April.

Enterprise, *Paladin* and *Panther* had rejoined the Eastern Fleet after rescuing *Cornwall* and *Dorsetshire* survivors. Before arriving at Port T, *Cornwall*'s unwounded and walking wounded survivors, clad mostly just in shorts given to them by the crew of *Enterprise*, were mustered on the quarterdeck and addressed by Captain Manwaring. *Cornwall*'s captain, bandaged and with his arm in a sling, was bareheaded and wore a white shirt and shorts. In the words of one of the survivors,

he looked like the typical story-book wounded soldier . . . and gave us as stirring an address as I've ever heard. He spoke for only a couple of minutes, but the morale of everyone present was boosted tremendously. If there had been any despondency among his men before he spoke, everyone wanted to fight the Japs by the time he had finished. He thanked and praised everyone for their courage and forbearance in the water, and also thanked *Enterprise* for picking us up. He was given three lusty cheers.

The survivors also gave three cheers for *Enterprise* whose Commanding Officer, Captain Annesley, stood next to Captain Manwaring.

A few men who died after being rescued were buried at sea, but the funeral service on the quarterdeck of *Enterprise* was interrupted when action stations was sounded as a result of a submarine report.

The Japanese 'Easter eggs' had taken a heavy toll of the 1,546 men who served in *Cornwall* and *Dorsetshire*, 424 (27.7 per cent) of them losing their lives during the bombing, going down in the ships or dying

in the sea or after being picked up. *Cornwall* lost 191, including ten
officers, and *Dorsetshire* 233, including 19 officers. The 'missing
presumed killed' or 'died of wounds', as they were officially listed,
included 23 of the 104 South Africans serving in *Cornwall* and 16 of
more than 100 in *Dorsetshire*.

On arrival at Port T the wounded survivors were taken to a storeship, which was improvised as a temporary hospital while waiting for a
proper hospital ship to arrive. The unwounded were distributed among
the four R-Class battleships to be taken to Mombasa and then in troopships to Durban. It marked a sad end to our association with *Cornwall*,
which had sailed more than a quarter of a million miles during her war
service. In little more than thirteen months since she had resumed
service after her refit at Simonstown, where some of us joined her, she
logged 123,000 miles, spent three hundred days at sea and crossed the
equator 29 times. Now all that remained was an unmarked grave in
the Indian Ocean, officially recorded as at one degree 41 minutes north,
77 degrees 51 minutes east.

11

The day before arriving at Port T Admiral Somerville received a signal
from the Admiralty in which they acknowledged that their hope that
the Eastern Fleet and pressure from America would discourage the
Japanese from making an incursion in force into the Indian Ocean had
proved in vain. As the Japanese force was superior in all respects to the
Eastern Fleet, the four old R-Class battleships might be 'more of a
liability than an asset'. They therefore gave the Commander-in-Chief
full discretion to withdraw them to the east coast of Africa. Furthermore, the Admiralty considered that the rest of the fleet should not
use Colombo for the present.

This was in accord with Somerville's views after the activities of the
past few days. After discussing the situation with his Flag and Commanding Officers on arrival at Port T on Wednesday, 8 April, he
replied to the Admiralty agreeing to their proposals and at the same
time emphasised his grim position if he continued to operate near
Ceylon. The Japanese had control of the Bay of Bengal and could
obtain local control of the waters south and south-west of Ceylon at
will. Because of the superiority of the air strength of the Japanese force,
the Eastern Fleet would have little security against air attacks in the
Ceylon bases at Colombo and Trincomalee and none at Port T.

The Commander-in-Chief decided to send the four old battleships *Resolution, Ramillies, Royal Sovereign* and *Revenge,* and the rest of Force B to Mombasa to help guard the vital convoy route to the Middle East and Persian Gulf and at the same time do some training. The faster Force A division, which included the two carriers *Indomitable* and *Formidable,* would for the time being avoid Ceylon and be kept in Indian waters to deal with any attempt by the Japanese to operate against shipping with light forces. Somerville commented that until the Eastern Fleet could be reinforced with more modern ships, he could only 'create diversions and false scents, since I am now the poor fox'. He emphasised, however, that 'the proper way to defend Ceylon is by shore-based aircraft, not the fleet'.

So at 2 a.m. the next day, Thursday, 9 April, Force B under the command of Vice-Admiral Willis, left Port T and headed west for Mombasa. Four hours later the Commander-in-Chief sailed north with Force A for Bombay. Captain Agar, who was with the fleet as a passenger in *Enterprise,* noted : 'It was several days before we reached Bombay because Admiral Somerville kept the fast division of his Fleet at sea, cruising off the Maldive Islands lest Nagumo should try another strike at Colombo and, unhampered by the slow division of battleships, he would have a chance to get in his counter thrust at night.'

At about the same time that Somerville's Force A got under way from Port T, ninety-one bombers escorted by thirty-eight fighters, commanded again by Fuchida, took off from the Japanese carriers to have another crack at Ceylon. This time their target was not Colombo but Trincomalee – and perhaps still hoping to find the Eastern Fleet in harbour.

When on course for the flying-off position the previous afternoon, part of Nagumo's fleet had been sighted by a Catalina flying-boat on patrol 470 miles south-east of Trincomalee. It reported seeing three battleships and a carrier. An order to clear Trincomalee harbour was made by the Commander-in-Chief East Indies, Admiral Arbuthnot, who instructed all ships to sail southwards and keep close inshore. The ships that sailed from Trincomalee included the aircraft-carrier *Hermes,* a destroyer, *Vampire,* a tanker, *British Sergeant,* and a corvette, *Hollyhock,* escorting the fleet auxiliary *Athelstane.*

The Japanese fleet was sighted again by a Catalina shortly after daylight on the 9th, but the flying-boat was shot down by Japanese fighters before it could complete sending a signal giving the position and composition of the enemy force. It did, however, enable a reasonably accurate estimate of the position of the ships to be made.

The approach of the Japanese aircraft was later detected by radar and twenty-one fighters – fifteen Hurricanes and six Fulmars – took off from Trincomalee in time to attack the enemy planes before they reached the naval base. Eight of the Hurricanes and one Fulmar were shot down and one Hurricane that was damaged crashed on landing. The Japanese planes were over Trincomalee and started bombing shortly before 7.30 a.m. They damaged the dockyard, airfield and two ships still in harbour.

Eleven Blenheim bombers took off from Colombo to attack the Japanese carriers, but two had to return with engine trouble. At 10.25 a.m. the remaining nine sighted the enemy force which, they reported, included three battleships and four or five carriers (there were, in fact, four battleships and five carriers). The Blenheims were attacked by Zero fighters protecting the Japanese fleet which made bombing difficult and only three near misses were seen. Five of the bombers were shot down and four, which were damaged, managed to get back to their base.

Unfortunately *Hermes* was seen by a seaplane from one of the Japanese battleships and a powerful force of about fifty bombers and twenty fighters was flown off to attack the old carrier which did not have a single airworthy plane. Her aircraft had been flown off at Trincomalee to augment the base's defence. In another crushing onslaught, the carrier was hit by about forty bombs in ten minutes. She heeled over and sank within twenty minutes of first sighting the enemy planes. Describing the attack, an officer in *Hermes* said it 'was carried out perfectly, relentlessly and quite fearlessly, and was exactly like a highly organised deck display. The aircraft peeled off in threes, diving straight down on the ship out of the sun'. The bombers then attacked the destroyer *Vampire*, which broke in half and sank. They also sank *British Sergeant*, *Hollyhock* and *Athelstane*.

Eight Fulmars sent from Colombo to defend *Hermes* arrived at the end of the action when *Athelstane* was sinking. They were able to engage the Japanese planes and claimed to have had some success for the loss of two of the Fulmars. Allied losses during the second Japanese attack on Ceylon were given as fifteen planes (eight Hurricanes, two Fulmars and five Blenheim bombers). Together with the three Catalinas lost on reconnaissance flights, this brought the total of losses in the Ceylon operations to at least thirty-seven.

The Japanese losses over Trincomalee included a Zero fighter whose pilot was apparently determined to anticipate the later exploits of the kamikaze suicide squadrons and deliberately crashed his plane into a large Navy fuel tank. The fire blazed for days. According to the Japanese, who were extremely conservative when it came to giving information about their losses, the whole Ceylon offensive cost them only seventeen aircraft.

The sinking of *Hermes* added 302 more deaths to the Navy's casualties during the Japanese offensive in Ceylon waters from 5 to 9 April. Nineteen of the men who died in *Hermes* were officers. Eight, including one officer, were killed in the destroyer *Vampire*.

Fortunately for the men from the five ships sunk on the 9th, a Royal Navy hospital ship, *Vita*, was nearby during the bombing and spent most of the rest of the day picking up survivors. The *Vita* rescued more than six hundred and took them to Colombo. A few *Hermes* survivors set off on a long swim to the Ceylon coast about five miles away. Seven of them were rescued by a fishing boat while hanging on to a buoy during the night. Three others reached an island and were taken across to the mainland by fishermen. While walking through the jungle they came across a local inhabitant who drove them by car to a police station. The next day they were put on a train to Colombo.

Vice-Admiral Ozawa's Malaya Force (one light aircraft-carrier, seven cruisers and several destroyers) had duly synchronised its operations in the Bay of Bengal with Nagumo's offensive from 5 to 9 April. In the waters north of Madras on the east coast of India, his force sank twenty-three merchant ships (112,312 tons).

Although he never found Admiral Somerville's Eastern Fleet, Nagumo must have been well pleased with his achievements in Ceylon waters. For the loss of only a few aircraft, his fleet had sunk an aircraft-carrier, two heavy cruisers, two destroyers, one corvette, a Navy auxiliary ship and a few merchant vessels. After the attack on Trincomalee, he took his victorious First Air Fleet east and left the Indian Ocean via the Malacca Strait at the same time as Ozawa's force left the Bay of Bengal on the same route. Fuchida noted that in the 'four hectic months' since Pearl Harbor, the First Air Fleet had sailed 50,000 miles in the course of its offensives, ranging from Hawaii nearly to the shores of India. It was an incredible record, none of his carriers, which were so carefully protected by fighter aircraft, suffering any damage.

When Somerville heard that there had been suggestions in the House of Commons that the Royal Air Force was to blame for the naval losses during the Ceylon offensive, he wasted no time in sending a signal to the Admiralty to make it quite clear that there had been no lack of co-operation between the Air Force and Navy:

The trouble was that the RAF had nothing suitable or sufficiently trained to co-operate with. What little they had, they did their best with. I've sent a signal to say that so far as I am concerned, there's no truth in the suggestion and the RAF did all they could to help. I added that TLs [Their Lordships] no doubt appreciated that the loss of these ships was in part due to a wrong appreciation on my part: (a) that the attack on Ceylon was postponed or cancelled, (b) that the attack would be on a relatively small scale with normal carrier aircraft.

PART SIX

In the Wake

I

The offensives by Japanese naval forces in the Indian Ocean and Bay of Bengal caused acute anxiety and alarm. After the fall of Singapore and Japan's other conquests, Ceylon became the key position in the defence of the Indian Ocean. If Ceylon had been occupied, two of the Allied lifelines in the war – the sea routes round Africa to the Middle East and the Persian Gulf with its vital oil resources – could have been cut. This would have had an incalculable effect on the progress of the war. At the time the Allies' position in the North African desert war was precarious. A severance of the supply route to Suez would have placed their forces in even worse jeopardy and eliminated the successful offensive that was to come at Alamein.

There was also the fearful possibility of a link-up of the Japanese with the German and Italian forces. The Eastern Fleet that had been mustered to oppose or deter an incursion in the Indian Ocean by the Japanese was woefully weak compared with their First Air Fleet with its vast superiority in aircraft. If the Eastern Fleet had clashed with the Japanese force, it would have been one of the blackest days in the Royal Navy's history and a major disaster for the Allies. As Admiral Somerville stated in his signal to the Admiralty: 'If the Japanese capture Ceylon and destroy the greater part of the Eastern Fleet, then I admit the situation becomes really desperate.'

In February 1942, Vice-Admiral Nomura, Japan's Naval Attaché in Berlin, urged that Germany and Japan should concentrate on knocking Britain out of the war. He wanted the Germans to attack in the Middle East and thus create favourable conditions 'for a Japanese thrust against Anglo-American sea routes in the western part of the Indian Ocean in the direction of the Red Sea and Persian Gulf'.

In a discussion with Hitler a few days later, Grand Admiral Raeder, Head of the High Command of the German Navy, predicted the early capture of Ceylon by the Japanese which, he pointed out, would have considerable effects on Britain's power in the Indian Ocean and on oil supplies from the Persian Gulf. He said only Alexandria, Durban and Simonstown would be available for the repair of large British warships, and an early German and Italian attack on the key position of Suez would have a decisive influence on the outcome of the war.

The High Command of the German Navy actually gave the German Naval Attaché in Tokyo details of suitable landing places in Ceylon. In mid-March Raeder told Hitler that the Japanese proposed to establish bases in Madagascar after occupying Ceylon. It was reported that Hitler said he did not think France would consent to Japanese bases in Madagascar. Apparently he did not show much interest in the proposal, which would also have required Germany's approval.

The Japanese offensive in Ceylon waters came at a critical time for Britain and her allies. Field Marshal Sir Alan Brooke, Chief of the Imperial General Staff, referred in his diary on 7 April (two days after the sinking of *Cornwall* and *Dorsetshire*) to 'the unpleasant situation created by entrance of Japanese Fleet into Indian Ocean' and added :

I suppose this Empire has never been in such a precarious position throughout history. I do not like the look of things. And yet a miracle saved us at Dunkirk and we may pull through this time.

In a message to President Roosevelt on 15 April about 'the grave situation in the Indian Ocean', Churchill wrote :

Until we are able to fight a fleet action there is no reason why the Japanese should not become the dominating factor in the western Indian Ocean. This would result in the collapse of our whole position in the Middle East . . . Supplies to Russia via the Persian Gulf would also be cut. With so much of the weight of Japan thrown upon us, we have more than we can bear.

While relaxing after a dinner at which he was the guest of honour at the British Embassy in Washington a few months after the end of the Second World War, Sir Winston Churchill was asked by another guest what he felt was the most dangerous and most distressing moment of the war. One of the guests on that occasion, Mr Lester Pearson, who later became Prime Minister of Canada, recalled Churchill's reply which must have surprised those present because he did not refer to Dunkirk, Rommel's advance in North Africa, the fall of Singapore or some of the other anxious times.

'He considered the most dangerous moment of the war and the one which caused him the greatest alarm, was when the news was received that the Japanese Fleet was heading for Ceylon and the naval base there,' said Pearson.

Churchill added that the capture of Ceylon, the consequent control of the Indian Ocean, and the possibility at the same time of a German conquest of Egypt would have closed the ring and the future would have been black.

As it happened, overtures for co-operation between Germany and Japan to effect a link-up from the Indian Ocean were bedevilled by mutual suspicions. Hitler was evidently not keen to have the Japanese encroach on his sphere of operations and was not interested in direct co-operation.

Sir William Stephenson, who had the code name Intrepid, and directed Britain's incredible wartime security organisation from headquarters in New York, stated : 'The Germans wanted the Americans to focus on Japan to give Hitler time to finish his initial schedule of conquest, and to make sure that when Japan did advance, she wouldn't advance too far beyond South-East Asia.'

In a broadcast a few months before the end of the Second World War, Admiral Somerville, who had been Commander-in-Chief of the Eastern Fleet, referred to his efforts to find the Japanese First Air Fleet in 1942. He said : 'It is curious how little use the Japanese made of their opportunity . . . I was waiting for that fleet south of Ceylon – waiting with a hastily assembled force which, as I found out subsequently, was not up to the strength of the Japanese Fleet and was deficient in that vital component of the fleet, the aircraft-carrier. The Japanese looked for me on that occasion and I looked for them. Both searches failed. If either of those searches had succeeded, I should not be talking to you at this moment; I should probably be, as sailors put it, in "Davy Jones's locker". But after this one sortie the Japanese retired into the straits [of Malacca] and never emerged again. I wonder why? They had the ball at their feet then with the goal wide open . . .'

Though it was not known then, the reason was that the incursions of Nagumo's First Air Fleet in the Indian Ocean and Ozawa's Malaya Force in the Bay of Bengal were never intended to be anything more than raids while the high commands in Toyko were considering in which direction the next major offensive should be aimed. So in retrospect – with hindsight – the period following the Ceylon crisis and the departure east of Nagumo and Ozawa's forces was an anti-climax in the Indian Ocean. Within a matter of days the Japanese and British fleets were thousands of miles apart.

But a detailed study had in fact been made by the Japanese of a proposal for an offensive to the west in the Indian Ocean to capture strategic points, including Ceylon, and destroy the British Eastern Fleet. The plan necessitated participation by the Army in amphibious operations against Ceylon. The Army strongly opposed the proposal and refused to take part because it felt it had to keep an eye on the Soviet Union for fear of an attack from that quarter. The Army also rejected an alternative proposal for an invasion of Australia to cut it off from supplies from the United States and prevent it being used as a springboard for a counter offensive by the Allies.

Fuchida and Okumiya explain that in theory the Army and Navy General Staffs, operating as a section of the Imperial General Headquarters, formulated strategic policies. In practice, however, the dominating influence of Admiral Yamamoto, Commander-in-Chief Combined Fleet, gave him the initiative in deciding on naval strategy. After the rejection of the proposed offensives, including another attack on Hawaii, the Naval General Staff favoured less ambitious plans to extend control over eastern New Guinea, the Solomons, New Caledonia and Fiji islands north and north-east of Australia to stop the flow of war materials from the United States. It was felt that at the same time this would bring out the United States Pacific Fleet and lead to the naval clash that was generally agreed to be the major objective.

This did not satisfy the Combined Fleet planners who were impatient for decisive action against the American Fleet. They proposed, in the face of strong opposition from the Naval General Staff, that the Navy would have to operate with the minimum Army participation and that the seizure of the island of Midway, only 1,130 miles from Hawaii, would be the best way to force out the United States Fleet, particularly the carriers, so that they could be destroyed. Yamamoto came out uncompromisingly in favour of this Midway operation in the east and the Navy General Staff reluctantly agreed. Ironically, this decision was made on 5 April, the day that Nagumo's fleet struck at Colombo and sank *Cornwall* and *Dorsetshire*.

The gambler Yamamoto played the wrong card this time. It was his last gamble and led to the 4/5 June Battle of Midway, the 'battle that doomed Japan', all four of Nagumo's aircraft-carriers taking part being sunk and Japanese naval supremacy in the Pacific destroyed.

One can only ponder with awe what the effect on the war would have been if the Japanese, instead of going east against Midway, had decided to conduct a large-scale offensive in the Indian Ocean in the west, captured Ceylon and knocked out the British Eastern Fleet.

In *The War At Sea 1939–1945* Captain Roskill summed up the position thus :

We were saved from disaster in the Indian Ocean, though more by good fortune than by our own exertions. For when matters looked most grim for us, the Japanese diverted their forces to the central Pacific. The advantage which they had gained in the Indian Ocean was thus never pressed home.

2

Were *Cornwall* and *Dorsetshire* decoys sent on a suicide mission ? Were they deliberately routed close to the Japanese Fleet so that they would attract the enemy's attention and distract him from the Eastern Fleet ?

These questions are posed because many survivors believe that the two cruisers were intended to be decoys which, if necessary, had to be sacrificed to preserve the main body of the Eastern Fleet so that it could get into a position to carry out a night attack with torpedo bombers.

It is clear from the track chart in official British publications, show-ing the movements of the Japanese Fleet and British warships that when *Cornwall* and *Dorsetshire* changed course at 7 a.m. on Easter Sunday from 220 to 185 degrees, they steered virtually a parallel course to the main Japanese Fleet which had turned south after the morning raid on Colombo.

The track chart also shows two Japanese carriers and three other ships in a position at 4 p.m. very close to where *Cornwall* and *Dorset-shire* were sunk. There can be no doubt from this that *Cornwall* and *Dorsetshire* sailed close to some of the ships in Nagumo's fleet while racing south in an effort to rejoin the Eastern Fleet.

A signal sent to Somerville from Ceylon giving the position of the Japanese battleships during the forenoon indicated that they were not far to the east of the track of *Cornwall* and *Dorsetshire*, but no anxiety was felt for the cruisers because it was estimated that they were about 150 miles farther south and increasing their distance from the enemy all the time. What was not known was that the Japanese bombers and fighters had a much greater range than was believed by the Allies.

Despite what Captain Agar has written to the contrary, there is reason to believe that both he and Captain Manwaring, Commanding Officer of *Cornwall*, were not happy about the course they were given when the cruisers sailed from Colombo and subsequently. But this is a grey area in the reports on the activities during Easter Saturday and Sunday.

In the course of corresponding with United States naval authorities, I received some interesting information from Professor Robert W. Love Jr, of the History Department at the US Naval Academy in Annapolis. He carried out research work for ten years with acccess to American, British and Japanese archives as well as private manuscripts.

It seems the report that the Japanese were to strike into the Indian Ocean in March-April 1942, came from an American naval Intelligence unit. It may have been passed personally by Admiral E. J. King, US Chief of Naval Operations, to Admiral Sir Dudley Pound, First Sea Lord and Chief of Naval Staff, while he was on a visit to Washington from Britain in March, or it may have been given to the British Admiralty Delegation in Washington.

Professor Love mentioned, however, that one aspect of the whole operation remained unexplained. He said there was substantial evidence to suggest that the track chart published in official British publications

of *Dorsetshire* and *Cornwall*'s fatal sortie is inaccurate and that, rather than sailing to rendezvous with the main body of the Eastern Fleet, Somerville had actually deployed them for a night attack on the Kudu Batai (the Japanese term for their main carrier task force). In such an encounter they could expect reasonable success. However, they were discovered by enemy aircraft before night fell. . . .

It is critical to remember that after the action Nagumo immediately reported this analysis of British intentions, his conclusion that the British had broken his 'Fleet Code', and his urgent recommendation that this code be changed immediately. Of course, this plea was ignored in Tokyo.

A letter to the Admiralty has not brought any further information beyond the statement that it has not been possible

to trace any evidence that Somerville intended to use the *Cornwall* and *Dorsetshire* alone as a night action group against the Japanese force. He had already decided that with his aged battleships and untrained carriers, his only chance of success would be to catch the

Japanese at night when they would be unable to use their air superiority. (He also, mistakenly, attributed poor night action response by the Japanese.) But such an action would have had to be with his whole force, not just two cruisers.

It is all very intriguing.

Is it possible that the Americans gained additional information as a result of Somerville sharing some of his thoughts with them after he was appointed head of the British Admiralty Delegation in Washington in 1944?

As for *Cornwall* and *Dorsetshire* being decoys, this does not hold water for either version of their movements. If, as the official track chart shows, they were on their way to rejoin Somerville's Force A, he obviously would not have wanted them to risk unduly being caught by the Japanese. Neither would he have wanted them to be jeopardised on their way from Colombo if they were to be deployed for a night action against the enemy carriers.

There is the point, though, that *Dorsetshire* and *Cornwall* could unwittingly have played the part of decoys and thus helped to preserve the Eastern Fleet. This aspect was dealt with by Captain Agar in a special message to an anniversary reunion of survivors in Cape Town some years ago :

While to the British nation and the Navy the loss of these valuable ships at the time came as a shock, we know now from the evidence and analysis of our own and enemy documents, that by taking the full force of the Japanese strike aircraft on that Easter Sunday, our cruisers *Dorsetshire* and *Cornwall* prevented the main Japanese carrier force from probing a further hundred miles to the west, where they would have had little difficulty in disposing of Admial Somerville's hastily assembled Eastern Fleet...

History alone can judge these events in their true setting, and without doubt will give the two cruisers full credit for being the means of preserving intact the Eastern Fleet in April 1942, to enable it to play its part in the later stages of the war. The ships' companies of *Dorsetshire* and *Cornwall*, therefore, can claim with justifiable pride that, while their ships were sunk in fighting an enemy striking from the air when they themselves had no aircraft or weapons to fight back with, the sacrifice thus made by the hundreds of our comrades who went down with their ships undoubtedly saved the Eastern Fleet from a very severe blow from which recovery would have been extremely difficult. Our comrades, many of whom were South African sailors, therefore did not die in vain.

3

Before the Eastern Fleet left Port T, the *Cornwall* and *Dorsetshire* survivors were each given some money which, I was told, was the result of a collection among the warships. I remember receiving fifteen rupees, which was the equivalent of £1.2s.6d. It was very welcome because the sole possession of many of the survivors was their belt with possibly a few coins in its pouch. Many of us among the wounded had our clothing cut off in the improvised Sick Bays on board *Enterprise* and did not even have a pair of shorts. At Port T we were also given facilities for sending a cable home but, as the cables had to be taken to Mombasa to be despatched from there, it was about two weeks before they were received.

In the meantime, on the night after the fleet sailed from Port T on Thursday, 9 April, the wounded on board the storeship, which was being used as a temporary 'hospital', heard on the radio the BBC's broadcast of the official communique announcing the sinkings :

The Board of the Admiralty regrets to announce that the cruisers HMS *Dorsetshire* (Captain A. W. S. Agar) and HMS *Cornwall* (Captain P. C. W. Manwaring) have been sunk by Japanese air attacks in the Indian Ocean. It is known that more than 1,100 survivors, including the Commanding Officers of both ships, have been picked up. No further details are yet available.

It was night time where we were out east, but afternoon in Britain and South Africa. This was the first news of the sinkings and it inevitably focused thoughts even more on our families and how they would be worrying. I learnt later that a family friend, Seau Minnaar, who was Field Marshal Smuts's private secretary and had advance information about the sinkings, tried to telephone my wife in Cape Town to break the news to her before it was broadcast. But by the time he was able to contact her she had just heard the radio announcement of the communiqué.

Our stay at Port T was extended to ten days because the naval hospital ship *Vita*, which had to pick us up, was delayed by having to rescue the survivors from *Hermes*, *Vampire* and a couple of other ships sunk near Trincomalee and take them to Colombo. *Vita* eventually arrived on 16 April and there was a cheer when it was announced that she would take us to Durban. The transfer of the wounded from the storeship to *Vita* was quite an operation. They had to be lowered on pallets by a crane into barges and taken across the lagoon to the hospital ship. The patients had their eyes bandaged to protect them from the tropical sun.

It was a relief to have proper hospital facilities after the lack of them at Port T where the doctors had to work under difficult conditions. But the big thrill came when we felt the throb of *Vita*'s coal-burning engines and knew that the ship was under way. She was an old vessel that had served in the First World War and cruised at only eight to ten knots, but she was going in the right direction and even at her speed, there was some sea breeze that cooled the wards and made them very pleasant compared with the heat, humidity and flies at Port T almost on the equator.

We called at Mauritius for a 24-hour stay during which people ashore sent gifts of cigarettes, sweets and fruit to the hospital ship and we were able to send cables. In case the censor would delete any reference to our destination, I used my own code in a cable to my wife, telling her merely to 'go to Twines', which she knew was a hotel in Durban. So when *Vita* arrived on 2 May – just one day short of four weeks since the sinking – Alice had already come to Durban from Cape Town.

When we were carried down the gangway, we were wearing pyjamas lent by *Vita* and, in most cases, our 'luggage' consisted of a belt and toothbrush, toothpaste, a packet of cigarettes and box of matches tied in a handkerchief. But within a couple of hours of our being driven to hospital, the Red Cross Society ladies arrived with suitcases filled with articles and comforts of all descriptions. By the time they left every sailor had shaving kit, handkerchiefs, comb, writing pad and envelopes, pen, ink, pencil, cigarettes, matches and a slab of chocolate. They called regularly to ensure that depleted stocks of necessities were replenished.

Young Paddy Keeping who became blind when *Cornwall* was sunk, received an unexpected gift a couple of weeks after arriving in hospital at Durban. One evening he fell back and bumped his head on the bed-post. The black-out he had endured since the Easter Sunday bombing suddenly gave way to light.

'I can see! I can see!' he cried.

Fortunately the optic nerve had not been damaged. It turned out that his loss of sight was due to psychological shock. So in his case what appeared to be tragic had a happy ending.

Not so happy was the experience of Chief Yeoman Sam Langford who had his left leg amputated soon after being rescued by HMS *Enterprise*. Because of his condition, he had to stay on board the cruiser and was taken to Bombay when Admiral Somerville's Force A left Port T. Later his right leg had to be amputated in hospital. He spent six months in St George's Hospital, Bombay, and while there was visited by the Commander-in-Chief of the Eastern Fleet and the Governor of Bombay. He was taken on a visit to Government House where he met the Governor's wife who arranged for meals to be sent to him in the hospital.

When he was sent home to England, Sam spent more than two years in hospitals before being discharged from the Navy with two artificial legs. He has since had to return to hospital several times to have further operations on what he quite cheerfully refers to as 'my stumps'.

Surgeon Lieutenant-Commander Glyn Rees, the popular Senior Medical Officer in *Cornwall*, was the victim in a particularly tragic sequel. After the war he settled in Cape Town where he practised as a gynaecologist. About sixteen years ago he was killed in a ghastly motor-car accident on the De Waal Drive near the Groote Schuur Hospital where he did much of his work and where the world's first heart transplant operation was performed by Professor Chris Barnard.

Glyn Rees will always be remembered for his dedicated service after *Cornwall* sank. He swam among the survivors attending to the wounded and giving morphia injections, a rating 'carrying his bag' for him. He then attended the seriously wounded cases in the motor-boat during the long wait before rescue ships arrived.

After surviving the *Cornwall* sinking, Lieutenant-Commander Geoffrey Grove was sent to the Mediterranean where he was in action in the battleship HMS *Valiant*, and was awarded the Distinguished Service Cross. But in 1943 he found himself 'in the drink' again when the troopship *Marnix*, in which he was taking passage back to South Africa, was torpedoed and sunk by an aircraft. He and other male survivors were picked up by a destroyer, put ashore at Philippeville on the coast of Algeria and, much to the consternation of the woman in charge, spent the night in a Young Women's Christian Association hostel.

There was an occasion in 1974 when a *Cornwall* sequel gave me a good laugh. My telephone in a newspaper office in Port Elizabeth rang and the woman on the switchboard said: 'It's a call from Cape Town.'

It was my cousin, Bill Dimbleby.

'Have you seen the story in *The Argus*?' he asked.

'Which one?' I inquired in reply.

Bill told me briefly what it was about and I could hardly wait for a copy of *The Argus* to arrive the next day. The story was a columnist's interview with a *Cornwall* survivor. It read :

He is Maltese. His name is Nazzareno Bezzina. But as manager of the Master Mariners' Club in Bree Street, Cape Town, he is known as Reno – and in the bar there, known appropriately as the Tavern of the Seas, he recalled the time he saved the life of Richard Dimbleby, the father-figure of British television whom South Africans remember well for his excellent wartime radio broadcasts.

Dimbleby, who died at 52 in December, 1965, had an intimate radio manner which won the hearts of millions, including members of the Royal Family. Had it not been for Reno, though, he would have been lost to the world at a much earlier age.

After recalling the sinking of *Cornwall* and *Dorsetshire* in 1942, the report continued :

Reno tells the story : It happened east of Colombo. There were about 400 Japs in the air when they suddenly came out of the sun. They dropped oil bombs and I saw Dimbleby, who was staggering around with his clothes on fire. I got hold of him and somebody else aided me and we threw him into the water.

There is no doubt that this saved his life. He did not forget me and many years later when he came to Cape Town and I was manager of a restaurant in Constantia Nek, he thanked me again. There is no doubt that he was my most satisfied customer.

I did not want to knock *The Argus*, a newspaper with which I had a close family and personal relationship. My grandfather came to South Africa from England just over a hundred years ago to join the *Cape Argus* (as the newspaper was named then), my father started his career in journalism on the *Cape Argus* and I, and then my brother Des, were the third generations to start on this Cape Town newspaper. But I felt a correction was needed because the columnist had obviously been misinformed. So I wrote a letter to the Editor in which I said :

You will appreciate my surprise when I tell you that Richard

Dimbleby was not in the cruiser *Cornwall*, and never visited Cape Town. It so happens that I was the Dimbleby in *Cornwall* when she was sunk, but my clothing was not on fire and when the time came I went over the side without assistance from Reno or anyone else. Furthermore I have never met Reno at his restaurant. To put it mildly, this must be a case of mistaken identity, otherwise the passing years have played havoc with Reno's memory.

Richard Dimbleby, to whose family I am related, was a BBC correspondent who served with distinction in other theatres of the war. I still correspond with his mother in England and she, having a keen sense of humour, will enjoy a laugh when she reads about Reno's rescue operation.

A correction was duly published.

4

There must have been many dramatic and tragic sequels among the survivors from *Cornwall* who returned to active service after recovering from the Japanese dive-bombingg. They went to various theatres of the sea war – the heat and sweat of the Persian Gulf and other areas out east, the freezing conditions of the Arctic convoys to Russia and the hazards of the Atlantic.

There is, however, one sequel I know about that stands out as truly incredible.

When 19-year-old Able Seaman A. V. (Tony) Large, of Durban, was rescued after the sinking of *Cornwall*, 27-year-old Henry (Ted) Dobson, of Lincoln, was serving in *Enterprise* which picked up the survivors. Large did not meet Able Seaman Dobson, who helped survivors on that day in April 1942. But fate arranged a meeting of these two sailors some months later in grim, fantastic circumstances.

Large, a tall youngster, who was shaken up but unscathed in the *Cornwall* sinking, was subsequently selected as a candidate for a commission and was drafted to undergo a course of training in England. He sailed from Cape Town on 29 August in the 19,695-ton liner *Laconia*, which had two thousand passengers, including 1,800 Italian prisoners-of-war, men from the Services and civilians.

The voyage was uneventful until the night of 12 September when the *Laconia* was hit by two torpedoes fired by a U-boat hundreds of miles off the west coast bulge of Africa and 850 miles from Freetown. Before the ship turned over on her starboard side and sank, some lifeboats and rafts were launched. Large and a few others managed to launch one of the boats and by the next morning it was loaded down to the gunwales with more than sixty survivors.

During the next four days they and some other lifeboats were taken in tow by a U-boat which was then depth-charged, but not sunk, by an American Liberator aircraft that had suddenly appeared on the scene. Large and some of the others from the *Laconia* who survived the attack were cast adrift and later taken by an Italian submarine to an empty lifeboat. Those in the boat included a civilian, a few merchant seamen, four Poles and members of the three Forces.

'We were fifty-one males, thrown together by inscrutable destiny,' Large told Louis Duffus, a leading journalist and doyen of South African Sports Editors when he retired.

In a memorable letter to his parents, Large wrote :

'In this badly equipped boat (it had been swamped and most of the gear lost) fifty-one of us found ourselves with one and a half oars, no rudder, no mast or sail, and three gallons of fresh water, 700 miles from land. We rigged a mainsail comprised of a raincoat lining and a dozen shirts. Our foresail was a blanket folded diagonally, the mast an oar. We used the half oar for steering. Aided by a steady prevailing wind we made about one knot forward and sideways in the general direction of the coast.

'We had to ration food and water very severely, and after a bit chaps began to get depressed. We managed to augment our food supplies with raw fish. There was a large shoal which followed us for days, and all that was necessary was to drop an unbaited bent nail over the side of the boat and wave it about. The fish, averaging five or six pounds apiece, did the rest.

'The procedure then was to cut the fish on the underside, just below the head, squeeze the blood into a tin, cut off head and get more blood, and drink it before it congealed. Get roe, if any, also liver and heart. Suck gills for blood and eyes for moisture, very like fresh water. We also skinned the fish and hung the stripped flesh to dry for the next day's consumption. You've no idea how good it tasted . . .

'Our ration of water was only half a tot a day and in spite of all warnings given, some began drinking salt water and urine. For a while they continued perfectly normally, but after a few days the stuff had its effect and they just gave in. Others died of exposure, depression and blood poisoning.

'There was a sailor, an English boy, going back to UK. He was a magnificent figure of a man and had been a butcher. "Butch" followed automatically. His undisputed billet was right forward in the boat. In the daytime he sat there stark naked except for a piece of cloth wrapped round his head. He washed himself religiously every few hours and was one of our finest fishermen. He threw live and wriggling fish into the mass of men who lay in the bottom of the boat, already overcome by lassitude, and watched the scrambling for titbits with malicious pleasure.

'Almost from the first he drank salt water. He drank a full pint morning and evening. He appeared perfectly normal for about a week and won many over to his philosophy. Combinations of Horlicks, pemmican, brine and urine were reputed to be harmless. Long before Butch went under himself his disciples began to go.

'One morning I woke up and "Satan" (a *Laconia* steward) told me that a Pole was running riot with an axe. I was stronger than anyone at this stage, but still felt no enthusiasm about disarming him. The Pole was mad and was hitting at the bottom of the boat. This was fortunately steel and as yet he'd done no serious damage. I told him to hand over the axe and he threatened me with it. Somebody attracted his attention from behind and as he turned I jumped in and pulled the axe out of his hand. Later he obtained the axe again and we had to throw him overboard. He cried a little and then swam placidly away from the boat. There was no alternative. It was a bitter, hard little world where there could be no turning back from reality.

'One morning when we woke up even Butch showed the usual signs. He was silly, doped almost, and would not get up. He clambered into the most inextricable position in the boat and died there. This was a general tendency. Men seemed afraid to die in the open and pushed thmselves into unimaginable positions from which we had a hard time extracting them. We grew callous of death. All it meant was that a body had to be lifted the agonising few feet to the gunwales and dropped.

'There were exceptions who died nobly and who were greatly missed. Such was a Canadian who went over the side one day. He was discouraged and tired but he went over to give the rest of us a better chance. We managed to stop him once but later on he slipped over the side and floated quietly away. A grown man wept openly when he heard that "Canada" had gone.

'An English Squadron Leader doled out the water. When he became too weak to do the job I took the water round each evening at sunset. It was in a rectangular gallon can which had been provided by one of the U-boats. I used to take soundings of the water each day and reckon out our future prospects. We never allowed ourselves very much. "Canada" had provided a tin which had once been a tropical film pack for a miniature camera, and somebody had scrounged a glass from the Italians.

'The best time to drink seemed to be sunset, but even in the cool placidity of those evenings the ration only came to half an inch in the glass and seemed dreadfully small. Some watched with round and wondering eyes as I poured, and some watched jealously. Some gulped the water, sweetish, rusty, beautiful stuff, in a single movement, and some took five minutes to sip it and ease it over their tongues.

'None tried to make me increase the daily ration. Things were getting pretty bad, but after "Canada" had gone I never confided in anyone. I told them there was plenty, but no one believed me. I told them that the destroyers would be here in the morning and some took courage. Occasionally someone would cry out, cursing bitterly, and a wave of despondency would run through the boat.'

In any community there must be a moral code, a code of life, some sort of rule of law. Even confined to a small boat almost devoid of the barest necessities in mid-ocean, the survivors made their own laws, with the death penalty for stealing water or food.

Large wrote :

'One day in the heat of the afternoon when we were most exhausted, there was a loud outcry. The water can was lashed under the stern benches where I perched and I woke to find a Cockney lad being accused of tinkering with it. He was a nice kid and I would not believe it. Then and there, with general assent, we decided that any person found stealing water or food would go over the side. The offence was too enormous to be envisaged.

'The Cockney denied the accusations vigorously, but was watched. Next day, about the same time, he was caught redhanded. He had a rubber tube and, dipping one end in the can, was sucking water through the other. This time there was no denial and mercifully he made no attempt to get away without punishment. He said he was very sorry, drank a lot of salt water from one of the tins and threw himself over.

'On the seventeenth night, when there were about thirty of us left –

and by this time none of us was strong enough to take the steering oar or do lookout – we sighted a ship. About half an hour before a fullish moon rose a merchant ship of about 4,000 tons passed us, about 400 yards away. This was the bitterest blow of all and people just gave up after that. Four days later there were only nine of us alive.

'We now had a day's ration of water left. I, at least, was too dry to eat any of our rations, except the chocolate, which I ate at night, taking an hour to get down one small piece – one inch by half an inch by a quarter of an inch. Our rations were three of these pieces a day, four pieces of Horlick's malted milk tablets, and a spoonful of Bovril pemmican. There were some biscuits in the boat, but these needed saliva and were out of the question.

'About the twenty-first day, with only nine of the total of fifty-one left, the wind dropped one evening and later, at about 2 a.m., it rained. Yes, real, honest-to-God, life-giving rain, and for the first time in my life I appreciated it. It was not a tantalising drizzle, but a gorgeous tropical downpour. I get excited now, as I think of it, standing out there shivering, feeling the strength coming back as I sucked water from thwarts and benches, from the sail, from tins, from anywhere. I must have drunk a couple of gallons that night as we filled our water cans and bottles.

'Four of the nine were too far gone to recover, and died, and one of the remaining five had a slight discharge from the ear and seemed to give up. He lived on for several days but would not eat anything. That left four of us, all RN ratings, and it strikes me as odd that out of the three Services represented in that boat at the start, more or less equally, only Navy should survive.

'The first and most interesting is Leading Seaman Harry Vines. He was a gunner on board the ship. In our boat he was in charge of navigation and seamanship, while I was in charge of food and water – "in charge" is a bit strong, but we had the last word. He's a vital, intelligent chap of twenty-four. Comes from Peterborough and was working in a grocery before the war. An ideal type to survive with, and it doesn't end there.

'Next is Ted Dobson, who is twenty-seven and regular Navy. He was in the *Enterprise* when we were fished out of the water after *Cornwall* had been sunk so we had a lot of common ground to go over. He's to be married as soon as he gets home to Lincoln. Next is Ted Riley from Liverpool who got sacked from his van-driving job for a laundry when a slump threatened and so joined the Navy.

'We four organised the food rations to give us about twenty-five more days, and now we fared quite well. After the rain bowels had worked for the first time since the sinking and as we could now eat the biscuits, a little bulk was provided daily. With the extra clothing we could rig up a sun shelter by day and keep warm at night. None of us knew anything about navigation. We used to time sunset and sunrise (when cloud permitted) each day with the mean time of three watches which continued to function throughout the escapade. Then with complicated (for our befuddled and unfed brains) calculations we'd work out how many degrees and the miles we'd sailed each day. I suppose that all the calculations were on the optimistic side, but it gave us something other than our extremely unpleasant prospects to dream about.

'It now rained fairly frequently and we scarcely needed to draw on the canned water, refilling bottles almost as soon as we'd emptied them. We were still very weak though, and used to have bad times bailing out after heavy rains. Once, too, we had an exhausting morning repairing our boom which had snapped. One always seemed to be climbing over thwarts and a four-foot obstruction after weeks in an open boat on meagre rations is no joke.

'Our daily programme was something like this: if it rained, arise at dawn and bale out, try to dry clothes, look round for a ship (dawn and dusk seemed the most likely times, somehow). If it hadn't rained, up at about eight o'clock and breakfast as slowly as possible, breaking up biscuit into tiny pieces and eating them one by one.

'After breakfast we would talk until the sun grew too hot. Then we would rig shelters with overcoats and try to sleep. Fourish, as the sun began to weaken, we would congregate to talk, read from the New Testament, eat at five o'clock and talk until nine o'clock. This was if the day was fine, but if it had rained we beetled for our shelters forward and aft (two in each).

'These days were not completely halcyon. Comparatively we lived like kings, and our chances of survival were bettered, but we lived too close together. Personal peculiarities and habits, however innocuous or minor, became matters of enormous importance. We were tremendously moody and it required great self-restraint not to come to blows over the most trifling matters. To amuse ourselves we used to spend hours delousing our clothes of the peculiar little white bugs that came to inhabit them. I was guilty of whistling Suppé's "Light Cavalry" *ad nauseam.* Riley whistled "A Whistler's Mother-in-Law" and nearly drove me crackers. Dobson would comb his beard for hours at a time. There was nothing at all to do but look, hope and talk ...

'Anger was exhausting and depression was worse. The combination left us gasping for breath with a knotted stomach.

'We were worst during the heat of the day. In the late afternoon when we had our session with the New Testament, had our meal and water, and told our oft-repeated tales, we became human and friendly again.

'That New Testament I mentioned, the property of an RAF sergeant who had died, gave me and the others, I'm sure, a lot of courage. After the rain I used to conduct our services and, odd and unorthodox though they were, they were still services. Disgusting how we turn to God only in distress. I must do my utmost to remain in my present state of mind.

'I was still confident that somehow, sometime, somewhere, we'd strike lucky. Then one morning we heard a plane, and though we didn't see him you can imagine the effect. Two days later – our thirty-sixth day in the boat – at about eleven o'clock a plane flew right over our heads and did not see us. On the same day we sighted new birds and oil fuel on the water.

'Next day we sighted a Sunderland in the distance and turned in feeling that at least we were getting near something. It rained at about 3 a.m. and we beetled for cover and "coma'd" till dawn, when I felt the need to stretch and go out. At that hour there were very dark layers of horizon cloud, and one very black spot that might have been something. I called my companion out and we saw it dissolve into nothing. We felt very optimistic.

'I went back into shelter and the rain stopped. Again the spot appeared on the horizon, again I was called out, and again it dissolved. I had a bad knee and went back to shelter again. My companion stayed outside and called me back again five minutes later. This time I grumbled because it hurt like blazes to move, but eventually I got out. There on our four-mile horizon were about a dozen pinpoints of masts, sticking up jet-black against the grey background. What's more, they were real masts, not the vague elusive things I had been seeing for the past five weeks.

'Convoy! I don't know where the strength came from, but I leapt up on a thwart to see better, and started waving madly with a blue jersey. We didn't dare wake the two who were sleeping forward because of the general depression it would have caused if the convoy passed us by.

'They were coming towards us and across, getting slowly closer. . . . Harry and I talking and praying in whispers. Can see funnels and upper works. . . . One ship turning either towards or away from us. Oh God! Pass one of those rain tins, Shorty (this is the thirst of excitement). Can see ships signalling to one another.

'Slowly she approaches and at last, when she's about a mile away, we can be sure. We wake the other two and they are unwilling to come out. "Don't joke about things like that," they say, but they do come out, and it's a pleasure to watch them.

'We collect ourselves and have a little service of thanks, gather up our precious souvenirs, all the gear and wallets, and wait, waving. She's an HM trawler converted from a fishing trawler, and she comes alongside throwing lines. . . . She's a grand little ship and her name (*St Wistan*) is engraved on my heart.'

The 39-day ordeal was over for the four men out of 51 who survived. It was a happy ending to an amazing feat of fortitude and endurance bolstered by faith. When rescued they were only eighty miles from the coast. The next morning they arrived at Freetown.

Tony Large was awarded the British Empire Medal. After the war he qualified as a dentist and emigrated to Australia.

5

On the clear moonlit night of 30 May 1942, a South African Air Force officer was invited to dine in the wardroom of the British battleship HMS *Ramillies*, which was berthed at Diego Suarez, the naval base at the northern end of Madagascar.

In the course of conversation in the wardroom after dinner, the South African airman expressed admiration for the way the men in the Royal Navy faced danger. His host, a Royal Navy Lieutenant, said in his opinion airmen lived a more dangerous life.

'No,' said the South African airman, 'you people are attacked by things you can't even see, such as torpedoes.'

The naval officer laughed and replied that he had always felt as safe as a house in a battleship. The next minute there was an explosion and the lights went out as a torpedo struck *Ramillies*.

The time was 8.25 p.m. There were more explosions as two corvettes dropped precautionary depth charges in the harbour and then another one at 9.20 p.m. when the tanker *British Loyalty* (6,993 tons), was also torpedoed.

The torpedo flooded one compartment in the battleship, which stayed afloat, but the tanker settled on the bottom of the harbour.

Those two attacks marked the start of a submarine campaign by the Japanese off the east coast of Africa. It was launched in terms of an agreement with Germany to harass Allied shipping.

The Japanese had considered using Madagascar as a base for operations in the Indian Ocean, which would have threatened the Allies' essential sea route around South Africa and up the east coast of Africa to the Middle East. The Prime Minister of South Africa, Field Marshal Smuts, was acutely conscious of this danger to what he regarded as 'the key to the safety of the Indian Ocean'. Early in February, 1942, Churchill said in a message to Roosevelt: 'A Japanese air, submarine and/or cruiser base at Diego Suarez would paralyse our whole convoy route both to the Middle and to the Far East.'

As Madagascar was under the control of the Vichy French, there was was always the danger that the Japanese would be allowed to use Diego Suarez just as they had been allowed to move into French Indo-China the previous year. To forestall any such move by Japan, a plan to occupy the strategically situated naval base by a seaborne British force, supported by the Royal Navy and South African Air Force, had therefore been put into operation on 5 May. Rear-Admiral E. N. Syfret, a South African by birth who went to school in Cape Town, was in command of the supporting ships and the battleship *Ramillies* was his flagship.

Meanwhile five large Japanese submarines of about 2,000 tons each had been assembled at Penang at the end of April. Three of the submarines carried midget submarines and the other two small reconnaissance seaplanes. They made their way across the Indian Ocean, refuelling from two merchant raiders, *Hokoku Maru* and *Aikoku Maru*, which also acted as supply ships.

The Japanese were more interested in attacking warships than merchantmen and on their way down the east coast of Africa reconnoitred the ports, including Durban on 20 May. They then sailed back up the Mozambique Channel to the vicinity of Diego Suarez. On the evening of 29 May the reconnaissance seaplane from one of the submarines reported that a battleship, cruiser and other ships were at the naval base. The next night, when the submarines were about ten miles from the harbour entrance, orders were given to launch the three midgets. Two of the submarines managed to launch theirs but the third could not get hers away.

The torpedoing of *Ramillies* and *British Loyalty* was an outstanding success for the midgets, but it would have been even more so if, instead

of the tanker, the ship next to her at the quay had been chosen as a
target. It was loaded with ammunition and a torpedo would have
caused a major disaster. *Ramillies* was patched up and escorted by a
cruiser, three destroyers and a tug to Durban where she was repaired.
British Loyalty was salvaged but in March, 1944, was again damaged
by a torpedo, this time fired by a German U-boat at Port T.

Three days after the Diego Suarez attack, two of a Japanese submarine's crew were shot when a patrol came upon them in the bush a
few miles from the bay. The wreck of one of the midget submarines was
found on 17 June on a reef where it grounded. The other one never
got back to its parent submarine.

The Diego Suarez attack was followed by a five-week campaign in
the Mozambique Channel by the Japanese submarines during which
they sank at least twenty ships totalling about 120,000 tons. One of
the captains involved survived a hat-trick of sinkings. When his ship
was torpedoed, he was picked up by another merchantman, but within
a few hours that ship was also sunk. He was picked up again but this
rescue ship was also torpedoed. A third ship took him on board and
this time fate was kind. After surviving the three sinkings in a matter of
a few days, he arrived safely at Durban.

At the end of their offensive in the Mozambique Channel, Japanese
submarines left southern African waters and did not return, but the
sinking of the vessel *Congella* by one of them in the Indian Ocean near
Ceylon the following year provided an epic example of the defiant
spirit of the Merchant Service in the Second World War. The ship
was gunned and the survivors pulled away in a lifeboat. One man was
still on board, alive but mortally wounded. He was the captain, Arthur
William Folster, who was well known in Durban.

Folster refused to leave his ship and was last seen on the bridge. As
the *Congella* sank, he 'tapped' out a V for victory on the ship's siren.
That was drama in the raw.

Captain Folster's memory is perpetuated by the plaque in the Mission
to Seamen's chapel in Durban.

6

It was New Year's Eve 1943 and one of the British trawlers requisitioned for anti-submarine work in the Royal Navy was on patrol off the
Natal coast. It was a boring routine, sailing up and down much the

same course with very little chance of an 'incident'. On New Year's Eve it was a particularly tedious and irritating job, with no chance to see in the New Year with an appropriate celebration.

So the Commanding Officer of the trawler – let's call the ship HMS *Trawler* for convenience – was thoroughly 'chocker'. He was a burly Royal Naval Reserve Lieutenant, a fisherman in peace-time, who had distinguished himself in northern waters earlier in the war (DSC and mentioned in despatches). He was recognised throughout the Navy as a 'tough guy' who was not awed by gold braid or U-boats. He called a spade a spade and bluntly aired his grievances to senior officers.

One could read his mind as he lamented his fate on that New Year's Eve. There he was meandering up and down a set course off Durban. He was accustomed to action. The Royal Navy had just sunk the German battle-cruiser *Scharnhorst* in waters that the Commanding Officer of HMS *Trawler* knew from peacetime fishing as well as the back of his hairy hand.

Orders were that radio silence should not be broken except in an emergency. Christmas and New Year greetings on the radio in wartime were strictly prohibited. But that did not deter the Commanding Officer of HMS *Trawler*. Very deliberately he wrote out a signal addressed to the Commander-in-Chief South Atlantic in Simonstown and repeated to the Commodore-in-Charge, Durban, the South African Naval Officer-in-Charge, Durban, the Extended Defence Officer and the Commander Auxiliary Patrols (the officer in charge of the patrol vessels and his immediate CO).

At one minute to midnight he handed the message to his signalman and this is what was tapped out from HMS *Trawler* to the five addressees on that New Year's Eve :

'Greetings. Tonight's big swell is ever in our favour. May it emulate greatly for our cause this coming year.'

In due course the Commanding Officer of the ship was asked, in true Service style, to state his reasons in writing for sending the New Year greeting over the radio while at sea.

The incorrigible Commanding Officer headed his formal reply : 'A well wished signal.' His letter read :

I ...., Skipper Lieut., RNR, DSC, RD, mentioned in despatches (twice), did make such a signal having previously heard of our Royal Navy's grand success in the sinking of the *Scharnhorst* in the waters around the North Cape, where I have been so often and knowing that the swell and sea there must be in our favour, also the Russians capturing Titonar forty miles from Poland's border and we at sea running with the swell, it came to me as how grand it would be were it ever to be in our favour for our cause to win and finish this blasted war which will be done because we all possess that grand gift of understanding.

I have the honour to be, Sir,
Your obedient Servant . . .

Presumably the authorities had 'that grand gift of understanding' because nothing more was heard of the incident – and in due course the 'blasted war' ended.

Peacetime Postscript

It was 1949, four years after the end of the Second World War. Although Sam Langford had lost both of his legs, he was by no means inactive, even if confined to a wheelchair. He was always a staunch enthusiast when it came to anything connected with HMS *Cornwall*, in which he had served as Chief Yeoman of Signals from the outbreak of war until the ship was sunk by Japanese dive-bombers in 1942.

Sam and another ex-member of *Cornwall*'s ship's company decided it would be a good idea if they could get survivors of the cruiser together to form some sort of association. After many months of correspondence with the Admiralty, Royal Marine Depots and individuals, they had got in touch with enough *Cornwall* survivors to start an organisation. Thus was established in 1951 the HMS Cornwall 1939–42 Association and the first reunion was held in the Embassy Ballroom at Welling, Kent.

Since then the Association has held an annual reunion as near as possible to 5 April, the date on which *Cornwall* was sunk. The gatherings are usually held on board HMS President, an old ship which is moored permanently along the Embankment near Waterloo Bridge and is a training ship of the London Division of the Royal Naval Volunteer Reserve.

The reunions are followed a few months later by a social evening which is attended by wives.

In addition to being Secretary, Sam Langford became Vice-President of the Association and corresponded from his home in Maidstone, Kent, with ex-*Cornwall* men as far afield as South Africa and New Zealand, some of whom have since attended the annual reunion in England. He was by no means confined by his disability and has flown to South Africa a couple of times to visit friends.

It was while sitting in the lounge of a friend's home in Cape Town in 1980 that he felt a tap on his shoulder. It was a stranger, Richard Tomczak, who had served as a Petty Officer in the German raider *Pinguin* until shortly before she was sunk by *Cornwall* in May 1941. Some time after the war he settled at the Cape. That was Sam's first meeting with a member of the German crew. Their friendship grew and, as a result, Sam was able to contact other *Pinguin* survivors in Germany who had also formed an association which holds reunions.

Four of the German survivors came to England in 1981 to attend the annual reunion of the HMS Cornwall 1939–42 Association at which they were warmly welcomed. That really started the ball rolling and Sam was invited to attend the Germans' reunion in Lutjenburg.

'The time there was a momentous one for me,' he said. 'I was treated like a long lost brother. I was wheeled everywhere by a German naval officer, Kapitän Leutnant Harald Wentzel, who explained everything to me in English. He is the son of a doctor in *Pinguin* who was lost in the action with *Cornwall.* We have become firm friends.'

The next year sixteen *Cornwall* survivors went over to Germany to attend the *Pinguin* reunion at Oberskirch.

'Many friendships have been made with the German survivors and their wives, and those who were once our enemies have become our friends,' said Sam. 'They are altogether a fine crowd of chaps and I feel chuffed that we old enemies are now good friends.'

It seems the motto under *Cornwall*'s crest is most appropriate – 'One and all.'

Appendix
The Raider *Atlantis*

A vivid description of a raider in action is given by a German officer who served in *Atlantis*, which had set out from Süderpiep near Wilhelmshaven on the North Sea coast of Germany on 31 March 1940. He tells as follows* how *Atlantis*, which was then disguised as the Japanese ship *Kasii Maru*, sank the freighter *Scientist* (6,199 tons), about 600 miles off the coast of South West Africa:

'It was on the morning of 3 May, quite suddenly and cutting across the everyday routine, that the cry came from our masthead look-out: "Ship in sight!" And a few minutes later we were steaming towards the British ship *Scientist*, the first of our twenty-two victims . . .

'As the alarm bells brought us to the guns we realised, even the dullest of us, that with the advent of the Britisher, a new sequence was beginning. ; . . We had worked out a drill for such an occasion long before our sailing, relying for procedure on precedents outlined in the histories of World War I. In certain respects the information they yielded seemed comprehensive enough – first a signal to stop; next, because it was deemed good form, a shot across the bows; and finally, a polite reception of gracious surrender. But we had an uneasy feeling that the historians had not devoted sufficient attention to explaining what went on between the sighting and the arrival of one's "guests" upon one's decks. In total war at least, we were prepared for something more, something different to fill up the interval between preface and epilogue.

'To the English ship only two men would be visible on our bridge, the Captain and myself, who, as officer of the watch, was responsible for transmitting his orders and supervising their execution. Not a glimpse would they catch of the Gunnery Officer and three ratings who lay crouched behind the canvas rail of the range-finder . . . So this was it . . . to endure two hours for the range to close, slow in passing. No great drama here, I thought, just a little steamer approaching you as you approach her, the whole thing developing so steadily that it was almost possible to predict the moment of our warning shot.

'A Leading Signalman stood by a cluster of bunting, the traditional

* Reprinted with permission of T. Werner Laurie Ltd at the Bodley Head from *Atlantis* by Sellwood and Mohr.

signal XL, "Stop or I fire", followed by another flag signal, "Stop
using wireless". The Englishman came on. I lowered my binoculars and
glanced interrogatively at the Captain. He nodded. The moment had
come. *Fallen Tarnung* (drop camouflage). The flaps roared up. The
crane became Number Three gun, and the hut on our stern yet another
5.9 inches as our battle flag shot upwards in the breeze. The whole
operation occupied precisely two seconds . . . But no reply came to our
signal . . . Instead a sudden hum QQQ . . . QQQ . . . "Unidentified
merchantman has ordered me to stop." He was using his wireless . . .
Everything seemed to be normal with still no sign of life on board her
except for the solitary figure on her bridge. Her silhouette had begun
to change. Before our eyes she was turning. She was making a run
for it . . .

'The guns opened up, the acrid reek of cordite filling our nostrils.
Momentarily the target was obliterated. When it cleared I saw four
white jets of foam rise from the sea round the steamer.

' "Again . . . again . . ." called the Gunnery Officer.

'She was still sending her messages.

' "Again . . . again . . ." called the GO.

'A great cloud of dust followed from the steamer, dirty black and
grey, like a carpet being beaten. Our shells had registered. "Again . . .
again . . . again . . ." called the GO. But this time the voice of our
signalman called : "Ship stopped sending."

'The merchantman now lay stopped. Her decks had suddenly become
alive with men climbing into the lifeboats. I was to accompany the
boarding party and set foot on British soil. As we cast away, *Atlantis*
made a lee for our boats and those of *Scientist* and soon I had my first
glimpse of our victims. My impression was one of surprise; surprise at
seeing so many dark faces, for I had never encountered Lascars before
and somehow I had expected to find an all English crew.

'One solitary figure remained on *Scientist*, and as I clambered up the
side of the ship he gave me a cold look and a short but correct salute . . . I
discovered that *Scientist* was a Harrison steamer. She was carrying a
cargo of ore, chromium, copper, hides, tanning bark, maize, flour and
jute, was on her way from Durban to Freetown where she was to
join up with a convoy to England.

'The formalities disposed of, I searched the Captain's quarters and
chart room for papers, wireless, codes, mails, logs, routing instructions,
anything that might prove useful, but the Captain had done his job
well and ditched anything that might have proved useful . . . My swag
was confined therefore to odd items such as binoculars, signal flags and

a chronometer . . . There is something inexpressibly strange about searching through cabins where pictures of girl friends and wives, mothers and children gaze down in mild reproach as one rifled through their personal belongings.

'Searching the officers quarters I was surprised to find how cramped they were, for *Scientist* was quite an old ship; even the Captain's cabin was half the size of my own quarters on *Atlantis* . . . The wireless room was an appalling shambles but the operator's only injury a wounded arm. Emerging on deck I came across a dead Lascar, his skull blown off. He lay huddled in a pool of blood. I felt sick. I glanced at the youngsters in our party. No time for soliloquizing now. To make quite sure of sinking *Scientist*, we opened her seacocks as well as planting our charges...'

Index

Index